[Partly reprinted from the QUARTERLY JOURNAL OF VETERINARY SCIENCE IN INDIA.]

A MANUAL

OF THE

DISEASES OF THE CAMEL

AND OF HIS MANAGEMENT AND USES,

BY

JOHN HENRY STEEL, V.S., A.V.D., F.R.C.V.S., F.Z.S.,
FELLOW OF THE UNIVERSITY OF BOMBAY,
PRINCIPAL AND PROFESSOR OF VETERINARY SCIENCE, BOMBAY VETERINARY COLLEGE,
EDITOR OF THE QUARTERLY JOURNAL OF VETERINARY SCIENCE IN INDIA,
AUTHOR OF SUNDRY WORKS ON VARIOUS BRANCHES OF VETERINARY KNOWLEDGE.

[Illustrated.]

INDIAN VETERINARY MANUALS, III.

Madras:
PRINTED AT THE LAWRENCE ASYLUM PRESS, MOUNT ROAD,
BY G. W. TAYLOR.

1890.

TO

J. H. B. HALLEN, F.R.C.S.E., F.R.S.E.,

INSPECTING VETERINARY SURGEON, I.V.D.,

GENERAL SUPERINTENDENT OF HORSE BREEDING OPERATIONS.

THIS

SMALL WORK

IS

RESPECTFULLY DEDICATED

AS A

TESTIMONY TO HIS

Long and persistent efforts to promote

VETERINARY PROGRESS

IN

INDIA.

LITHOG: FOR LAWRENCE ASYLUM PRESS, MADRAS,

BY ALEX. BARREN.

THE CAMEL MARKET, - ADEN.

PREFACE.

When I brought out the companion work to this, on the Elephant, an ingenious critic rated me soundly because I had not detailed information on diseases of the mighty pachyderm comparable on even terms with our knowledge of the surgery and medicine of the horse, ox, and man. That critic will have lots of scope in scarifying me over this book, for Cameline Pathology is sadly in arrears and the English in India, the Russians in Central Asia, the French in Algeria, and the Arabs in North Africa and South-Western Asia are but slowly accumulating exact knowledge of diseases of the Camel. Had I chosen to bring pure theory to bear I might have posed as a grand promoter, indeed as the originator, of Cameline Pathology and have given a full and elaborate account for correction hereafter by practical observers. Such has not been my object; I have aimed at "holding a mirror up to nature," and have painted Cameline Pathology "with all its warts;" for I believe that by making the utmost of what we *do* know, by systematic arrangement, and by scientific expression I best prepare the subject for future advances. It is no slight step forward when we learn our ignorance of a science!

J. H. S.

Bombay, 1890.

ILLUSTRATIONS.

PLATE 1. Aden Camel Market° ... ... Frontispiece.
„ 2. One and two-humped Camels in good condition To face p. 2
„ 3. The forehand of a Soudanese Baggage Camel° „ „ 6
„ 4. A Soudanese warrior on a Sowari Camel° „ „ 8
„ 5. The Stomachs of a Camel opened longitudinally* „ „ 60
„ 6. Histological diagrams of various structures* „ „ 67
„ 7. Gastric mass of a Camel (Colin) and some anatomical and histological details* ... ... „ „ 68
„ 8. Temporal glands and Female generative organs* „ „ 83
„ 9. Sarcoptes Cameli* ... ... „ „ 92
„ 10. Various Surgical details:—
(*a*) Method of tying down the Camel (after Gilchrist).
(*b*) Serwan's implements (after Leach).
(*c*) Ligature for bleeding, and splint for lower jaw (after Gilchrist).
(*d*) Structure of the humps (after Lombardini).
(*e*) Histology of the humps (after Lombardini) ... ... „ „ 103
„ 11. Heart bone and diaphragm bone of Camel* Skeleton of the Camel* ... ... } ... „ „ 114
„ 12—19. Diagrams illustrating dentition ... ... „ „ 161
„ 20. Map of Camel distribution ... ... „ „ 164

* After Lombardini. ° From photographs casually obtained.

TABLE OF CONTENTS.

TRODUCTION : General Essay on the Subject ... ... pp. ix—xvi

CHAPTER I : *The Camel as an animal of Transport.*—Opinions on the camel vary. Uses of the different parts of a camel after death. He is *the* transport animal for certain countries. *Varieties :* Afghan, Pahari, Bactrian, Scindi, Punjabi, Beloochi, Bikanir, North-West Provinces and Oudh, Taloocher, Persian, Asia Minor, and Mesopotamia. The two-humped camel, Turkestani (Tuya). Russian experiences. Algerian varieties; want of judgment in selection of varieties of camel for service. Europeans do not understand camels. Camel as an animal of Transport seldom properly cared for. Qualities which affect his value as an animal of Transport, effects of rutting or "must," hardihood—loads—pace—advantages of camel convoys. Want of versatility; use for guns and in harness. Care in management of camels, Arab and Turkoman experiences. Effects of state of road on progress of camels. Crossing rivers and nullahs. Food and feeding. The regulation ration—grazing—fodders. General routine of camel management. Watering. How often should camels be watered? Inspection, arrangement of lines, night guard. Care of saddlery and other gear—loading—jhools—camping grounds. Castration. Selection of camels for public service. Dentition as denoting age. Method of examining a camel as to fitness for Transport service. Age limits to efficiency. Attendants—the gait of camels—procurability. Nunn on names applied to camels of different sizes. Breeding. Natural history of the camel ... ... pp. 1—32

CHAPTER II : *General considerations on diseases of the Camel.*—Special features of cameline pathology. Information resulting from Veterinary Science. General symptoms of ill health. Fever. The pulse. Internal temperature. Respirations. State of excreta—prognosis. Treatment ... pp. 32—38

CHAPTER III : *Cameline Therapeutics and Materia Medica.*—Mussauls. Nahass or snuff. Lapes or ointments. Unjuns or lachrymants. Firing. Bleeding ; general and local. Fomentations. Laxatives and cathartics. Enemata. Sedatives. Stimulants, &c. Doses. Methods of administration. Means of restraint. Miscellaneous considerations ... pp. 38—45

CHAPTER IV : *The Blood and its diseases.*—Anatomy and physiology of the blood. Anæmia or debility. Surra (Khanhog and Doaia), Anthrax (Chhalie). Fatal but obscure disorders of camels. Haslam's record from Suez. Foot and mouth disease. Rinderpest. Camel pox *v.* Variola cameli (Mata, cheechuk). Glanders. Pinsee ka murz. Pakdar. Strangles. Rabies Tuberculosis. Rheumatism. Zerbad. Hydatid cysts. Hæmatozoa. Poisoning. Problems to be solved concerning blood diseases of camels. ... ... pp. 45—59

CHAPTER V : *The Digestive system and its disorders.*—Anatomical peculiarities of the alimentary canal. The teeth, pâlu, stomachs. Colin on the dimensions of the Alimentary Canal. Gahasha or Inflammation of the Pâlu. Sore throat, three forms. Parotiditis, glossitis, vomition; Hoven or flatulent colic; Impaction of the Rumen. Enteritis (Bhao, one form), Ascites; constipation or costiveness; Diarrhœa, purging, dysentery. Lombardini on the digestive system of the camel. Teeth. Tonsilar concretions. On the functions of the water sacs. Umbilical Hernia. Indigestion. Vahee golah (Gilchrist). Intestinal parasites. *Appendix.* The pancreas. The liver. Congestion of the liver. Hepatitis Hydatid invasion of the liver ... ... pp. 59—71

CHAPTER VI : *Circulatory system.*—The heart. Burke's rapid cirrhosis. Anatomy. Venesection ... ... pp. 71—72

CHAPTER VII : *The Respiratory apparatus.*—Nasal catarrh (Khoorka). Laryngitis, cough. Kapaulee and obscurity of its pathology. Ulceration of the nostrils. Nose peg injuries. Maggot in the nose. Œstrus cameli or the camel Bot. Diseases of the chest. Pneumonia. Pleuropericarditis (Lombardini). Pulmonary Apoplexy. Strongylus filaria. Chronic lung disease. Hydatids. Tubercular Phthisis ... ... pp. 72—81

CHAPTER VIII : *Urinary disorders.*—Retention of urine. Dysuria. Hæmaturia (Soozark). Renal and urethral calculi. pp. 81—82

CHAPTER IX : *Generative apparatus.*—Temporal glands and their secretion. Larrey's observations on genetic furor. Pendulous penis. Castration. The generative organs of the female and their functions. *Appendix* 1. *On the diseases of young camels.* Ulcerative Stomatitis. *Appendix* 2. Analyses of milk of female camels ... ... pp. 82—84

CHAPTER X : *The Nervous apparatus.*—General remarks. Megrims; Vertigo. Tup Surga (Leach). Murghee ka murz (Gilchrist). Cumaun ka murz (Gilchrist) "Cold Struck." Cerebritis. Ahren bhao (Gilt). Cænurus cerebralis. Paraplegia (Jolay). Tetanus. Hewa or Heat Apoplexy ... pp. 85—88

CHAPTER XI : *Cutaneous system.*—Mange or itch (Kharisk). Its varieties. Eczema, the non-parasitic form. Preventive treatment. Cure. The "mange insect," Sarcoptes cameli. Communicablity of true mange to mankind. Causes. Symptoms. Treatment: preventive and curative. Various methods: Leach's, Haslam's, Clayton's, Yaldwin's, Gilchrist's, Bennett's, Montgomery plan (Nunn), Carbuccia's, Lombardini's. Major Elliot on the problem of treatment of skin disease of camels on service. Other diseases of the skin. Eczema, Agheen bhao. *Ectozoa.* Jehun (lice). The Seroot fly, The Debab fly ... pp. 88—102

CHAPTER XII : *Minor Surgical conditions.*—Wounds in general; bullet wounds. Branding sores. Contusions. *Galls.* Of nose. Injuries to tail. Ulceration of the tail. Crupper galls; injuries of the jaw and mouth. Elbow gall. Boss or pad galls. Soreback or saddle gall, its causes and treatment. Hump injuries and Cancerous disease. Abscess (phora) : of neck glands, of chest, of groin (el magoub), outside thigh, over eye, gomri or kapaulee, subcutaneous boils, chandri or chhahliyan ... ... pp. 102—113

CHAPTER XIII : *The Locomotary system.*—Description of the leading peculiarities of the skeleton. *Fractures and dislocations.* Anchylosis. Bone spavin. Anchylosis of Vertebræ. *Sprains* (*Lutchuk*), levelled legs, swollen joints, sprained shoulder, atrophy of limb muscles, laceration of the ham muscles. *Tumours* rare. Fibroma ... ... pp. 113—115

CHAPTER XIV : *The organs of the Special Sense.*—Paucity of our knowledge. The *Ear*, canker of the ear. The *Eye*, injuries. The *pedal apparatus.* Postures of the camel, paces, structure of the foot. Diseases of the foot: overgrown toe nails, inflammation of the elastic pad, whitlow (quittor, guzmah, tahkne), sarpo, mooroos, pedal fibroma ... ... pp. 115

Notes and Appendices. [These have been gradually collected while the chapters of this book were passing through the press, and could not well have been inserted without interference with the simplicity of the original work, which there are strong reasons for retaining].

APPENDIX I.—Notes on Camel Corps, after Burn 181

" II.—Records of the Suakim Camel Corps 124

" III.—Camel notes at a Camp of Exercise (Steel) 125

Para. 4. The feeding of camels on grain. Camel attendants; Ectozoa, Musthi, wound treatment and complications. Illustrative cases. Arguments for castration. List of more important cases. Diarrhœa due to parasites. Need of Veterinary supervision for camels.

APPENDIX IV.—Notes and additions 131

Note 1. *Products of the camel and his uses in various parts of the world.* The wool, skin, bowels, and bones, as articles of trade. The flesh as human food. Boisse's information on this subject.

„ 2. *Different kinds of camels, their peculiarities and designation,* sources, and distribution :—Bactrian. Influence of marsh land. Arabic names for camel. Dromedaries from Scinde, Bikanir, Oman, Kathiawar, &c.

„ 3. Camels employed along the Nile (Burn). Range of the Camel in Africa, Europe, America, and Australia.

„ 4. Camel losses on service.

„ 5. Procurability of camels.

„ 6. Walters on camels in the Soudan Campaign (1885).

„ 7. Fenton on camels of the Suakim Expeditionary Force.

„ 8. *Camel loads of the world* (Lord and Baines).

„ 9. *Camel guns.*

„ 10. *Camels as a means of Transport for the sick.*

„ 11. *Transport of camels by rail and sea.*

„ 12. *Opinions as to the value, relative and absolute, of camels for transport on service* :—Queriple, Pringle, Poyser; outcome of experiences up the Nile.

„ 13. *Watering of Military camels.*

„ 14. *Saddles* by Burt and other Veterinary observers.

„ 15. *Camel Management on service,* swimming across the Nile. (Queriple).

„ 16. *Average rations.*

„ 17. *Sample rations* for service.

„ 18. Camel grazing at Suakim (Smyth).

„ 19. List of plants eaten by camels (Watt).

„ 20. Precautions against skin disease.

„ 21. Clothing and bedding.

„ 22. Weight and dimensions of camels.

„ 23. *Examination as to soundness* :—According to Burn and "Snipe."

„ 24. Minor notes on camel sickness.

„ 25. Poyser on an outbreak of disease.

„ 26. Danakil Equine Typhus fever or African Glanders (Hallen).

„ 27. Soudan Catarrhal Fever.

„ 28. Rheumatism.

„ 29. *Parasites* : Filaria Evansi (Lewis).

„ 30. Cobbold and Colin on camel parasites.

„ 31. *Poisoning.*

„ 32. Formad and Vedernikoff on enzootic disease,

„ 33. Lady Anne Blunt on camels in Arabia.

APPENDIX V.—Dentition as indicating age 161

„ VI.—A few notes on the History and Literature of the camel, principally after Lombardini 164

„ VII.—Megnin on Sarcoptes Cameli 166

„ VIII.—Materia Medica and Therapeutics 167

1. List of Medicinal Agents (Pharmacopœial).
2. Do. do. do. (extra Pharmacopœial).
3. Samples of prescriptions for camel treatment.
4. Formularium.

INTRODUCTION.

(The following elementary paper on the Camel, as read before the Bombay Natural History Society, on 10th July 1889, will lead up to our subject by giving a sketchy outline of its popular bearings. It has been reprinted by kind permission of the Society.)

In dealing with a subject so large and so interesting as the camel one hardly knows where to begin and where to leave off. It is extraordinary how various estimates have been formed of his value. Mahomed says of him that he is the greatest of all the blessings given by Allah to mankind; recent writers have represented him as ugly, spiteful, unreliable at work, stupidly phlegmatic, malodorous, and endowed with all the bad qualities under the sun; his very virtues, especially steady endurance of excessive toil, being attributed to want of sensibility and of even the faintest gleams of intelligence. The songs of the Arab of the desert are about the camel, as one of the most beautiful of created beings; the remarks of the British soldier and transport regimental officer about his baggage camels are not suited to ears polite! Who is right and who is wrong?

We can have no hesitation in taking the side of the Arab. Still there is some excuse for the recent military opinion on this subject, because undoubtedly in the Soudan, along the Nile, and in Afghanistan, camel transport has not been a success, and the poor beasts have died wholesale as a rule. The Russians in Central Asia, the French in Algeria, and, recently, the Italians in Massowah, have been quite as unsuccessful as we in our various campaigns as regards keeping camels in health and efficiency. Individual officers have solved the problem of how to keep camels at work and to prove them valuable on a campaign; but our troops have most certainly not been successful; however, surely, if overladen animals have not their saddles removed for a fortnight, we cannot wonder to find horrible sores on their backs; if animals remain ungroomed and tied up in lines or on the march for months together, we cannot wonder if they get mange in an aggravated form; and if animals get no food nor water for a week, we cannot wonder that they at last fall and die under their heavy burdens. To sum the matter up in a few words. If men have in war emergency suddenly to deal with an animal about which they know nothing whatsoever, the animal must not be blamed that the results are not altogether satisfactory.

The knowledge of the camel possessed by the untravelled Briton is easily summed up. Firstly, he is certain that the animal is the "ship of the desert." Secondly, that it has something to do with the eye of a needle. Thirdly (and most positively) it is a sort of travelling reservoir, consisting of inexhaustible water tanks and never needs to drink. Fourthly, it has a hump and long legs and neck. Finally, it is an uncanny brute of strange habits, suited only to the wandering Bedouin of the desert and the inimitable Barnum. When called on in the emergencies of service to take charge of camels, the principle an Englishman works on is to treat them as much as possible like the beast of burden with which he is most familiar, the horse. Where this has been carried out thoroughly the results have been not unsatisfactory, for when groomed regularly the camel does not get mange, when properly saddled and loaded he does not get sore back, and when properly fed and watered he remains serviceable and does good work. It is when one soldier is given several camels to take care of, and is aided only by a lot of lazy, cowardly coolies, who know as little about a camel as he does and have no intention of trying to do anything whatsoever for their pay, that the poor camels fail.

The water-tank theory is an unfortunate one. Certainly a

camel can go for seven days without water when properly cared for, but he ought to be watered once a day whenever possible and stinted in this respect only in extreme emergency. There are pouches in his stomach, and they are frequently, after death, found to contain fluid; but that they are reservoirs pure and simple is doubtful; and it is very certain that the parched traveller who has to cut open his dying camel and obtain its accumulated stores of water, will thus procure only a very little fluid, of a temperature of about 90° Fahr., a mawkish sub-acid flavour, and an unpleasant odour. It is evident that the time-honoured water-tank theory needs much modification, and is a dangerous one to insist on as a guide to practice during campaigns.

As a matter of fact, the active and special services of camels in war and peace have been most extensive and valuable. That they have been associated with enormous losses is due to our ignorance and mismanagement, and is decidedly not the camel's fault. In Afghanistan, the Punjab, Sind, and Beluchistan; in Abyssinia, Egypt, and the Soudan, the camel has been essential to success of the operations; and it is certain that when we need to fight in China, Central Asia, Western Asia, Arabia, and North Africa, the services of this extremely valuable baggage animal will be again called for. The camel is, I believe, under a cloud now in official estimation, but, like the Royal Marines, he has done good service on many an occasion, and is always ready to do it again and sure to turn up when there is hard work going. Although the camel spits and grumbles when being loaded, though he makes unpleasant noises in the camp at night, and though he is generally considered unlovely in the extreme—and certainly no European nose can appreciate his odour—these unpleasant habits and conditions are to my mind more than redeemed by the undaunted and plucky manner in which he plods on with his load until he actually falls dead, by the stolid manner in which he remains quiet after a mortal wound until he rolls over on his side to die, and by the way in which he steadily plods on mile after mile under his heavy load until the halt is called, even for a march of considerably more than regulation length.

The peace services of the camel are not less meritorious than his war services. His function as ship of the desert is gradually being taken away from him by the spread of railways, as in Rajputana, Scind, Central Asia, and Egypt, and we have historical evidence that his range has been limited to an extent since the time when the westward and eastward waves of the Mussulman invasion extended from Spain in the West to Southern India and China in the East. A few representatives remain in Spain, very few in Mysore, and in Europe practically the only camels are the stunted race of Pisa, which seems to have been introduced somewhat recently from Tripoli. I believe there are camels in Constantinople and European Turkey; I observe that General Gordon writes of them in Turkey. I noticed recently in the Royal Dublin Society's Museum a sowari camel on a real and antique Irish harp as its prominent decoration: how it came there I cannot surmise!

I have somehow arrived at the impression that in Asiatic Russia, and in the Caspian region and Crimea especially, of European Russia, the range of the two-humped camel is becoming restricted by railway development. Expansion of range is taking place in the Southern States of America, where imported camels have done well and are multiplying rapidly, and in Australia, whither they have been imported from India, and where have been established breeding stations. It is considered that the camel will prove specially valuable in opening up Central Australia. In Mongolia, Western China, the Central Asian Desert, the Khanates, Afghanistan, Beluchistan, Persia, Asia Minor, Arabia, and the whole desert area of Northern and Central Africa the camel reigns supreme as a means of transport for goods and travellers. Tradition has it that the camel invaded Africa by way of the Isthmus of Suez; he has invaded America and Australia by sea.

It is reasonably surmised that the camel is decreasing in numbers; one of the Caliphs, for example, is credited with assembling 120,000 camels for a journey to Mecca. Here we are face to face with one of those difficulties constantly appearing before naturalists. Some allowance must be made for oriental exaggeration in the actual statement of numbers, and for unintentional multiplication in quality and quantity by *laudatores temporis acti*, people who systematically run down the present in comparison with the past. The two-humped or Bactrian camel is much less frequent than the true dromedary or one-humped species. Palgrave, the celebrated traveller, is responsible for introducing serious confusion between the terms dromedary and camel. He has tried to restrict the former to the hygeen or running camel, known to us as sowari, and to make it out to be a distinct breed. This is not correct. The fact of the case is, that wheresoever camels are freely used and bred there are found well-bred light animals suited for sowari, and heavier, coarser-bred individuals suited for baggage duties. According to the requirements of the locality the former or the latter predominate. There are very many local *varieties* of the camel, but only two species *(a)* the Southern, Arabian, one-humped camel, or true dromedary, and *(b)* the Northern, Bactrian, two-humped, or "true" camel. Where the two meet is the line of the Euphrates and Tigris; a few Bactrians have passed into Arabia, and I believe the two-humped camel is the one which has been imported into North America by the United States Government. In Northern Persia and Afghan-Turkestan the two species are found, and sometimes they cross and produce a hybrid. It is the one-humped camel which has invaded Australia, that of Bikanir in Rajputana, which shares with Jessalmir the honour of being the best places in India for camels. The Bactrian camel is very tolerant of cold, he works across snow on the Steppes, and is said to eat snow when he becomes thirsty; the dromedary is intolerant of cold, but will stand a remarkable amount of heat. Moisture in the air is probably the condition of climate of which the camel is least tolerant. No animal will travel better over sand, for which the peculiar structure of the foot, the deliberate action, and the length of limb well suit him; mountainous passes are trying only to plain camels; even deep rivers with sandy bottoms can be forded by this animal, but a clay bottom and slippery soil proves very trying to him, especially under a heavy load; and deep ditches or cracks in the soil prove serious impediments, because camels cannot do much in the way of jumping, except occasionally performing some awkward and grotesque gambols.

One great desideratum in a transport animal is that he be capable of use in various ways; the camel can hardly be considered very inferior in this respect. Besides sowari and pack work he carries small guns or will drag larger ones; he is used in high, peculiar, double-storey carriages (in the Punjab for example). General Gordon writes that camels are used for ploughing in Turkey, and that they make excellent tramway animals! The products of camels are most useful—fuel, milk, excellent hair for shawls, cloths, and various fabrics, both coarse and fine, are obtained from the living animal; flesh-food, leather, bones, and various other useful substances from the dead. No part of the dead camel should go to waste. In camel countries these animals are used to afford amusement by combats, running races, or are trained to special performances, such as dancing. The adaptations of the camel to the desert which is its home are numerous and evident. Among others they are his height giving wide range of vision; his length of neck enabling him to reach far on either side of the track to the shrubs suited as food; ears very small, and nostrils capable of closure to keep out the sand; eyes prominent and protected by an overhanging upper lid, limiting vision upwards and guarding from too powerful rays of the sun; his horny pads to rest on when he lies in the hot sand; his peculiarly cushioned feet; his hump or reserve store of nutriment; his water reservoirs in connection with the stomach; his patient, plodding habits. It is a great mistake to consider the camel ugly. "Handsome is who handsome does" applies well in this case; but it is universally admitted that though a mangey dromedary in a show or transport lines is not handsome, a well kept camel in his native place is not ugly but quite the reverse! In the loneliness of the desert travellers recognise the camel and his movements not only as suitable but sometimes as graceful, and even grand. We have this opinion in many well-known works of travel. It is well worth the while of any of my hearers who has not looked into the eye of a camel, to do so on the earliest possible occasion ; I particularly admire its rich colour, its large size and clearness, and the stern aspect produced by the overhanging brow. Camels are much blamed for objecting to their packs being put on, but they are as a rule fully justified in doing so, for the loads are (as they have almost invariably been found in the past) uncomfortable in the extreme, not unfrequently absolutely cruel. The peculiar arrangement of the camel's teeth makes his bite very formidable, and gives him a specially ferocious expression. He alone of ruminants has incisor teeth in the upper jaw, but in many other respects he is an aberrant ruminant, many of his anatomical details more resembling those of the horse than of the ox.

Here I am in a position (through the kindness of Mr. W. Home, of Jodhpore, and Mr. Phipson) to exhibit a most remarkable specimen—a horn taken from the forehead of an Indian camel. This may be a simple keratoid tumour accidentally occurring in this situation, but it gives scope for the general conclusion that the camel may, very occasionally, be found with a horn, indicating his zoological affinities with other ruminants. This will not seem very far-fetched if we remember the undoubted fact that horses occasionally have frontal horns. The shape of skull of both horse and camel is such as would lead the zoologist at once from it to conclude that the animal was hornless. Even in cattle and sheep, when the temporal fossæ become very large, the horns are shed by a species of natural amputation. Charles Steel records having observed in Afghanistan that the Bactrian camels sometimes have an extra rudimentary toe, and so are specially sure-footed.

The hump of the camel resembles that of the ox in structure, but is much less muscular. The one-humped camel has a rudimentary second hump, so that this distinction is not so very considerable after all. In camels low in condition the hump almost disappears, the animals are described as "living on their humps."

Finally, I trust I have succeeded in establishing to the satisfaction of my hearers that the camel has been much and undeservedly maligned by Europeans, and that the Arab's estimate of him is more just and in accordance with the services he has rendered to mankind in the past and continues to render in the present. I can honestly say that my personal and professional contact with the camel in the course of journeys, on the line of march, in camp, and in cantonments, has impressed me with a high sense of the value of these long-suffering and most useful animals.

CHAPTER I.—THE CAMEL AS AN ANIMAL OF TRANSPORT.

There is a tendency among Europeans to despise Camels and to ignore the important services which they have rendered us in our wars in the East. Some few observers have, in the interests of Military Service, given the Camel special attention; others have somewhat studied its diseases, and it has been found that under suitable circumstances and conditions the camel proves the most useful of Transport animals, but under unfavourable surrounding influences he is the most unsatisfactory beast of burden with which we have to deal. Though he is unsavory, unlovely in body and mind, and considered very liable to disease, yet Mahomed has written "The Almighty has created nothing as an animal preferable to the Camel" and Daumas, in his work on the Horses of the Sahara, quotes the Arab aphorism

"Horses for a dispute,
Oxen for poverty,
Camels for the desert."

And shows that, apart from his services as the "Ship of the Desert," the Camel affords in his *fleece* material for making tents, ropes, and clothes; in his *skin* leather for shoes and saddles; in the *milk* a nutritive food and pleasing drink especially valued as a very nourishing food for foals*; in his *dung* a useful fuel; and in his *flesh* a valuable meat food, the hump being a great delicacy; similar uses of the animal are made in Turkestan, where a sucking camel is highly prized and occasionally indulged in by the rich—but the camel is too valuable to the Arab to be utilized in these ways unless he be sick or incurably injured. We must accept M. Vallon's conclusion that "his good and bad qualities render him essentially *the* Transport Animal of the desert. This

* "In the autumn season with good milking the female camel will yield 2 or 3 Shtoffs (square bottles containing about 1/10 part of a bucket-ful) in the 24 hours, but she will not give more than 60 pailsful in the whole year" (Kostenko).

has been amply proved in several ways. Recently Giles found that in crossing the Central Australian desert camels "travelled splendidly"; Napoleon in his Egyptian Campaign of 1798-9 raised a Camel Corps in Egypt which did excellent service against the Arabs; and (the best proof of the suitability of any animal for army transport purposes) there are numerous parts of the world in which camels supersede all other animals used in ordinary trade—such places are unsuited for draught work, deficient in water supply, and, as a rule, level and sandy, but there are varieties of the camel which are used in uplands and even in mountainous countries such as Afghanistan and the Tell in Algeria. Central Asia, the desert of North Africa, Turkish Arabia, Asia Minor, the western parts of China, and Scinde are the centres of distribution of the camel. The Afghan Campaigns have thrown much light on the varieties available for use in operations on the North-Western Frontier of India, some of the conclusions from the observations of different writers may possibly prove useful for reference in future emergencies :—

1. *Afghan Camels,* as obtained from the Kabuli traders of Northern Afghanistan, are small in consequence of the shortness of their stout, large-jointed limbs but remarkably robust—with wide chests, strong loins and quarters, long fleeces almost black, and sleek soft skins. They may be obtained from Ghilzai traders, also from Koochees or pastoral nomads. They are good climbers, stand cold well, hardy, and capable of living on herbage only. They are very tractable being accustomed to travel in flocks and without nose ropes. They are devoid of odour (except the must male), and did excellent service in the Kuram Valley (Oliphant).

2. *Paharí or Hill Camels* have enormous hind extremities and are very hardy. Some of them used in the Kuram Valley were Jowakís, the property of the Afridis, being big, bulky animals, of a light colour varying from brown to a fawn tint (sometimes almost white). They were taken up among the hills during the hot weather and marched in the cool of the evening or at night (Oliphant).

3. *The Bactrian Camel* (with two humps) is seldom seen in India. It is found in Oran (Algeria), Asia Minor, and the Crimea —and can be crossed with either of the one humped varieties, which are correctly speaking Dromedaries. A few Bactrian

Fig. 1. The ONE-HUMPED CAMEL in full coat and condition.

Fig. 2. The Bactrian or TWO-HUMPED CAMEL in good condition.

LITHOG. BY ALEX. BAKREN, FOR LAWRENCE ASYLUM PRESS, MADRAS

Camels are kept in Southern Asia Minor to be crossed with Arabian Dromedaries, the product constituting the most useful form for this part of the world (Anderson) and cross-bred animals are said to be preferred by the Arabs as having much vigour of constitution. It is said that if the dam be a dromedary and the sire a camel the progeny works well in a cold climate, but if the dam be a camel the offspring is ill-tempered and intractable. This conclusion has not been proved.*

4. *The Scindí Camel* is a large animal with well developed, in fact enormous, forehand, noble looking, with short fine coat, but extremely susceptible to climatic changes, being very much affected by cold and not hardy. His long limbs suit for journeys over sandy plains and he can do much work in a dry land under a hot sun but the mortality of animals of this variety in Afghanistan, especially with the Candahar Force, was enormous, few of any other kind were used in South Afghanistan (C. Steel).

5. *Punjabí Camels* are very similar to those found in Scinde. The best are procurable West of Jhelum and the kind known as Bajrí found near Hissar is especially good. Camels fit for transport used to be procurable in serviceable numbers on the North Western Frontier but few can be obtained there now. In the Punjâb desert camels known as " Bár-ke-unt" are found but they are of inferior quality (Yaldwin). "The Camels of the Punjâb are much more surefooted than those of the lower parts of the Bengal Presidency and, if moderately loaded, will travel in very rainy weather over slippery clay soil quite as well as horses" (Meyrick). The information given recently about camels in the Punjab District by V. S. Nunn is of great value. He shows that Shahpur is the great camel breeding ground of the Punjab, both in the Bar and Thall are found large fine animals with light hair, and the breeding of which is denoted by a depression between the nasal and frontal bones. These are available in large numbers, they carry salt from the mines and the males are let out by their owners in strings to merchants but the females, are kept at work near home with a view to their utilization for breeding. The Thull Camels are used for pack, any required for riding purposes are imported from Jesselmeer and Bikaneer; Stud Animals, also

*The two humped species is almost the only one seen in Mongolia (Prjevàlski).

are imported. In Montgomery are found three kinds; *Sohává*, brown, with long lips, medium sized head and thick skin; *Ganda*, grey, with large head, small mouth, and thin skin; (the best variety); Hazára, red, with a very small tail (the worst variety); *Bagga*, white; and *Ratta*, red or bay; these two latter are inferior. Here, also, Sowarí Camels are imported from Bikaneer and Jesselmeer. In the Hazara districts are few camels and these have come into use since the British occupation led to making of roads. A few are bred in the District, but most, called "Beloochies," are imported from Kalabagh on the Indus in Bannoo. They are large, thick-set animals with long dark hair and probably come from Afghanistan.

6. *Bikaneer Camels* come from Rajpootana, those of Bagrí and Harotiya being considered especially good. Like those of Punjâb and Scinde these camels suffer much from cold. Rajpootana supplied the camels used in the Siege of Delhi.

7. Some *Camels are bred in the North-West Provinces and Oudh* but are not of much value for transport purposes. Those from Thull, near Bahawalpore are useless, meanspirited beasts, although to all appearance very fine. They are called by the natives *Taloocher* and do not make good baggage animals.

8. *Persian Camels* resemble those already described as Paharee or Hill Camels. Col. Stewart (Lecture before Royal Geographical Society, Proceedings, September 1881) notices the *Seistan Camels* ridden by Beloochí marauders of the Persian frontier. These camels are remarkable for their speed. "They can go 70 or even 80 miles a day, carrying one and sometimes two men and a little food" * * * * These camels require water every other day and can on a push last three days without water; they "find enough grazing in the less arid spots of the desert to support life, assisted by a little food supplied by their owners in the form of barley meal mixed with just enough water to make a paste. A camel can exist in this way for a few weeks only while the foray lasts." The Beloochis generally water their camels at lonely springs in the desert every second day. (*Marvin's Reconnoitering Central Asia*).

Dunlop Anderson tells us that Camels are not numerous in the Northern parts of Asia Minor where the dense forests and generally clayey soil cause the mud to remain long on the ground, making travel dangerous to these animals. The Camels of Turkish Arabia are very good and as procured in Mesopotamia cost between seven and eight pounds sterling each. A number of Arab Camels were carried to the Crimea in 1854 and they *all* died without being able to do any work in the cold climate. The two humped variety is used in waggons and under pack by the natives of the Crimea. This, known as the *Tuya*, is the most common camel of Turkestan. Col. Hamley mentions them as "especially fine animals; large, well fed, sagacious looking and covered with smooth brown hair, very different from the gaunt mangy dromedaries of Barbary." Burnaby, in his "Ride to Khiva," contrasts with the huge sleek ships of the African Sahara or the Libyan sands the "undersized shaggy camels with lionlike manes, provided by nature with every requisite for resisting a bitterly cold climate, which can stride through snow four feet deep where horses would not be of any avail," as found on the Steppes of Kirghiz.

The Russians in their invasion of the Turkoman Country captured 1,200 camels in one day from the Akhal Tekkes, and utilized them in carriage of ammunition boxes and water casks; they lost fully as many in the Tekke country as we did in Afghanistan. In Mongolia the best camels are bred among the Khalkas; "the stubborn camel becomes the Mongol's docile carrier" (Prejevalsky). The Tartars use the camel very extensively for trade purposes in the Mantchu country (Fleming), and the earliest known work on the diseases of the camel is in the Chinese Language. Col. Malleson, in his work on "Herat," tells us that "Andhko (in Afghan Turkestan) is a relic of the past. Less than a century ago it possessed camels of a very remarkable breed called Nér, distinguished by abundant hair streaming down from neck and breast, a slim slender figure, and extraordinary strength. This rare breed of camels is fast disappearing." It is sometimes still seen in Turkestan, but only in the south, as it endures frost badly; at Tashkand a camel costs about 6 guineas.

Kostenko tells us that during the Khivan Campaign of 1839-40 more than 10,000 camels were procured for the Russian detachment at 10 Roubles (£1¼) apiece, and that for the Khivan Expedition of 1873, 8,800 camels were equiped for the Turkestan detachment alone, and to these another thousand had soon to be added. The Kizil Kum Kirghiz furnished most of these animals; but some hundreds were sent by the Amir of Bokhara.

The contract method of Camel Transport has proved to be the best in Russian experience, but General Ivanin advocated a permanent Camel Train as more secret and as affording also the requisite number of camel men (Lautchís). However a Committee decided that this arrangement would be too expensive. The French keep up permanent camel train of 500 animals with drivers in Laghouat, the most southernly post of Algeria, which suffices for a flying column available for quelling insurrections.

Prior to the Khivan expedition the requisition system was brought into play by the Russian military authorities in all Steppe Campaigns; the camels thus obtained were paid for at so much per head, at rates determined by Local Administration, and the natives were expected to provide one man for every seven camels. But the worst and weakest camels were supplied and the poorest men who had never owned a camel and were, therefore, ignorant and devoid of interest in their charges were sent as Drivers causing great difficulties in the way of transport and much loss of camel life.

The Turkestan Detachment in the Khivan Expedition (1873) obtained camels by requisition and had no little trouble; the Orenburg Detachment by contract transport and did well. The latter system was expensive, but expense is a secondary consideration in war (*Journal United Service Institution of India, XII. No. 56*).

M. Vallon found two varieties of Dromedaries in common use in Algeria, (1) a small and active kind, used for riding across the desert (such as we, in India, would term the sowarí), and (2) a large strong beast found especially in the plains, suitable for heavy pack work. Some of our most valuable information about the Camel in health and disease has been obtained from the Veterinary Officers of the French Army of Algeria. This has been recently, to an extent, supplemented by experience gained in Egypt and the Soudan by British Veterinary Officers. I. V. S. Walters has confirmed the value of the Sinde Camel, as obtainable through Karachi, for desert warfare; the camels from Aden and Berber were very serviceable but less powerful, those from the Nile Delta were quite unsuited for work in the Desert.

From perusal of the above details as to varieties of the Camel

LITHOG. FOR LAWRENCE ASYLUM PRESS, MADRAS. BY ALEX: BARREN.

the reader will conclude that *there is scope for the exercise of judgment in selection of the best breed of Camels in accordance with the probable field of military operations*—and that many of the failures of camels as Animals of Transport depend on a want of care in choice of the best variety. The mortality in Afghanistan was notoriously among the large desert camels such as were brought up from Scind and the Punjab, they were overcome by cold and mountain work which the Paharees were exposed to with impunity; again in the Crimea the local two humped variety worked and thrived while the exotic Arabian Camel died, whereas had the field of operations been Egypt or the Sahara the Crimean Camels would have died and the African Dromedaries done good work! The valuable rule, to use the trade animals of the country, was not entirely adhered to either in Afghanistan or the Crimea. The French have learned the same lesson when trying to use the hill camel of the Tell in the plains of Algeria, and the Russians found the Kirghiz Camel unsuited for the Turcoman desert country. Further, *the Camel is an animal which Europeans do not understand*; a state of affairs most uncreditable but undeniable. I. V. S. Oliphant and Lieutenant Martin, R. E., in their notes on the Kuram Valley Operations, have forcibly brought this fact under our notice; V. S. C. Steel in Southern Afghanistan and M. Vallon in Algeria noted the same fact. Also, *the Camel as an Animal of Transport is seldom properly cared for*, because he is disliked on account of his want of sociability, his ugliness, his strange habits, and his unpleasant odour. He is despised as fit only to be managed by natives. He is not understood either in health or disease, for which we have no excuse, as the opportunities of observation are ample, we have some literature on the subject available for our information, and our knowledge of the management of other ruminants in health and disease is so advanced as to warrant us in applying it to the Camel rather than trust him to the tender and uncontrolled mercies of the Serwan and Native Camel Doctor. We cannot subscribe to an opinion which has been recently published "that the safest course for a Veterinary Surgeon with a sick camel is either to leave him alone or to allow the natives to treat him in their own way which is often effectual, although apparently brutal," without its qualification that these courses are to be resorted to only when the Veterinary Surgeon "does not see clearly the proper way to treat the sick camel," in other words, does not know his business! With such a peculiar animal as the Elephant the qualified practitioner may plead some want of special knowledge, but his science ought to render him competent to deal with a sick camel with more prospects of success than an ignorant and superstitious native driver can possibly have! It is not fair to urge that the camel is unfit for use in Army Transport on active service because he has succumbed to bad management in countries unsuited by geography and climate for him; nor that we are unacquainted with his management although we have much information accessible; nor that we dislike and despise him. These arguments are more than counterbalanced by the facts that in some countries the camel is, under intelligent and sympathising appreciative management, the most reliable animal for Transport in War and Trade.

We must now *treat seriatim the qualities of the camel which affect his value for Army Transport*:—(1). He is patient and enduring, remarkably tolerant of thirst and of exposure to the heat of the sun. He is a very easy animal to feed under the emergencies of a campaign for he will put up with all sorts of food unsuited to other herbivora and "he alone can nourish himself with hard prickly plants like cactus leaves" (Vallon). (2). He is docile under proper management but most intractable and obstinate when handled unskilfully or imposed upon by a too heavy load. We very frequently hear such expressions as "a camel is never in a good humour," which probably arise from the remarkable expression of the animal and the pliability of feature which the camel exhibits certainly to a greater degree than any other herbivore. We are unprepared for this in a vegetable feeder, we do not anticipate seeing sharp teeth in the front of the upper jaw which are fully exposed by the opening of the cleft in the upper lip. When we look at the sharp fangs, the split lip, the long downward bent muzzle, and the narrow nostrils of this animal our preconceived ideas of what a beast of burden should be receive a shock, and we conceive a dislike to the camel and call him unlovely; we hate his gawky limbs and ungainly gait. His skin pads look as though they were disease. As horsemen we object to his long, narrow, ewe neck and the dispropor-

BY ALEX: BARREN.

LITHOG: FOR LAWRENCE ASYLUM PRESS, MADRAS,

tion which is generally observable between his fore limbs and his hind. We look upon him as a "washy" brute, and we say of an ugly useless horse that he is "like a camel." But in our narrow-mindedness we are apt to forget that the very qualities and points we as "horsemen" object to, as "camel-men" we might have reason to admire and find of value. The narrow nostril, which the animal can close at will, excludes sand and prevents rapid evaporation from the Schneiderian membrane during the journey through deserts, thus increasing the tolerance of the animal for dust-storms and journeys through a parching atmosphere. The split lip, long ewe neck, downward bent muzzle, and sharp teeth adapt the camel to obtaining nourishment where a horse or ox would starve and from substances unsuited to ordinary herbivores, and they enable him to grasp and retain food stuffs while he continues on the march, in a manner eminently conducive to the support of his "staying" powers. His long limbs and his foot-pads adapt him for travelling over sand with an easy and long stride as well as for traversing rivers with sandy bottoms; indeed it is found of advantage in dealing with such an impediment to the progress of an army as the latter to send the camels over first, in order that they may consolidate the sand and thus render it easier for draught (Wolseley). When we look carefully at the body of the Camel we remark that for a ruminant he has a remarkably small belly and a very equine chest, that is to say he has some of the endurance of the ruminant combined with some of the excellent respiratory capacity for which the horse is pre-eminent and at the same time the upward arch of the spine and the flatness of the sides are points which we like to see in a pack animal. The skin pads indicate, and probably (by evolution) result from, the useful habits of camels lying down to receive their loads and assuming the recumbent posture without removal of the load during halts, the former tending to our convenience and the latter to the animal's powers of endurance. What we are at first sight apt to consider unsightly features, thus, examined from a utilitarian point of view, are found to be beauties. (3) Although the camel is peculiar in his likes and dislikes, this may be so met by a knowledge of his habits as to prove no detriment to his value. The French found in Algeria that "he easily becomes used to Europeans" and our soldiers have recently managed him very fairly in the Soudan, but Galton urges that men attach themselves to horses and asses, less to mules and oxen, but camels are never made friends of. However, it is, on the contrary, a matter of every day experience in India that many Serwans are very kind to and careful of their camels and the latter know their own attendants and are tolerant of them, which is the cameline way of showing pleasure and affection. It has been urged that camels require skilled attendants, but what animals do not? Let it be remembered that before the mules could be utilized in Abyssinia specially trained Indian muleteers had to be sent, and the bullock batteries often remained useless during the Mutiny in the hands of British drivers whom the bullocks would not obey. Galton gives a piece of information which ought to be remembered in convoy duty, "mules and camels must never be taken together—they have mutual aversion which time will seldom, if ever, overcome" but all animals have their pet aversions, which little peculiarities must be respected and will be overcome in time; it is not often that the one under consideration will prove a serious inconvenience. Camels are quarrelsome and apt to bite one another offensively or defensively. They are amorous and the males should not, therefore, be worked with the females, however this rule only holds during the time of *rutting* or *must*—when the animal is apt to yield to irresistable charms of the female and bolt, forgetful of load or rider. With regard to vice, occasionally the camel indulges in a far-reaching and very forcible kick and some are apt to lie down suddenly "without forewarning motion" in the manner facetiously described by Burnaby, who, however, is very far from the mark in saying "It should be well understood that the camel, far from being the hardy convoy carrier as stated in the stories of our youth, is a very delicate tender beast of burden only calculated to perform a certain amount of work at a very slow pace, not suited to accompany any army." This paragraph is contradictory to a previously quoted statement of the writer and is misleading and inaccurate both in sentiment and expression. (4) *The camel is a hardy animal*—certainly in the endurance of privations, and we have no evidence that he is specially obnoxious or non-resistent to disease. Vallon found that "Although camels do not appear susceptible of easily taking the acute diseases which decimate Equidæ, nevertheless the fatigues of expeditions cause a great loss of them." Although we have had ample proof of this we must remember that there has never been a campaign in which camels have been placed under competent and experienced veterinary management or indeed experienced European supervision of any kind (except, perhaps, the recent Suakin Camel Corps, which had little trial of service)—and no animal could withstand such mismanagement and perversion of its natural habits as the camel on service is generally subjected to. It was remarked in Afghanistan that the officers' baggage camels and those under regimental charge and so receiving special care and attention seldom died; and I. V. S. Meyrick records his opinion, based on considerable experience, that camels when well fed, rationally worked, and properly tended seldom suffer from disease. That a camel when reported as diseased usually dies, even under the care of a veterinary surgeon, is an indubitable fact, but he is seldom so reported until the serwan has exhausted his list of nostrums and the animal, as being in a state of collapse, is quite unable to go a step farther on his journey. Thus skilled medicine very seldom gets a fair chance and the camel is described as incapable of withstanding disease whereas, in fact, he fights against it with such pluck as to work until he drops, while the ignorant, careless, or wilfully neglectful camel-man does not observe or report that anything is wrong.

(5) *The Camel is capable of carrying loads which are heavy, and most awkward to convey on other animals (often even in carts),* such as tents, tent-poles, scaling-ladders, and pontoons; and also ammunition trunks and capacious medicine chests are carried by him with facility. 400 lbs. is a fair average weight for a well laden camel, about equivalent to that carried by two mules. The regulation load in India is 5 maunds; Yaldwin estimates 4-8 maunds as the carrying power; Tassy puts 330—660 lbs. as the weight of load for a large Algerian camel, and 220—330 lbs. for the small running camel of the Sahara. Galton estimates the *net* carrying weight for a camel at 300 lbs. which may be considered reasonable as some allowance must be made for weight of trappings, also for the exigencies of service and the difficulties of the road. Martin tells us that the large Bactrian will often carry 10 maunds —but the "Handbook for Field Service" is most misleading in

estimating as a camel load 4 cwt. (448 lbs.) for a long march to be increased up to 9 or 10 cwt. for a shorter one—for a four or five year old animal. It is contrary to regulation to purchase a camel under 6 years of age, be it remembered for the information of the authors. The Turcoman camel seems to be a valuable weight carrier; Burnaby found that "although a strong beast will carry 800 lbs. day after day for a short journey, he very soon breaks down if you should increase the march. Even with so *light* a load as 400 lbs. I had great difficulty in making 16 miles per diem," and Potto in his "History of the Steppe Campaigns" says that the load, should be limited to 700 lbs.—which is to be diminished in spring, when the animals are changing their coats, and increased when there is plenty of forage and no great speed required, to 800 or 880 lbs. which is about what is carried in traders' caravans. "In the case of trade caravans the load is a fixed one amounting to 16 *puds* (lbs. 576), or for the one humped Khivan camel (*nar* or dromedary) as much as 18 *puds* (lbs. 648). During the movement of troops the several loads are reduced to 12 *puds* (lbs. 432)" (Kostenko). The ordinary camel load of the Arabs is about 550 lbs. (2 *tellis* of wheat).

(6) *The camel, although a slow and deliberate worker, can traverse much ground daily and keep up with an army.* His average rate of marching is 2 miles per hour, and varies from 3 miles on a good road to 1 mile per hour in a close country. This rate of progress can, if the animal be allowed to browse as he walks, be sustained in case of emergency for 10 or 12 hours—a march of 17 or 20 miles *per diem* is not too much for a reasonably-loaded, well-fed camel but it must be remembered that as a rule after arrival at the halting place these animals have to collect their own fodder.* Halts during the day's march are a mistake, they are not required for camels and the animal is only the longer kept under the load and the arrival in camp delayed. On the other hand camels must not be hurried—the nose rope should be kept neither slack nor too tight to prevent browsing. The camel of the desert travels, at his fastest, 5 miles per hour for 8 to 10 hours per diem (Warren). The French found that the large Algerian Camel will do 25 miles (40 kmrs.) as a maximum daily journey, whereas

* Pringle advocates halting for two days per week when marching with camels to give them grazing (Report in No. 13 of Q. J. V. S. in India).

the small Saharan running camel will do (80—100 kmrs.) 50—65 miles per diem. Young camels scarcely yield to horses in the quickness of their gallop. Kostenko puts the rate of a camel's trot at 6⅔ mile per hour; Daumas says "If not overdriven the camel can go from dawn to sunset, if allowed to pluck herbage from the roadside as it passes, it will cover 10—12 leagues (24—29 miles) in 24 hours and every fifth day must be permitted to rest." When used with caravans 20⅓—26⅔ miles is the length of the average stage. The ordinary Kirghiz summer daily move amounts to 16⅔ miles (Kostenko). We may agree with Leach in his estimate that 12 to 15 miles per diem is the proper distance for camels on service to march. Martin's estimate 17 to 20 miles can apply only when traversing level sandy country. Thus the camel is the slowest paced animal we ordinarily use for transport and so should be taken neither on flying columns nor on long imperfectly protected lines of communication with a rapidly moving front, but he is eminently useful as a pack animal with an army advancing slowly and securing its lines of communication carefully.

(7) *Camel convoys are capable of long daily marches, and, considering the weight carried, they comprise few attendants and occupy a small space.* 500 camels in Indian file occupy one mile whereas mules or ponies carrying the same load would occupy two miles; also 2,500 maunds carried by camels in lieu of ponies lessens the number of attendants by 293 (Yaldwin). These are most important considerations as indicating:—(*a*) A marked reduction in the number of noncombatants to be protected, fed, and carried when sick and wounded. (*b*) Also in the number of combatants to be diverted from work at the front to protect the convoy. Some camels, as those from the hills of Afghanistan, will work in a drove, but this, however advantageous for protection, is generally inadmissible in a convoy and the ordinary method of having the camels in strings of three, the nose ropes of the second and third being attached to the tail or saddle of the first and second respectively, is found to be best. It is well when opportunity offers to march on a broad front when the country traversed is hostile, but the drivers prefer to go in long train and will take up this formation unless made to arrange themselves otherwise. It is remarkable that the French in Algeria consider that for the general purposes of army progress the camel is the "swiftest by

far of our draught animals and that even while picking up nourishment by the way he can go as fast as most of our pack animals." This, of course, refers to progress over sand or loose ground where the elastic cushion-like feet of the camel stand him in good stead. Ordinarily on the march in India when the semi-dry sandy bed of a river has to be traversed the camels come into Camp first (elephants always excepted) and the bullock carts last; but where there is no impediment of this kind the mules arrive in camp first and the camels last.

(8) *The most serious drawback to use of the camel in Army Transport is his want of versatility*—in that he is essentially a pack animal, suited for certain climatic and geographical ranges only, and working at a disadvantage except on certain kinds of roads. (*a*) We have shown that the Camel can carry an enormous pack-load for a considerable distance; he can carry small guns, such as the gatlings suggested by Col. Maxwell and those used in the Aden Battery. Lieut. Elliott of the 3rd Bengal Cavalry, in a paper published in the *Journal of United Service Institution of India*, mentions some occasions on which Camels were utilized in war emergencies for purposes other than Transport. "In 1842-3, Sir Chas. Napier mounted a Company of 13th Light Infantry on Camels, each soldier being seated behind a native Camel driver. In the mutiny of 1857 and for some time subsequently two Camel Corps were organized, one Company from the Rifle Brigade and another from the 92nd Highlanders. At the battle of Calpi, in May 1858, the Rifle Brigade was brought up opportunely on Camels to relieve the hard pressed line." The Punjab Frontier Force, Guides, and Hyderabad Contingent, as well as many of the Native Armies, have Camel Sowars attached in the present day, mainly for use as swift orderlies. The camel is used extensively in Arabia similarly, indeed the running camel of the desert is very different from the slow beast of burden, and has sometimes, in the conveyance of despatches, done good service in covering a wonderful distance of desert in a very short space of time. In some parts of India camels are used in carts for draught work but for this their habits, slow pace, and figure render them thoroughly unsuited. Kostenko, however, tells us "The Kirghiz often harness this animal to their carts, the shafts of which are attached to cords fastened to the foremost humps.

When so made use of the Camel will draw a weight of 720 lbs. and this as an ordinary rule; when harnessed to a properly constructed cart a Camel can easily draw from 1800—2160 lbs. weight."

The camel then is essentially a pack animal, but in emergencies of hunger or thirst he has been slaughtered to afford flesh or fluid for men—in the latter respect he is entirely special, and probably there is much exaggeration in the stories we read of Camels slaughtered in the desert saving their owners' lives by the supply of water from the pouches of the stomach. The camel, it may be concluded, is not, like the mule or ox, available for draught as well as pack—he is not, to express the matter roughly, "such a good animal all round" for Transport. (*b*) Nor can he withstand vicissitudes of climates and stress of bad weather, or change of country, so well as most other Transport animals. No doubt this is largely due to a want of precautions in transferring camels from one climate to another and in taking proper care of them, still it cannot be doubted that the adaptibility of the camel to changes of climate is slight—all our evidence goes to support this view. The Arabs find that much care and experience is necessary in camel management "after 15th April they are not sent out to feed until the afternoon because it has been remarked that the grass is covered with a sort of dew that lays the foundation of fatal diseases" (Daumas). Also they are prevented eating what remains in the morning of the small quantity of grass given to the horses over-night. Throughout the whole winter, the end of autumn, and the beginning of spring they may be permitted with advantage to browse on shrubs with a salt flavour, but in the beginning of April and at the end of May they must not be allowed to do so for more than 5 or 6 days. The Arabs of Tell take their dromedaries into the interior annually at the approach of the winter months and they annually give them a turn at the Salt Lakes (Letang). The Camels of Turkistan moult in the beginning of the spring, hair remaining only on the head, lower part of neck, and thighs; leathern jhools are then put on them. In summer jhools are found absolutely necessary to protect from gad-flies. The country along the central and lower course of the Sir, and even at the mouth of the Amu, is so infested with these pests that cattle simply cannot exist there in the summer season (Kostenko). In June the camels sweat on the neck and under the saddle, and gall easily, for the whole coat is then shed, and the animal should be sent to graze for 3 months. They generally die or remain permanently in bad condition if worked in the summer months (Martin).* Oliphant was informed that the natives are of opinion that Camels cannot live through a summer in the Kuram valley. In this want of adaptibility to climate the camel is inferior as an animal of Transport to the ox or the mule. (c) Different kinds of roads influence the progression of camels variously. On a level sandy road camels will travel as fast as any other animal, and they will continue at work for a greater length of time and under a hotter sun than any other Transport animal; under such circumstances the large plain Camel is the most useful but proves quite unfit to cope with the difficulties of an uphill or downhill road across a pass, which can be traversed with facility by the Paharis. Most camels are bad climbers and unsuited for journeys over undulating or mountain roads and must be given only short marches and judiciously halted to rest before the fatigues of a long ascent commence. Stony roads are an impediment to camels if the stones be rounded and liable to roll under their feet, on the other hand sharp stones are apt to injure the foot-pads. But over shingle or where stones are frequent but not large, sharp, or rounded, camels go well. Moisture impedes progress and sadly diminishes the value of the Camel Transport; it was found by the French that in the mountains and valleys of the Tell a day's rain or snow suffices to stop a whole convoy of camels. The moisture renders rock and clay slippery and falls are frequent and serious among the laden camels,† which become rapidly tired in consequence of the difficulty in keeping on their feet. Yaldwin tells us that the Bactrian Camel has a sort of claw or toe projecting beyond the pad of the foot which enables him to go over ice and snow safely. With regard to the ordinary impediments met with in travelling through those countries in which the camel is principally used, he can traverse deep fords, which

* But the Tartars of Kirghiz use them during the summer with light loads which they gradually increase as the animals regain condition.

† In passing slippery places the Serwans pass a rope round the hind legs in such a way as to allow of only short steps being taken and to prevent divergence of the limbs so abruptly as to "split the animal up," one of the most frequent accidents to camels on the march.

he does with caution, stepping very high. If he gets into a quicksand he is apt to "lose his head" and exhaust himself seriously in his struggles—but places which have a shifting sand bottom are often passable by mules, oxen, &c., only after the bottom has been hardened and rendered firm by the passage of a number of camels; when the bottom is slippery the camel is apt to get into difficulties. When the water is very low and practically the river is but a wide stretch of sand the camel traverses it with facility. Over deep wide rivers they may best be conveyed in long boats, they will kneel down transversly in a row and remain very quiet. With regard to swimming camels, it is much better to ford a river if possible. This may be attempted even when the water is 3 or 4 feet deep if the bottom be good and the current not too rapid. As even a narrow trench will absolutely check the progress of camels, it is always advisable to, as was found essential in Afghanistan (Martin), carry on the leading camels gangboards 8 ft. by 3 ft. to act as Camel-bridges; many a very vexatious and prolonged delay will thus be prevented. A camel weighs about 14 maunds with 5 maunds as load, we must, therefore, have somewhat stout boards with which to make these bridges.

(9). *The Camel is an easy animal to feed and requires only simple management while on active service to preserve him in working order,* but even this has not been granted to him in recent campaigns. Martin tells us that in the Kuram valley "a very large number of camels perished. The camel appears to have remained a comparatively neglected animal and his diet, treatment in sickness, habits, capability of marching, &c., appear to be only partially understood. When camels were attached to regiments as Regimental Transport they fared better than when on general duty. The Sepoys and Camel-men foregathered and the beasts and their drivers obtained a larger share of consideration, the officers of the regiment naturally interesting themselves in them." It is very evident that Camel Transport has never had a fair trial, for it has never been under good management, as ensurable only by adequate european supervision. It is to be anticipated that things will be much improved under the present Transport Organization for India which supplies experienced Transport Officers and Non-commissioned Officers, but, unfortunately, not in sufficient numbers.

Food.—It is extraordinary what a variety of common plants can be used by the camel as food and under what emergencies he will obtain enough to support life. Tassy urges in his favour as an animal for army transport that "the Dromedary will find nourishment where a horse or ass would starve and will during 20—30 days do 36—40 kilometers daily with only such food as he can pick up. If required to go longer a small amount of corn or a few dates will suffice." The French allow Dromedaries in Algeria a daily ration of 4½ lbs. grain while on the march; in the Crimea 9 lbs. barley meal and 12 lbs. chopped straw was given daily or in lieu of the latter 9 lbs. barley, manifestly an improper diet for a ruminant; but the results of Camel Management in the Crimea were such as to prove instructive in forewarning us against similar errors in the future.

The Regulation Diet of Transport Camels in India is:—

Conditions.	Grain lbs.	Fodder—either.			Salt.
		Dry.	Green.	Bhoosa.	
In Cantonment.	4	25 lbs.	40 lbs.	20 lbs.	One drachm.
On Command...	6	25 lbs.	40 lbs.	20 lbs.	......
At Graze ...	2	...	...	...	......
At Sea ...	3	20	...	...	One drachm (Water 8 gallons)

In Bengal 2½ annas per mensem is allowed for mussals. Provision is evidently made in the article of fodder for the substances obtainable by browsing on the road and by grazing around the Camp. Camels will remain alive and capable of a certain amount of work on the food obtained by grazing alone, but on service they have not sufficient time to procure fodder, also they require grain food, as they are doing hard work and because they arrive in camp too tired to procure their living by grazing. If a tired camel is turned out to graze he is liable to poison himself by eating everything that comes to hand, but an absolutely fatigued camel will remain hungry rather than get up and feed. However it seems that camels turned out to graze seldom pick up poisonous herbs; perhaps, also, they have an instinctive knowledge of what branches and shrubs are best suited to their state of health, as most other animals seem to have. Nunn informs us that in

Shahpur camels browse on the bushes in the Bar and get no other food. Nim and Burgot are considered very good food; Peepul and Babul are stimulant and specially suited for the cold weather. Yaldwin mentions also the following as useful fodder :—Goolur, Kateela, Phulai, Behr, Jhana, Jhari, Goolalee, Hees, Kurrul, Jawassa, Karouda, Kair-Lana, also Kusseel, Mote in any stage of ripeness, Sarson, and Tara Mera in seed, each in its season. Martin tells us that Jowasír (the Camel Thorn) and Falai (an acacia) and other acaciæ constituted the principal fodder in Afghanistan and nourished the camels well. Leach mentions Gocru and Missi as used near Roorkee during the rains. Gilchrist considers that the use of Peepul combined with Banyan leaves causes colic. "The animal can pass three days without food. But either deprivation of solid food for two days, or of liquid food for four consecutive days, greatly weakens it, and in order to prevent it perishing under such privations its load must be immediately and very materially reduced, the full weight not being re-imposed until the lapse of a week from the date of the restoration of the named necessaries" (Kostenko). It is evident that our knowledge of the fodder required for Camels is very general at present and we must rely to a great extent on the instinct of the animal in determining what is suitable and what ought to be rejected—we shall seldom, if ever, have to regret having done so. The fodder must be varied in character, and sufficient in quantity to give the bulk essential for the due performance of Rumination. We must never, as was done in the Crimea, imagine that increased amount of grain can compensate to a herbivore, especially a ruminant, for loss of its fodder. Camels maybe given *grain or pulse food* of various kinds. The Arabs object to barley as liable to bring on diarrhœa in a few days; and Yaldwin, in writing of his observations in Afghanistan, expresses his opinion that barley is a poor substitute for gram or mote. He considers a mixture of wheat flour with ghee and ghúr excellent, or barley flour may be used made up into balls with mutton fat, and urges the necessity for weekly administration of stomachic mussauls. There is reason to believe that these latter are beneficial especially for camels kept on bhoosa and other non-stimulant forms of fodder. At certain times of the year the camel men apply for Kharisk or Itch mussauls, which are of a more tonic character and also should be considered admissible to keep the animal in fair health while shedding the coat and to render superfluous the change of air which the Afghans and Arabs seem to consider absolutely essential to health. Grain should, generally, be prepared either by crushing or soaking to render it digestible, otherwise much of it escapes mastication. Even when the coolthee is prepared by soaking I have observed that much remains unutilized not nearly so much, however, as in the case of ox. Each camel in Madras carries a hide (Chursah) in which the gram is soaked and which is carried over the saddle and jhool on the march to protect them from wear.

The *General Routine of Camel Management when on the march* consists :—in unloading immediately on arrival in camp. It should be arranged, if possible, that this take place at about 8—9 A.M., so that the camels are not unnecessarily exposed to the sun and are on the move during the cold time just before and after dawn; the day's march of 12—18 miles may have been completed before nine o'clock. Then a little bhoosa should be thrown down before the animals or they may be turned loose to graze. In any case the saddle should be removed in about an hour's time. The natives have a prejudice in favour of leaving on the saddle from one end of the journey to the other, but this is a very bad plan to work on, it hides the falling off in condition of a camel which is being robbed of its grain and mussauls, it prevents our noticeing the hollowness of flank which denotes deficiency of fodder, it hides galls as caused by bad saddling and sadly aggravates them and increases their number by a part pressed upon gaining no ease; finally, it is quite enough for the camels to carry their gear while at work.

Before being brought in from grazing, at 4 P.M., they should be *watered*. Much has been written about the tolerance of thirst exhibited by the camel and his powers in this direction have been exaggerated and it has been supposed that camels of all kinds can rely on their internal accumulations of water. This is an important error to start with. Again, it seems, from Colonel Warren's observations, that if the camel "has for a month or two been employed where he can get water daily he will drink sufficient for only one day and nothing will persuade him otherwise. Consequently some camels, although true desert ones, are apt to be lost on first starting into the desert. They require to be trained to taking in a four days' supply." This is done by men pouring five or six gallons down their throats; but a Bactrian camel can only lay in and retain half this amount (Yaldwin). The Arabs say that in winter the camel never drinks (Daumas), but Charles Steel records as the opinion of an experienced Serwan that in Afghanistan during the hot weather they should be watered daily and in the winter at least every third day, and states that if deprived of water for five days the camel will die. However, Giles, in crossing Australia, found that once when he could get no water for his camels for ten days only one old cow camel died, and she succumbed just on reaching the water; he thinks that in summer the camel can go four or five days without drinking water and in winter much longer; we may conclude that camels should be watered once daily—at about 4 P.M.. They should not be allowed to drink from streams when they cross unless very hard pressed—contrary as this may seem to our general management of animals on the march there is reason in it and we must guard ourselves against the somewhat common mistake of finding fault with Serwans for not letting their camels drink.* They know very well that if the animals are watered daily it is superfluous to allow them to drink while on the journey, that there is a special natural provision for moistening the throat and retaining moisture while on the march, and, lastly, that a drink of water tends to bring on rumination and the animal becomes lazy and tries to lie down and chew the cud. The Arabs encourage tolerance of thirst on the part of the camels by never allowing them to drink until they reach a camping place. Some camels will not drink before noon —by which time the chill is taken off the water; still water is much preferred and a marked dislike of running water in cold weather is exhibited, although, according to Kostenko, the camel "will drink every kind of water, no matter how brackish, stagnant, or putrid."

After watering, the camels should have a small amount of fodder thrown down before them and be groomed. This process consists in carefully rubbing down the animal and scraping him over "with a wooden comb like a large blunt paper knife to excite the skin and to remove all dust, knots, and tangle, especially from

* Yaldwin, Journal of the United Service Institution of India, 1880, Vol. ix, No. 43.

the parts under the saddle" (Yaldwin), or, preferably, an ordinary mane comb and one of those hand gloves known in India as Copois. In hot weather (and annually in Arabia) camels are sheared,* one shear per 25 camels being allowed by Government; an allowance of oil to protect the body surface from the sun is also given.

The Camel should after grooming be carefully examined as to freedom from galls, bruises to the feet, thorns in the foot pads, or sole overworn, and other contingencies frequent on the march. This, too, is the time for careful inspection of the animals by the officer in charge or responsible for their condition; apart from the general appearance of the animal reliance must be placed on the fulness of the depressions above the eyes, plumpness of the hump, and absence of a "tucked up" look and traces of diarrhœa. The nose should be examined as to its freedom from lacerations, and the skin pads as to the absence of bruises. The animals should then be fed with their allowance of grain. The whole amount may be given as one feed, it is not sufficiently bulky nor allowed in such an amount as to cause inconvenience to a ruminant. In permanent lines mud troughs may be made for the animals to feed from but on service all camels should be formed up in one or two lines, the ration of each placed before him on the chursah and those which do not get on very well may be hand-fed; the Serwan taking a full right handful, placing his left hand on the camel's nose and throwing the grain in when the animal turns its head and opens its mouth as it will do when ready for another mouthful. All the grain having been thus given, the camels may be fastened for the night, their saddles put on, and, left with fodder before them. It is advisable to put the saddles on overnight before it gets dark, because they cause no inconvenience to the animal, if adjusted in the dark of the early morning galls would be more frequent from hasty and careless work, also loading camels is a matter of time and if the saddles be left on ready for the morrow's march the camels need be disturbed fully half an hour later than if they had to be saddled. Again, sleeping in the saddles keeps the camel warm and there is no greater enemy to the efficiency of a camel transport than cold nights and imperfect protection from rain.

* In the Punjab camels are shorn in March and give about 3 lbs. of hair.

During the day time each Serwan should see to the GEAR of his three camels and keep it in repair. It consists of:—

Pulán or pack saddle, composed of a wooden tree and panels or pads of taut stuffed with bhoosa, coarse grass, or rice straw, the latter is the best form of cheap stuffing—the grass is cut into pieces one foot three inches long and laid horizontally in in the pulan. The culm of this grass (Sínk) must not, however, be used, as it is too hard (Leach). The tree must be kept tightly braced, to this end the Arabs cover it with raw camel's hide which they allow to shrink on it. Martin advocates that, when a numnah is not obtainable, the saddle have an undressed sheepskin fixed in it with the wool inwards. He also insists that the pads shall have no sharp points, the corners being turned up and rounded by stitching; an opening (9 in. by 15 in.) being in the centre to keep it clear of the hump, produced by three tightly drawn stitches through the pad and round the central horizontal stick of the tree. This weighs 21 seers inclusive of the *Fastening Ropes*, three in number:—Goorband or throat strap; Dumchi or crupper; and Tung or girth—which is a thin rope running behind the Rahafay or breast pad. "Each camel should have its own saddle, as the pads very soon take the shape of the animal's back, and if put on another would rub it" (Leach). The *loading rope*, by means of which the load is fastened on the saddle weighs about four seers. The *head collar, leading rope, and nose string* together, one seer; the *jhool and suleetah* each 8 seers. The total appointments weighing 1 maund 2 seers, for which allowance must be made in telling off the weight to be carried. A margin, also must be left for such contingencies as tents getting wet and roads proving extra-difficult to traverse either in consequence of impediments or as the result of a shower.

In LOADING, the greatest possible care should be taken to have the load evenly divided and well balanced. The pulan having been found to be placed over the hump, squarely and evenly adjusted, the animal should kneel down to receive the load and not be caused to get up until it is necessary to move on. If, in the course of the march, it is essential to halt for any length of time the camels should be allowed to kneel down and rest themselves. When a camel will not rise with his load, before forcing him see that the load is not excessive and also that it is properly adjusted so as not to hurt him. It is a most painful thing to see a camel which has attempted to rise under an excessive load lying in agony with his thighs stretched horizontally one on each side. When the ground is somewhat slippery camels are apt to fall suddenly into this position and lacerate the muscles of the inner side of the thigh. We read of camels serving in Afghanistan so weak as to be unable to rise with their loads, and, accordingly, laden while in a standing position. Of course the emergencies of active service compel us to exact from animals all the work they can do—but if the regulation, which lays down that 10% spare camels shall accompany a force and that these shall not be unnecessarily laden, be attended to, it will generally be possible to subject animals only to loads which they can bear. This will prove in the end much more effectual, not to touch upon the question of humanity, than that terrible want of system which sacrifices camels in large numbers to overweighting. Except under very extreme emergency every sixth day a halt for resting purposes should be given to the camels. "One *Jhool* per camel is required; usually made of tât lined with blanket or numnah. To make a jhool two pieces of tât, nine yards long, nine inches broad, and half a blanket are requisite" (Leach). This jhool is to be carried over the saddle in cold weather (and as part of the load in hot) and covered by the grain hide while on the march; it is absolutely essential in cold weather. The Arabs after shearing their camels in the latter part of April compensate for loss of the fleece by use of a jhool, which not only serves to protect from cold but also from the attacks of insects. When camels have to work in the sun the head may advantageously be protected by a wadded cloth, as suggested by Gilchrist. On the march a high ground* sheltered to windward if the weather is cold, with good natural drainage, should be chosen on which to picket camels—in hot weather topes, if not damp, are to be preferred (Gilchrist). "During winter moves great care is required on the part of those in charge of camels because this animal cannot rest where there is snow. In such cases the ground must be thoroughly swept and cleared beforehand, otherwise the heavy perspiration which

* The Tartars avoid localities where stagnant water lies and generates moisture in the atmosphere, for they find moisture most prejudicial to the camel.

exudes from this animal would quickly cause it to catch cold, moreover the moisture generated by this exudation would, after cooling, freeze the animal's hair and fasten it to the earth, from which it would be difficult to disconnect it" (Kostenko). All stones should be carefully removed as being liable to bruise the animals when they are lying down; it is to be remembered also that care must be taken lest, in loading or unloading, camels kneel down on stones. Martin suggests that in standing-camps the ground should be picked up to the depth of one foot when it becomes hard baked, and carefully swept. Yaldwin prefers picketing in circles facing inwards as economising space and sentries, and he tells us that a circle with a radius of eleven paces will contain 50 camels, with their food, gear, and attendants. This, doubtless, is the best system on a campaign, Leach advocates it in preference to placing them in parallel lines "as it is what they have been accustomed to, and custom should never be needlessly interfered with either in the case of camels or their drivers." From a sanitary point of view picketing in parallel lines is preferable, but, as the attendants must be accommodated somewhere, it is questionable whether there is any economy of space. However objectionable it may seem at first sight to have human beings and camels huddled together in the circular picket, we have no evidence that it does harm in movable camps and the men like it and pay more attention to their camels than if bivouacing farther away from them. In the Madras Presidency on the march the Serwans voluntarily live among their camels and picket them in no regular order each animal to a single peg not far from the others. Males and females must be encamped separately and well apart from one another, the females being some distance to leeward and out of sight of the males. They must be kept apart also on the line of march, and according to the Bengal regulations the proportion of establishment to be kept up for troops is $\frac{2}{3}$ males, $\frac{1}{3}$ females, but males and females in equal proportions may be told off for duty.

The necessity for these precautions might easily be obviated in the case of camels by castration. The Testes (occupying the position of those of carnivora) are easy to remove. The Mongols castrate regularly at three or four years of age, with a view to rendering the males more tractable, better workers, and to prevent indescriminate breeding. The periodically recurrent sexual desire of the male is termed *Must*; it necessitates the special precaution of tying the tail round to the saddle lest it be continually switched about and thus urine when passed be sprinkled over drivers, loads, and other camels (Leach). Indeed the provision of nature whereby the urine is expelled in a backward direction often against the tail seems not very satisfactory. It has been urged that thus the animal is to an extent prevented from having to stand with his hind feet in a puddle of urine such as would soften their horn and cause disease, but the male elephant, which has more tender feet than the camel, urinates forward. It certainly is a great advantage for camels not to have to take the first step after a halt from a slippery patch of ground moistened by urine. The Serwan judiciously whenever possible moves his camel a yard or two to either side of the place where he has urinated directly he has completed the act. These experienced men halt their camels regularly about every ten miles to allow them to "make water."

The camel averages eight feet in length, and it is estimated that 500 in single file occupy one mile. In Bengal hired camels are procurable through Government for the use of military officers.

We are told that, in loading, bags are to be preferred to boxes, but camel trunks are supplied by Government for medical and veterinary stores, and prove very capacious and convenient.

When camels and mules are both available, the former are to be used for baggage and heavy loads. Public camels are to be branded in letters three inches long on the near side of the neck with the last two figures of the year of purchase; care is to be taken to avoid blemishing, and carbolic dressing is allowed to keep off flies from the brand marks while healing; cast animals are branded on the buttock.

Camels when purchased for the public service are to be between six and eight years old, and not less than 6½ feet high at the shoulder. The Russians make their camels work with loads from two years of age upwards—the full load being attained at five years, when the camel is considered full grown—but he becomes worn out early by age and ill treatment. In the Montgomery District young camels are broken to the Nakala (nose string) when three years old, and usually put to work at four years with three maunds this being *gradually* increased to the full load of eight maunds. The age may be determined by the teeth, I. V. S.

Oliphant has carefully examined this matter from a practical point of view. He found that of camels sent up the Kuram Valley, 35°/o were unserviceable as being either too old or under five years of age. V. S. Chas. Steel found out of 70 dead camels at Quetta 26 under two years of age; evidently camels for the last Afghan War were very badly selected. To prevent too young or too old animals being rushed across the frontier with a view to their owners obtaining compensation for loss, Mr. Oliphant gives the following information for officers appointed to select camels:—DENTITION OF CAMEL AS DENOTING AGE—At two years of age there are of the front teeth two temporary in the upper jaw and eight in the lower. At three years of age they are more worn, so that by four years old the lower ones become simply peg-like fangs wide apart in the jaw and discoloured. At about five years the first permanent incisors are cut, the animal is now called *do uk* (previously *chatri*); at about six years the lateral permanent incisors appear (the animal becoming a *chowga*); at seven years the corner incisors are obtained (the camel being a *chiga*). Between seven and eight years the lower tushes are cut and are quickly followed by the upper. At eight years they are even with the incisors which form a level series the corner pair, only, being unworn (the camel is now termed *nesh* or *jewan* and is in its prime). The two upper secondary tushes are cut later and are somewhat irregular in their time of appearance. The true tushes at first slant forwards, then become upright and finally curve backwards; in very old animals they become worn by mutual friction. The incisors become indented by wear on their sides and tops, the latter caused possibly by friction in the act of jerking the head to break off foliage in browsing. The condition of the teeth of the animal between four and six years of age renders him little fit for grazing and certainly unfit for active service (*Veterinary Journal*, Vol. xi. Page 244).

The following is the best routine *Method of Examining a Camel as to Fitness for Transport Service*:—

(*a*). Determine age.

(*b*). Height.

(*c*). Condition and general state of health (especially freedom from pregnancy).

(*d*). Strength, as shown by rising and sitting down under a fair load without undue trembling.

(*e*). Paces good, and free from lameness.

(*f*). Nose not torn; pads sound and free from sinuses; back, sides, &c., free from galls; no elbow brushing*; feet neither over-worn, bruised, ulcerated, nor otherwise diseased; tendons firm and clear; hump well nourished.

(*g*). Eyes good and sound.

The camel lives about 18 to 25 years according to the Arabs and Turkestanis, but in India attains a greater age (40 years in Montgomery, Nunn). Nothing will induce Mongol camel owners to use their camels under a certain age, the Arabs bring the males into work at the fifth year, when they attain the state of puberty, after which they fill out, and the hump becomes fully furnished at seven or eight years of age.

One *Attendant* is allowed, now, for every three camels. Unfortunately, although it is urged as an objection to the use of camels that they require skilled attendants, in time of emergency, when careful management is especially required, men who are not Serwans, mere kahars or common coolies, are hurried up and the camels entrusted to their tender mercies in spite of the facts that they do not know how to handle or manage camels, ill treat them and rob them of their food and clothing, desert in numbers when danger threatens, and pilfer stores on every available occasion. The Russians find the same difficulties in dealing with camel drivers as we do. "They comprise a disorderly set of great numerical strength, possessed of no discipline, ready to desert at any moment, prone to plunder, and a source to demoralization to the troops themselves. In the expedition of 1839-40, under General Perovski, there were with the detachment, numbering 3,000 men, 2,000 drivers, who immediately they got to the Steppe took to flight. The General was therefore obliged to shoot two of the number who were caught. Desertion was thus stopped, but the worry with these men continued, and to such an extent that *the detachment became, so to speak, an escort for its own camel drivers*" (Kostenko). True Serwans are hardy, useful men, of sufficiently high caste to necessitate you being careful lest your long shadow fall on the food they are cooking at evening stable time and render it polluted and unfit for consumption. They are shrewd, careful men as a rule and very kind to their animals,

* An especial point to look to in purchase of a camel is that the elbows be well turned out otherwise the loading rope galls them (Nunn).

which good feeling is reciprocated. There is a prevalent idea that camel men suffer from spine disease and die young, but I don't think we have sufficient evidence of the correctness of this. "The gait of camels is peculiar," says Burnaby, "they go like a pig with the fore and like a cow with the hind legs. The motion is decidedly rough." Another writer sums up the feelings and sensations induced by a camel ride across the desert as "very different from the exhilaration produced by riding a horse; this is soon replaced by a feeling of extreme discomfort." Possibly the latter remarks refer only to the heavy caravan animal, and the light sowarí dromedary, travelling his ten or twelve miles an hour over the desert, may impart a less tedious and trying sensation to his rider—at any rate the motion seems to be one to which people soon become used but a tight Kămăr bănd is very necessary for the rider.

The question of *Procurability of Camels* remains to be dealt with. In this respect India labours under no difficulty—sufficient numbers of camels to meet all our requirements for trade and war can be obtained from internal and foreign sources of supply if reasonable system be exercised. But this has not been the case hitherto. When an emergency has arisen animals of all kinds have been accepted for transport; thus camels old and worn out, too young, pregnant, physically unfit, and incapacitated by disease were hurried towards the front in Afghanistan after having been subjected to examination not even by a competent transport official, much less by a Veterinary Surgeon. Now transport officers are gaining considerable experience in camel management, some steps are being taken for animal census in India with a view to information as to where animals available for transport are procurable, and we may note with satisfaction the success of camel supplies to the Soudan from India recently as contrasted with the unsatisfactory local supply from the Nile Delta.

As yet no measures seem to have been taken for regulation of the breeding and repression of communicable diseases among camels. Very much might be done to improve the breeds in different parts of India and to encourage native breeders to obtain animals of the most useful stamp and to castrate weedy males—possibly a stud system for obtaining a valuable breed of sires would be a great gain to the country. Something in this direction, has, we believe been tried at the Hissar Cattle Farm, but there is good scope for more extensive operations of this kind. Camels are not expensive animals to buy, they are capable of doing an enormous amount of pack work, they are inexpensive to feed on service, and only in very few countries has fodder to be carried for them. When properly selected for service and well managed they withstand the exigencies of a campaign fairly well. Thus there is much to be said in favour of camel transport, but I. V. S. Oliphant strongly advises that "if occasion should arise in the future only 'local' carriage be used, the animals remaining in the hands of their owners and carriage paid for by weight." It was proved that the government drivers took little or no interest in their charge in Afghanistan and the owners of the hired class were little better—preferring compensation to carrying out their contract. The system suggested by Mr. Oliphant, too, would do away with the costly, ponderous operations of a "Camel Compensation Committee," greatly to the advantage of Government.

Nunn informs us that the Bikaneer Camel in the Shahpur district is worth Rs. 200, and other breeds Rs. 80—50 according to their carrying power, but the price has much risen since the Afghan war. In Montgomery a *ganda* (or grey camel of superior class) is worth Rs. 100—120, and an inferior camel Rs. 90—50. He gives (*Vide* Quarterly Journal of Veterinary Science in India, Vol. III, p. 162,) the following:—

Names applied to Camels of different sizes:—

		MALES.	FEMALES.
Months	... 4	Lihare or Lihara Todi ... *General term,* Toda ...	Todí.
	... 6	Mahata	
	to 12	Kutela	
Till 3 yrs. or after weaning	...	Mayat	
Years	... 3	Trihan, Trehan, Tehak ...	Paraf, Parafí.
	... 4	Chhattar	Paraf, Liharí.
	... 5	Doyak	Dachí, Pahlan, Troker.
Second Incisor cut.	... 6 ...	Chauga	Dachí, Dugan, Troker.
	... 7	Chhigga, Chiga.	
Third Incisor and Tusk cut.	... 8	Vesh, Nesh.	
	... 9	Armosh, Arut.	

With regard to BREEDING, Nunn informs us as to the detail in the Montgomery District of the Punjab. The females are not put to the male until they are three years old; they "come in season" in March; one will produce nine or ten calves at intervals of two years, the calf being carried 12½ months. The calf sucks for one year; he is allowed only very small quantities of milk for the first fifteen days, and afterwards to please himself as to amount, he begins to browse when about three weeks old. When he is weaned the udder of the dam is tied up in a bag called "Jáli." The owner milks half the udder twice a day and leaves the rest for the calf; a good ganda gives about 12 seers per diem. This milk does not give butter, it is laxative in its effects on man and used in cases of enlarged spleen, but is the best kind for rearing foals on, as the Arabs also have observed.

The natural history of the camel is singular in this important respect that nowhere in the present day is he known to occur in the wild state. The two forms of camelus find their nearest Zoological allies in the Llamas of the new world but, in conformation of their limbs especially, they prove interesting from an anatomico-physiological point of view as affording transitional characters between the horse and the ox. There is, perhaps, no animal in the world which can be looked on as domesticated more thoroughly than the camel, he lives among men and in company with human beings only, he is mentioned in the earliest written records of the race of mankind. The Chinese have some literature of the camel and his diseases, Arabian works (ancient and modern) deal with his management and uses in a semi-religious manner from which the facts can be extracted only after the most elaborate research. The French, with their usual enlightened policy in matters of science, on occupation of Algeria called on experienced veterinary officers of the army for reports on the diseases of camels among other beasts of burden used in the recently conquered country and thus much valuable information has been obtained and recorded, probably that which from a scientific point of view is the most valuable available on Cameline Pathology. The records made by officers, veterinary and non-veterinary of the army in the Indian empire are of the greatest value from a pratical point of view but they are much scattered in periodicals, pamphlets, and inaccessible works of reference; some of the few special works on the subject are not to be had by the general public. The anatomy of the camel is casually touched on in works of comparative anatomy and is dealt with in a few memoirs reprinted from the proceedings of the Zoological and other Societies. The physiology has been mainly worked out in France through the labours of the learned Professor Colin. The diseases have been dealt with in the obsolete work of Gilchrist and the brief sketches by Oliphant, Leech, C. Steel, and the Algerian veterinary officers. We have to search far and wide for information as to medicines for the camel and the special features of their action on his system. Thus our knowledge of the camel has not been focused in the form of literary production; it is to remove this extremely unsatisfactory state of affairs, which may fairly be considered an opprobrium to the veterinary profession in India, that this work has been prepared.

CHAPTER II.—GENERAL CONSIDERATIONS ON DISEASES OF THE CAMEL.

As the diseases of the ox are better understood than those of other ruminants that animal must be considered as the standard for comparison in study of disorders of other species which chew the cud. It will be found that in pathology, as in anatomy generic resemblances are very close up to a certain point, but that there are many practically important matters in which differences can be noticed. These differences depend not only on special features of anatomical constitution but on the life conditions to which the species are subjected, and, especially, the uses to which they are put by man, thus the length of neck of the camel seems to entail on that animal a liability to certain forms of epilepsy and of injury to the cervical region, dislocation and fracture, not seen very often in the ox. Also it will be found that certain ill-explained disorders of the nape of the neck and upper part of the throat are not unfrequent in the camel and, again, broken back, lacerated thigh muscles, and galls, demand special attention in Cameline Pathology, for they result from abuse of the camel as a beast of burden. It must be confessed that as regards the various branches of comparative study of disorders of the ruminating apparatus we are sadly deficient in knowledge; that the camel suffers much from disease of the alimentary canal will be evident to the most superficial observer. His diet differs from that of the ox in these important respects, that his fodder is largely composed of the leaves of trees and of prickly shrubs, and that he receives little grain food and practically no roots, as a general rule he is left to shift for himself entirely in the collection of his food. The remarkable tendency in the camel for wounds to take on suppurative action and to become complicated with lymphangitis is one of the first matters which attracts attention in Cameline Pathology, it is probably due to constitutional tendency to a very great extent, but cannot wholly be set down to that cause, being often due to malpraxis in the treatment of wounds, and perhaps also to the irritant properties of urine, saliva, and other secretions of the camel which probably prove as offensive to a healing wound as they do to the nostrils of any one unused to be among these animals. Abscesses occurring in the positions occupied by lymphatic glands are commonly described as special distinct disorders of the camel, but they may almost all legitimately come under the head of lymphangitis and carefully conducted examination of the animal will generally show that they depend on some unhealthy wound. Thus the question early comes up for careful consideration whether there is in the constitution of the camel any intrinsic and special tendency to unhealthy action in wounds; in considering this it must be remembered that very many of the patients which come under our notice are in extremely low condition from under-feeding which materially lessens the reparative powers of the constitution, that in many cases it is almost impossible to secure anything like cleanliness of the wounds, and that generally, in the absence of our immediate personal supervision, simple dressings are discarded, and, either openly or surreptitiously, the Serwan applies the acrid medicaments which native practice sanctions; we have as yet no evidence that the flesh of the camel is peculiarly obnoxious to repair. RAYMENT is right in his estimate of the extent of the knowledge possessed by natives as to treatment of Camel Diseases.* Every Veterinary Surgeon with Indian experience can confirm his views and finds that the empirical knowledge

*"*A theory, which should be exploded as soon as possible, is that natives understand the treatment of these animals in sickness.* To mention some of their curative measures, let us take Dementia:—They tie the patient down, cover him up with blankets, light two fires before and two behind him, if

acquired and handed down from many centuries of camel treatment contains here and there the germ of a sound practical truth but that the chaff so abounds as to obscure the grain and warrant us in drawing information from native sources only after most careful consideration.

The habitat of the camel being as a rule dry hot countries of a desert character he is considered peculiarly susceptible to changes of temperature and the influences of climate, the various effects of a "touch of the sun" certainly are seen in the camel; rheumatic disease, "cold-struck," and respiratory disorders affect him frequently and readily when exposed to damp. Accidents of various kinds occur when the desert animal is removed to hilly, stony, or slippery places, his high centre of gravity renders him liable to falls but is counteracted in this respect considerably by the amount of ground the animal covers, the stoutness of his limbs and the considerable size of his footpads. These latter are liable to injury as being much less of the nature of hoofs than the horny pedal organs of other ruminants, resembling rather the hoof slippers of the elephant. Thus it is very evident that the uses to which the camel is put must be considered as the cause of by far the larger portion of the disorders from which he suffers. If sore backs, lacerated nostrils, and foot injuries be removed from his list of diseases the latter will be found to be very short.

The surgical conditions of the camel have been known and treated from time immemorial, but with them were confounded certain derangements with which we shall hereafter have to deal in a more extended manner under the heading "disorders of the blood." It may be claimed for Veterinary Science that it has thrown light on the special character of some disorders hitherto considered ordinary in their nature; camel-pox, anthrax, surra, and foot and mouth disease are additions made by scientific observers to the list of camel diseases from cases which were previously known as skin disease, colic, debility, and sore feet. Cameline Pathology at present presents the interesting spectacle of a branch

---

there is in addition a hot sun all the better! Again cow's urine is a favorite draught, indigo is rubbed over wounds, sinuses are filled with common salt, a slit is made in the ear for colic, &c., &c. That real Serwans understand the treatment, dieting, &c., of camels in health is of course undeniable, but we have now many Transport Officers and Subordinates who do so just as well." (Quarterly Journal of Veterinary Science, April, 1886).

of medical science in the act of emergence from empiricism, every scientifically observed case is of value, however simple it be, apparently and not unfrequently careful observation is rewarded with most remarkable and valuable results. The methods of science must be brought to bear on disease in camels and it rests with Government to give Veterinary Surgeons in India the opportunities required in this line of research.

The GENERAL SYMPTOMS OF ILL-HEALTH in the camel are obscure to all but the experienced camel manager, whether Native or European. The camel works almost until he falls dead, and once he gets down he must be considered in a very bad way, not, however, certain "never to rise again" as has been taught; refusal of food and loss of the cud are very important general signs of disorder; a dull, heavy, listless appearance of the eyes, very different from the naturally bright vigilant aspect of these beautiful features of the camel's face; a tendency to remain persistently with the head and neck stretched straight out and resting on the ground; a dry, hide-bound, unthrifty appearance of the skin; increasing debility as denoted by, besides the falling away in condition, the tottering and trembling of the animal when it attempts to rise. When FEVER is present we find, according to Gilchrist, that there is a cold stage followed by a hot. In the former shivering, restlessness, and general stiffness are present, and the limbs are cold; in the latter (which supervenes after a couple of hours) the urine is scanty and high coloured, but little dung is passed, respiration is quick and laboured, there is mucous discharge from the nostrils, lachrymation, and extreme thirst causing the animal when loosened to run to water and lie down in it after drinking. This condition is considered due to exposure of the animal while heated but is rare, and all mention of it seems to have been excluded from Gilchrist's later editions. Leach speaks of a form of Sun Fever, under the names Gurmi Mangaya, and Sarh-ki-bimari resulting from exposure in hot weather. The animal is dull and off feed, his skin hot and dry, and his breathing quick but the disorder soon yields to ordinary febrifuges or a stimulant dose daily. Natives treat it by stimulating mussauls and they apply stimulants to the eyes, sternutative powders and liquid applications to the nostrils, they foment the body and keep the animal in a sheltered place. This treatment is evidently directed to removal of symptoms, Gilchrist advises the withdrawal of from ½–1 gallon of blood from the jugular and purging with five drachms of aloes and two of calomel made into a bolus with jaggery. Here we see a noteworthy absence of recommendation for use of febrifuges and one hesitates considerably before following either method; experience tends to the support of the native system, that of *sustaining the strength of the animal as much as possible,* which will be found a rule of great value in dealing with all diseases of the camel. The tendency of medical science in the present day is to throw considerable doubt on the alleged occurrence of fever as a disease *per se* especially in quadrupeds. Irritative fever the result of extensive wounds and injuries, and symptomatic fever in blood diseases and severe internal phlegmons is very common but the general term fever is losing its original meaning and becoming the name for a collection of symptoms, just as dropsy, diarrhœa, and colic are they no longer conveying so precise a meaning as to meet the accurate diagnostic requirements of the present day.

The PULSE, taken at the heart, averages 54 beats per minute according to Gilchrist, but Colin puts the pulse of the camel at 25 to 32. The beats of the central circulatory organ may best be felt, "though not always distinctly, when pressure is made with the hand between the top of forelegs in front of the chest * * * no artery about head, neck, or extremities is to be found possessing a distinct and easily recognisable pulse." This fact seriously diminishes the value of pulse records for diagnostic purposes, but it must be remembered that the pulse of ruminants is so affected by physiological processes, especially digestion and pregnancy, as to render its indications but little reliable.

THE INTERNAL TEMPERATURE is a much more reliable and exact method of determination of the presence of Fever than is the pulse. The results afforded by my observations, as published in Vol. XX, of the Veterinary Journal, p. 80, are that the average internal temperature taken at the rectum in the morning is 99°F.; the maximum reading obtained was 102·6°F. "but the animal was probably the subject of some fever (he died the following day of Anthrax) since only in two other cases was the temperature over 100°F." The minimum reading obtained was 98·2°F. I should put the health limits at 98°F. to 101°F. The camels are made to "sit:" occasionally, in resentment of manipulation of the anus, they try to bring the buttocks to the ground or violently attempt to bite or to rise. Two assistants are necessary, one to hold the tail and the other the head. Often a number of ectozoa are collected beneath the tail; sometimes dung balls in the rectum prevent free introduction of the instrument; occasionally there is spasmodic closure of the anus. The thermometer should be kept in for four minutes each observation.

The RESPIRATIONS vary much in frequency in accordance with the conditions of the animal, being nearly double as fast in the heat of the day as in the morning or evening; as with other quadrupeds they, therefore, do not afford us much guidance in diagnosis, although the character of the efforts may point to important abnormalities. Laboured breathing, quick beating of the flanks, and panting are found in the extremes of respiratory effort, but it is often wonderful what an amount of exertion a camel may perform when on the eve of fatality from chest disorder. This renders *auscultation* especially necessary as a guide in cameline diagnosis and it should be resorted to in all cases of obscure disorder of the camel. Various sibili and râles will be found in lung disorder, conditions quite incompatible with a free, open state of the air passages. It will generally be necessary to use a stethoscope for these observations, because of the numerous parasites and the dirt in the coat of most sick camels. Cough and nasal discharge (especially when the latter is of a rusty colour) will direct our attention to the organs of respiration. The indications of *percussion* have not yet been sufficiently worked out.

The STATE OF EXCRETA must be carefully noted. The small round dung pellets expelled without effort in health, the urine passed freely in a backward direction, the animal "camping" himself for its expulsion and occupying a very long time in the process (the stream being very small), must be carefully looked to in diagnosis, and much must be learned from general observations on the state of the skin, coat, and visible mucous membranes.

PROGNOSIS in serious disorders of camels is generally unfavourable in the extreme. It is hard to get proper nursing for the animals; if the sick be moved to some place where there is shelter from the sun and any other violent climatic influence, such as considerable rainfall and high cold wind, it is generally thought the invalid is being well and sufficiently nursed. Again it is not observed that a camel is unwell, generally, until he is "in extremis" which, of course, is a matter which seriously hampers our curative measures and renders their effect unsatisfactory. It is constantly assumed that the camel has no power of resisting disease but this is by no means well established. It is an assertion made of every animal until our knowledge suffices for diagnosis of its diseases in any but their latest stages ; however, it must be admitted that in many cases of treatment when the disease has been promptly and well handled, and if the patient had been a horse we might reasonably have anticipated recovery, death ensues. It is to be feared that such unsatisfactory result depends more frequently on imperfect and unskilful handling of remedial agents than on specially fatal tendency of disease in the species Camelus.

Treatment must for the present be to a very great extent experimental, is so far as the use of drugs is concerned. We have as yet no accurate and carefully conducted therapeutic observations made on the camel. Still the organism of this animal does not differ so radically from that of the ox as to prevent our having some knowledge of the action of remedies, at any rate as to which may be given with the possibility or probability of good result and the certainty of doing no harm by their administration. Armed with this information and with the principles of pharmacy and medical treatment, any Veterinary Surgeon is more competent to prescribe for a camel than can be an absolutely ignorant individual told off to the care of camels in health, and than the experienced Serwan who wields traditional nostrums and shrouds his complete want of scientific knowledge in mystery.

Chapter III.—CAMELINE THERAPEUTICS AND MATERIA MEDICA.

The details of the subject of this chapter will be dealt with when we are writing of individual diseases, and as regards general principles there is but little to be said except that most *recent experience has amply proved the superiority of the stimulant tonic method of treatment* adopted by the natives, the outcome of their experience, as compared with the depletory methods adopted by Gilchrist, who objects to the native remedies as "at best, inert" or "useless, if not positively injurious" or (in some cases) as not having "even the negative character of doing no harm" but "being positively injurious, feeding the disease instead of subduing it." Examining carefully native treatment as derived from various sources we find it may be divided into mussauls, nahass or snuffs, lapes or unguenta, and unjuns or lachrymants.

The Mussauls consist of numerous ingredients, almost all derived from the vegetable kingdom, generally of a stimulant tonic character, in doses very similar to those required for the ox, and to be given in the form of a *bolus* about the size of a lime twice a day or every morning. Or else the form of *drench* is suggested, and we know that this is much preferable to a ball for a ruminant animal; water, milk, and wine are used as vehicles. It is evident that when a dose is made up of so many as fifteen ingredients, the practice of the prescriber is very much on the "hit and miss principle." We observe the same peculiarities in native prescriptions for the elephant and bullock; with regard to the latter there can be no doubt that European practice is far ahead of the native systems, and, so, we are in a position to expose the utter ignorance of natives in treatment of diseases of the ox; it is reasonable to infer that the same ignorance and presumption which prevails in native treatment of cattle does so also in the case of both elephant and camel, and all the evidence we have bearing on the matter tends to prove that such is the case. We elsewhere deal with Cameline Materia Medica *in extenso.*

Nahass or snuff consists of aromatic substances, not so numerous generally as those composing mussauls, powdered and blown into the nostrils. Examining the first of these which comes to hand we find it extremely bulky and unwieldy for this form of administration, weighing a tola each of the following powders, barringtonia, alum, galls, calombo, long pepper root, cloves, and assafœtida; this to be given twice a day; which sounds rather "rough" on the camel. There can be no hesitation in concluding that the blowing of about three ounces of irritant powder twice a day into the nostrils of a camel suffering say from Pneumonia must speedily terminate the case, by death of the patient, therefore this line of treatment as suggested by the natives must not be copied by officials in charge of Transport animals.

Various Lapes or Ointments are constantly recommended, they are either of the nature of poultices or of ointments proper. A very short experience with medicines suffices to show that these native prescriptions have absolutely no special advantages as compared with the corresponding preparations of the Veterinary Pharmacopœia, and they are usually so complex in composition as to be difficult to remember on emergency. Their special recommendation is that only bazaar medicines are required in their preparation, but the skilled pharmaceutist once informed what remedies are procurable in ordinary bazaars in emergency can combine them with efficiency greater than that of the unscientific recipes of the Serwans. The native recipes which seem of special value will be enumerated hereafter and it will be found that the value of lengthened experience in management of camels under disease has been neither under-estimated nor over-rated.

Unjuns or Lachrymants seem in much favour with Serwans. They are pastes, powders, or unguents applied to the eyelids on the inner surface; they, of course, irritate the animal much and produce a profuse flow of tears but it is very doubtful whether they are of *any* benefit whatsoever in the disorders for which they are used, certainly they have no more than a slight derivative action. They have long been discarded from all occidental practice except for local treatment.

Firing constitutes an important feature of treatment of animal diseases by natives, who usually like to leave *(and their clients to see)* distinct evidences that remedial measures have been adopted. In almost every case the unfortunate patient is extensively scored with the hot iron and it is seldom we see a camel which has entirely escaped this heroic measure, adopted either for cure or prevention of disease. We are constantly urged to score with the hot iron over the haunch and neck, on the head, along the sides and around the navel, from the ears to the shoulders, on the buttocks, and so on. Leach gives us some interesting details about the after treatment in cases of application of the actual cautery. "Three days after branding, a mixture of wood or cow-dung ashes and camel urine should be applied daily for seven days, when it will be found that the scab resulting from the firing has peeled off and that the abscess, if it has not already burst of itself, is ready to be lanced." Great virtue is attributed to the form of iron mark, thus the palmyra leaf pattern is called *kajuria dágh,* it is best for an abscess of the chest, but if the abscess occurs between the hind legs the cart-wheel brand *(choufulli dágh)* is required. It is quite unnecessary to dwell further on this matter, for the effect of the iron is the same whatever form it is made to design during application.

The use of setons, blisters, bandages, fomentations, cold water applications, and other valuable methods of treatment of diseases of lower animals seem to have been introduced into Cameline Therapeutics by Gilchrist, who also insists on the value in treatment of alteratives and the depletory method. Thus, his recipés comprise calomel, tartar emetic, and aloes in ordinary or very large doses and bleeding (with physic) is insisted on for all forms of internal inflammation. BLEEDING is to be performed to the extent of ½ to 3½ or 4 gallons. This operation can be accomplished with facility, as the neck is long and its jugular capacious (being between 2 inches and 2½ inches in diameter) and very superficially placed. The animal is made to sit down and the knees tied in the bent position each by several turns of a rope round the flexed limb binding the metacarpus against the fore arm; the rope passes twice over the neck and is then tied, whereby the animal is prevented rising. A cord is then tied round the neck at the inferior part of the superior third, moderately tight, the jugular fills speedily "at the site most eligible for incision and is opened by means of a common horse fleam, used in the same manner as for bleeding a horse. A gallon and-a-half of blood is a full bleeding, and in inflammatory cases the quantity should, in the first instance, be abstracted; afterwards a gallon, or only half, may be drawn off according to the urgency of the individual case." It was found that a healthy camel lived a few hours after 90 lbs. of blood had been, experimentally, abstracted from the jugular. Leach describes *local bleeding from a branch of the facial vein,* as follows:—Two men hold the head down and rub the back of the neck with a stick, which causes the blood to circulate freely and a vein just above the nostrils to stand out. This should be lanced. The blood is first of a dark colour, but changes to bright red when a seer or so has been taken. The bleeding should now be stopped by placing a wet rag folded so as to form a kind of pad over the incision. *Slitting the ear* is a primitive method of venesection adopted in emergency, and the superficial abdominal vein is sometimes opened. In the present day it is accepted that bleeding seldom need be resorted to in treatment, yet when undue excitement exists or a tendency to fatality from congestion of brain or lungs a prompt and effectual impression may sometimes be induced by this means, which, therefore, must be considered a valuable resource in emergency.

In abdominal and thoracic disorders of severity, free FOMENTATION with hot water must be tried; either the *ordinary method* of applying a blanket steeped in boiling water, covered by another blanket, to the chest or belly, and renewing the heat by pouring in water almost at the boiling point, must be adopted, or the *native method* of applying hot mud and water or cowdung and water beaten on to the skin by means of rags tied on the end of a bamboo; there is, of course, no special virtue in the lattter process but it is as effectual as the former and better understood by natives.

Considering the frequency of occurrence of a lax state of the bowels of the camel it might be supposed that our list of LAXATIVE and CATHARTICS would be a long and valuable one. As a matter of fact the case is just the reverse. Gilchrist finds benefit from only two substances, aloes and calomel, four to six ounces of the former in one to two seers of cow's milk, which much assists and increases its action. Calomel is more reliable and should be given in ball in half ounce doses. Gilchrist found that neither Epsom nor Glauber's Salts in doses of three to four pounds, repeated on consecutive days, proved effectual; ghee and castor oil given separately each in Ojss doses also had no effect; croton seeds in an ounce dose morning and evening produced no aperient or other visible effect; common salt given in doses of a pound was inert, and enemata did not act as laxatives, thus a clyster of water a gallon and-a-half, common salt a pound, and castor oil, one pint had no effect. These experimental results were, evidently, obtained subsequently to the issue of his first edition in which besides most of the substances already enumerated amaltas, indrayan, euphorbium, jungle soapnuts, mustard, and tamarind are placed on the list of the "most useful of this class of remedies." The common dose for laxative purposes is a seer of warm ghee.

ENEMATA, simple and medicated, constitute a means of treatment which must not be neglected in camel practice. It must be remembered that they act as internal fomentations and local applications, and so, even apart from any slight laxative effect, have a distinct value. With regard to substances having a direct SEDATIVE action, it must be understood that we have no distinct evidence as to effectual action of the compounds of antimony. The sulphurets, so extensively used in native medicine, are obtainable in the bazaars only in most impure state and their action is either negative or most uncertain. Tartar emetic has been the subject of an interesting experiment by Gilchrist, in which he gave 25 ounces in eleven consecutive days without any appreciable effect, the animal feeding freely all the time in the ordinary manner. However it is concluded that though this drug has no emetic effect it is useful as an alterative in doses of ʒss-ʒj combined with similar doses of calomel. *Stimulants, antispasmodics, tonics, and narcotics* are the agents principally relied on in treatment of camel diseases. The crude bazaar forms of these may in many cases be usefully supplanted by the purified drugs, but there are many agents of much value obtainable in the bazaars and most effectual in emergency. *It must be taken as a leading principle in the treatment of Indian Transport Animal that the drugs recommended be such and in such forms as are most readily obtainable on emergency in most Indian Bazaars.* With regard to DOSES, we can only repeat the rule elsewhere propounded that, when not otherwise specified, *the amounts suitable for the ox should be given to the camel.*

METHODS OF ADMINISTRATION of internal remedies offer some points of interest. Where speedy action is not required the dose may be mixed with the feed, or given as Boli about the size of a lime, but in more urgent cases the agents should be given in the liquid form for immediate absorption, milk being a convenient and much appreciated vehicle. The attendants give these drinks through the mouth by means of a hollow bamboo drenching appliance. It is to be remembered that most of our remedial agents are of the form of Carminative Massauls and that, therefore, the animal will take them by ordinary hand feeding from the Serwan and *much benefit medicinally may often be gained by alteration of the diet of the animal,* the naturally varied nature of which gives us great facilities for action in this direction except under the emergencies of a campaign.

MEANS OF RESTRAINT are few in number; the camel bears pain

well in the course of operations. His means of resisting the infliction of pain consist in biting, lateral movement, and, very occasionally, kicking. The head is held firmly by two or more men, and the attention of the animal diverted by jerking at the nose peg; it is preferable, however, to tie up the head as the animal is in the couchant position. Much camel surgery may be done while the animal is sitting and retained in that position (for slight and rapid operations) by the camel man standing on the forearm, in other cases by fastening the fore legs in the bent position, as described for bleeding. The double shackle to the hind legs is necessary in cases of abscesses of the groin and other parts of the hind limbs, otherwise the patient treads impatiently sideways on to the toes of the operator. However, absolutely the most formidable offensive means of the camel is his teeth. The bite of a camel is notoriously severe and liable to be followed by extensive loss of tissue and blood poisoning; the effects of which the natives compare to leprosy and very much dread. It is, therefore, very carefully guarded against, and when a man has been bitten his wounds should be promptly cleansed from the offensive and irritant secretions of the mouth and, with advantage, thoroughly cauterized. As a rule, however, the latter process is more or less imperfect, for the wounds are jagged and deep. The flicking of the tail bespattering the operator and the freshly cut surfaces with acrid urine is also to be guarded against by tying up that organ or having it firmly held. The operator soon gets used to the grunts, gurglings, and discontented utterings of the camel, which are apt to distract the attention of the inexperienced. As a rule to be constantly enforced we must "*never 'lose a chance' with a camel,*" avoid approaching him except when properly held by the man in charge, and generally he should be made to kneel before our approach; these, of course, are matters soon learned from experience. In the treatment of external injuries of the camel the greatest difficulties are experienced in keeping the parts clean; thus bandages, protective coverings, and boots for foot injuries are found especially necessary. Camphorated oil to protect from flies is of great value; and experience has proved that it is often absolutely necessary to form an artificial scab over the abraded surface by means of the actual or potential cautery. As a rule error is made in excessive dependence on blue stone, hot pitch, and other caustics. It must be remembered that camels are in case of irritation liable to lacerate the itching parts by biting and scratching, measures must therefore be always taken to lessen irritation of wounds and skin eruptions by the use of substances having a local anodyne action. Recipes for Kharisk or Itch especially need to be anodyne in their influence, for this disease seriously upsets the natural stolidity of the camel. *Stimulating applications* externally applied best assume the form of lapes, simple blisters are very liable to be torn and so generally are dispensed with or use of the hot iron substituted. *Cooling mussauls* are febrifuge, antiphlogistic, diuretic, and laxative in action. They find but a small place in the native pharmacy aud in respect to them cameline therapeutics has much benefited by the introduction of European methods of treatment and medicines, whiich, in a negative way has also proved beneficial by exclusion of urine, fæces, and even more objectionable excipients, from the Pharmacy.

Chapter IV.—THE BLOOD AND ITS DISEASES.

There is a peculiar bluish tint about the blood of the camel which results probably from the fact that his red corpuscles present the peculiarity so noteworthy among mammals, of being elliptical. This resemblance to the corpuscles of fishes, and reptiles does not seem to entail on Camelidæ any appreciable correspondence in habits or structure with non-mammalian vertebrates. The globules are 1-233rd of a millimeter (Colin) in mean diameter, thus resembling those of other mammals to a fair degree of approximation being smaller than those of the Elephant (1/100 mm.), Dog (1/139 mm.), Ox (1/168 mm.), Horse (1/181 mm.), and Sheep (1/209 mm.), and larger than those of the Goat (1/250 mm.). There will be noticed a marked tendency to the formation of yellowish clots in the blood vessels of the camel *post mortem* probably due to the frequent occurrence of anæmia in this species generally resulting from imperfect nutrition or prolonged attacks of unrecognised exhausting disease.

Anæmia or Debility is denoted by the animal being very thin and its hump very small, having difficulty in rising with its load, shivering when attempting to rise or to lie down, being sluggish and dull and evidently weak and unsuited for work. He sometimes sits for day after day in the same place refusing the most tempting morsels of food, and looking a perfect picture of emaciation until he stretches his head out or bends it round and dies quietly. This condition, known among the natives as Dhoobla, is often associated with diarrhœa, dysentery, and, especially, mange. Dropsy (Zharbad) combined with paralysis (Jolay) generally supervenes before death or the attack of anæmia assumes this form from the commencement. On post mortem examination a considerable amount of serum may be found present in the serous cavities, partially white clots in the larger vessels and heart, gelatinous matter replacing the fatty material in the grooves of the surface of the heart, complete absence of adipose material, and, very frequently, numerous hydatids in liver, lungs, or spleen. In these cases arrangements must be made for feeding the patient by himself (as the disease sometimes results from his not getting his fair share of the food given for the three camels of one driver) under reliable supervision on palatable fodder, such as neem and burgot, in as large amounts as he will consume, and on boiled oodoodh instead of ordinary gram; excuse him from all work but give exercise daily; groom freely and thoroughly and administer vegetable and mineral tonics, for which milk will in extreme cases be found the best vehicle.

This disorder in camels is often merely the most marked indication of the disease known as SURRA, which recent researches have proved to be Relapsing Fever due to the presence of spiral organisms in the blood. Yaldwin speaks of Surra as very common and fatal—the result of overwork in the sun and want of water. As indicated by loss of crispness of the hair and by looseness of the hair of the tail. He termed the disease "Heat Struck," and suggests its treatment with one pound of Ardawa daily or a handful of green Tel soaked with a little salt all night and given in the morning. Dr. Evans added materially to our knowledge of this disease. He drew attention to the very considerable losses in camels experienced of the Punjab Frontier Force annually from this disorder, thus for example, in 1878 the 4th Sikhs lost 29 camels almost all from Surra, in the following year 41, and in 1880, 28. The disease was well known to natives in charge of the animals and attributed by them to a fly, Búra Dhung, which in May comes from jungle land that has been under water, is very numerous in June and July, but at the commencement of October is obtainable with difficulty. It bites cattle and donkeys without ill effect, men with the result of a painful swelling at the seat of attack, and horses and camels causing the disease known as Khanhog, Doaia, Surra, (in its various stages), and Phipri in camels. *Khanhog* is the first stage of the disease; the animal is off feed, sluggish, and his urine is high coloured, if he be treated early he may recover from the disease at this stage. In *Doaia*, the second stage, the patient swells all over the chest: in the third stage there is dropsy of the abdomen and legs and progressive anæmia. Recovery is now almost hopeless, but if it occurs the animal is useless for two years, the urine becomes high coloured during the hot season but is natural during the cold weather. The attack occasionally lasts only a week and seldom exceeds four months in duration. Dr. Evans found that the Surra parasite lived longer by some hours in the blood of the camel after its removal from the body than in that of the horse. This disease has not yet been recognized among the few camels found in Southern India, but there can be little doubt that it is much more widely spread than has been hitherto supposed and that Evans is right when he attributes much of the extraordinary fatality among camels in our Afghan Campaigns to Surra. As we are still quite in the dark concerning the origin of this affection the views of natives attributing it to the bite of a fly deserve some attention and investigation. It is, in so far as we know, impossible to cure Surra, and considering the number of diseases (anthrax, dropsy, simple fever, &c.), with which it has been confounded we must accept the opinion of its curability with reserve. Its prevention consists in sound hygiéne for camels, care in avoidance of stagnant drinking water, and protection from vicissitudes and extremes of climate.

Anthrax (*Chhalie*) is described by Nunn as destroying in Shahpur District only hundreds of camels annually and by Oliphant as "a very serious malady in the camel which caused immense loss in the space of a few weeks in the Kuram Force spreading rapidly and running its course in a very short time." The latter officer records that at one station out of 919 camels 419 died in seventeen days (22nd July to 7th August), and the camel column of the force was annihilated, 1,400 animals dying in July,

August, and September. Recently Burke has studied the disease at Cawnpore in Transport Camels* noting a fatality of about 18°/₀ of animals grazing together in churraees or jungles and of about 50°/₀ of cases affected; this outbreak seemed clearly traceable to contagion but the period of incubation was uncertain, also the duration of persistence of virulence. It was observed that some animals which recovered suffered from a second attack often not many days after the first. Nunn mentions two forms of anthrax as occurring in the Montgomery District, termed respectively *Bil* (Dysenteric) and *Barr* (Apoplectic); Burke divides the disorder into internal and external forms, he finds that the latter often recover. Oliphant "noticed but few cases in which the effusion was in the areolar tissue in immediate contiguity to the skin but found generally tumours of extravasated coagulated blood on the surface of internal organs especially the lungs and spleen. Gilchrist does not record this disease as a distinct pathological state but he probably had seen cases and noted them as zaarbadh, jolay, apoplexy, and so on. It has been supposed that camels do not suffer from anthrax but experience has amply proved the incorrectness of this view; the characteristic organisms have been seen in the blood, in the tissues of aborted fœtuses, and even in the milk (Burke). The disease is most frequent during and after the rains—it is protean in its manifestations and not unfrequently has run its course unobserved so that the patient seems to fall dead suddenly or after having been for an hour or so in distress. As a rule the first signs noticed are dark coloured urine, the animal refusing food and drink, and becoming suddenly and rapidly emaciated. The internal temperature will be found high, rumination suspended, and the limbs apparently stiff and rigid. In external anthrax the skin becomes affected with boils and eruptions of various kinds which Burke has by observation of Bacilli in them demonstrated as true features of the disease. Diarrhœa and hæmorrhagic evacuations, sometimes associated with protrusion of the rectum, occur in some cases and a peculiar putrid and offensive smell of the animals before death with rapid decomposition of the carcase after death (Nunn). The disease under this latter form has possibly been confounded with rinderpest. Burke

* *Quarterly Journal of Veterinary Science in India*, No. 14, Vol. iv., p. 224.

has found that pregnant animals abort either during the attack, during convalescence, or even after recovery: the milk in this disease is thick and scanty and contains blood from the first. A not unfrequent feature is the occurrence of local swellings, especially involving the posterior part of the body, and an interesting question for solution by future enquirers is whether the camel, like the ox, suffers from a form of true external anthrax (Emphysema infectuosum) due to a distinct bacterium differing from that of the internal form of anthrax. Sooner or later in the attack, after continuous shivering collapse sets in, the animal lies on the ground raises its head occasionally or bends the neck and throws the head backwards, maintaining that position persistently until death occurs. *Prognosis* is always unfavourable. The natives consider the disorder quite incurable, although they give certain medicines such as gugal, gur, aromatic substances, and the seeds of Lepidium Sativum. They sometimes try the effect of the actual cautery, burning a line all round the body or branding across the spine, and a certain amount of curative virtue is sometimes found in the fresh blood of a goat. European methods for treatment of blood diseases have hitherto been but little tried for the camel, Burke considers he has obtained good results from use of carbolic acid and oil but his views need to be confirmed; he has pointed out an interesting secondary condition worthy of attention in the treatment of this affection in that there occurs a "fever of re-absorption," the temperature rising to 101°, 102°, and 103° on the third, fourth, and fifth days after apparent recovery (Veterinary Journal, January 1886). Often there is absolutely no time for treatment the animal being admitted in the moribund state. *Treatment* of a preventative nature is, therefore, more to be relied on than curative measures. Pasteur's system of Anthrax Vaccination has not yet been tried with camels, in so far as I am aware, but Government ought to at once attempt to reduce fatality by this means. The methods suggested, and enforced in so far as the emergencies of active service would allow, by Oliphant in the Kuram Valley are as follows:—(1) division of the total number of animals into several herds, (2) strict attention to cleanliness and a general sanitary condition of the camel lines, (3) supply of green food, (4) destruction of diseased animals, and (5) the disposal of their carcases by fire. To these may be added disinfection of localities, attendants, and affected animals; whenever possible removal of the camels still unaffected to a fresh locality where there is good range and plenty of fodder, and it must be remembered that this disease affects other animals also and is communicable to them especially by carcases and inoculation. Every care should, therefore, be taken in avoidance of places where post mortem examination or burial of anthrax carcases has occurred, and in making a post mortem examination the operators should adopt every precaution against their being inoculated. It is said that during the Horse Plague in Egypt in 1876 many camels died from anthrax and it is not at all improbable that camels and other transport animals have in many cases acted as unsuspected sources of anthrax conveyance to troop horses. Even under present arrangements it is wonderful how long even extensive fatality may be going on in the transport lines of a station, especially among camels, before the Veterinary Surgeon of the British troops at that station receives any notification of it; things were, however, much worse before the transport was made a separate branch of the Commissariat.

Post mortem Examination shows, generally, amber-coloured fluid in the serous cavities, especially the peritoneal sac, blood extravasations either as petechiæ of serous membranes, or masses of coagulated blood in the substance of parenchymatous organs. Emphysematous diffused patches of sero-sanguinous fluid may be found in various parts of the body, and gelatinous deposits at the sublumbar region and replacing the fat around the heart. In some cases there are no appreciable abnormalities and the appearance of the blood differs little (if at all) from its normal purple colour.

It is not unfrequent for outbreaks of a very fatal but obscure nature to occur among camels especially on service. One of these has been recorded by Veterinary Surgeon Haslam in the December 1885 number of the Veterinary Journal, and its facts are well worthy of notice. It seems there was a certain amount of doubt as to whether the animals did not succumb to poisoning, anthrax, or sunstroke, but the conclusion arrived at that "It is a fact that *ad libitum* watering immediately after a large meal in this climate will cause enteritis, peritonitis, and death in otherwise healthy camels" must be considered as not proven. V. S.

Haslam records that a severe fatality occurred among camels at the Desert Camel Camp, Suez, in June 1885. He found the gait difficult and painful, movements slow and tottering, lying down, quietly rolling on to the side; bending back the head or looking round at the flanks; an uneasy helpless look of the eye; no violence; pulse frequent, weak, and full; great tympanitis, breathing laboured, flanks drawn up; gradual exhaustion; ultimately stoppage of respiration and circulation and death in 6—8 hours after last meal. Fifty-six dead ones lay on their left side. Rumenotomy proved successful in slight cases; in others Mr. Haslam tried very gentle exercise, one pint warm water every two hours as a drench and feeding on warm bran-mash. Sixty-four camels died: post mortem examination showed diffuse inflammation of the alimentary canal from cardia to anus, diffuse peritonitis, stomach full of *unchanged* food and water with much gas (chiefly CO_2). Brain and spinal cord unaffected. In about 40°/₀ the heart had undergone partial or total *mucoid* degeneration (the right side generally, sometimes even the left ventricle was attacked). All but twenty-seven were in poor condition. Some cases disembarked on the day previous to death were suffering from pneumonia, but not sufficient to account for death. Division I. Disembarked after a six days journey, marched to the desert and watered on following morning shortly after a full meal of bhoosa and barley. Twenty-one deaths occurred within 16—24 hours after disembarkation, some on the line of march, some after arrival in camp. The distance traversed was four miles in the hottest portions of a not excessively hot day. Death took place more by shock (Syncope) and exhaustion than by the inflammatory state." A few of these suffered from scabies: simultaneously in Camp 43 died, but most of them 26 in number, all suffering from scabies, had disembarked on 25th and marched up on 26th. Those animals which had not marched up lately were the weakest and most severely affected with scabies in the camp; of them twelve were suffering from severe wounds, skin inflammation, fever, &c., and were unexercised. Five of the camels were strong and well. These camels were watered in the morning on account of the unusual heat of the day and a Khamsin wind commencing to blow which caused the camels to get loose and obtain drinking water freely. Some were watered at the fresh water canal where they got embedded in the mud and struggled severely.

FOOT AND MOUTH DISEASE undoubtedly affects the camel and proves a source of considerable losses especially on service. Gilchrist seems to have observed it for he speaks, under the heading *zillay baaz,* of ulceration of the mouth and tongue of an aphthous character; the animal being off its feed and feverish. The vesicles become pustules and then ulcers, and in severe cases the nostrils are invaded by them. The tongue is very white and rough from enlargement of papillæ. The treatment adopted was a cathartic internally, camphorated oil and astringents locally. Pringle (Veterinary Journal, September 1880) has given us an interesting account of this disorder as it prevailed in Afghanistan. The *symptoms* are those of fever, and a tendency to kneel facing the sun was observed. The feet swell all over, not in the cleft only, and are sore, as showed by the animal's gait. On the *third day* the entire foot is much swollen and seems to sweat, the skin is glistening and its hair on end. The mouth is less affected than the feet, being swollen and red inside, there is profuse salivation. On the *fifth day* very small vesicles appear in a circle all round the foot, in the cleft and to three inches above the border of the sole. Then vesicles in the mouth appear, rather like boils; they burst and leave nasty sores and an acrid discharge. The hair drops off the feet and the skin of the affected part peels off leaving a red coronary band which from a short distance "looks exactly as if small bundles of little red berries had been hung round them. At this stage the animal seems to suffer pain in all his joints." The fever usually subsides in eight or nine days. In bad cases the sole pad sloughs off. Even in health, scars in the mouth from prickly herbs in the food may be seen, these must not be confounded with foot and mouth disease ulcers. Fatality in this disorder occurs from inanition the result of inability to collect green food, from high fever, or from exposure to the sun's rays. The disease is communicable from and to other transport cattle.

RINDERPEST is recorded by Nunn as occuring among camels in the Punjab. The ordinary dysenteric form is called *Zahmat* or *Zahmat osat* in Montgomery District, *Mori* in Hazara. Animals so affected are not treated, for the disease is considered due to Kismut and, so, allowed to take its course. This disorder corresponds to the Murrain in Europe and affects also Indian bullocks and is known as the Burra Azar. Gilchrist gives a good description of the disease from which we learn that the serous and mucous membranes of the head, lungs, and bowels are the seats of the affection, the lungs and air passages being, also, most commonly disordered. The symptoms observed are those of apoplexy, the animal has a wild look and becomes delirious then falls, breathes stertorously, and dies. Sometimes at the commencement of the attack there is lethargy and confused demeanour the patient walks round and round its picket and attempts to lie down without doing so until the lethargy becomes great, then he falls heavily, breathes stertorously, and dies from pressure on the brain. Sometimes the nostrils are affected there being mucopurulent discharge and the animal frequently rubbing the nose against the ground or some neighbouring object and being restless and uneasy and uttering a guttural sound. In other forms the throat, uvula, and lungs are affected. When the bowels are the main seat of disorder there is purging, the evacuations being fœtid, slimy, often bloody. The belly is swollen and rumbles freely Tongue pale and dry. Animal is off feed and restless. Autopsy shows one or all of the following lesions, effusion on the brain, pneumonia, congestion of the brain or lungs, and inflammation and thickening of the bowels. Gilchrist completes his notice of this important disorder by recommending in the way of treatment prompt bleeding, sedulous fomentations of the body, good nursing, and purgation (if the bowels are the principal seat of the disorder), or common salt in four ounce doses.

Camel Pox or Variola Cameli has been observed frequently and seems to vary in severity much in different places. Hodgson describes it, under the name *Oheechuck,* as a slight disorder from which camels soon recover without treatment. A few cases of confluent small pox were destroyed in Afghanistan. The disease is known to the natives as *Mata,* and in one case, certainly, proved communicable to man (Oliphant). Masson has shown that children inoculated from affected camels show a more or less general eruption which usually is malignant and occasionally is mortal, the eruption being like that of cowpox in mankind; Agnelli states that the Arabs protect themselves from small pox by camel pox inoculation. The disease seems to be frequent in Algeria (Fleming).

Glanders has not yet been recorded as affecting the camel.

Tassy tells us that the Arabs have seen Farcy but not Glanders, probably the disease referred to is nonspecific lymphangitis. Gilchrist describes, as not common a disease, *Pinsee ka murz*, of which the cause is not very apparent. The membrane lining the nostrils becomes hyperæmic and then the seat of confluent ulcers with a profuse, fœtid, and sanguineous discharge. Sometimes the ulceration involves the outer wall of the nostrils. It yields to stimulant and detergent ointments but generally camphorated oil is necessary to prevent the appearance of maggots. This disease may be nonspecific and no experiments seem to have been made hitherto on the conveyance of glanders to the camel by inoculation.

Pakdar, Pockdarie, Phitgaya, Purana purgaya, Dalon se nikle gaya, and other names have been applied to an epizootic form of inflammation of the lungs, the exact relations of which with pleuro-pneumonia zymotica of the ox have not yet been established. Leach found it prevalent in Afghanistan and that but few animals recovered from it. It was considered contagious and conveyed from diseased to healthy animals by the medium of the picketing grounds. The diagnosis is difficult, but Leach tells us that "a certain method of recognizing it is to examine the urine by wetting a handful of clean earth with it and then smelling it If the animal is diseased the urine will have a fishy smell, although not differing in appearance from that of other camels." The disease is denoted by staring coat and slight ulceration of the lips (?) Animals suffering from it often start on the line of march apparently quite well and shortly afterwards simply lie down and die. Prompt segregation of affected animals is necessary; infusion of Babul bark and a mussaul consisting of aromatics, salt, and haobarang are used in treatment. The isolation, it is stated, should continue a month after recovery.

STRANGLES.—Sore throat with abscess is of frequent occurrence in the camel but whether of a specific nature and pathologically identical with the pyogenic fever of horses has not been established. Nunn mentions it as frequent, among riding camels especially, in Abbotabad and known as Khúk or Huk, whereas in Shahpur it is known as Hubbi. Apparently this is the same disease as was described by Gilchrist as Mumps, Choodee, or Cuppray. The leading symptoms are swelling and soreness of the throat, sometimes associated with ulceration of the lining membrane of the pharynx and fauces. The swelling generally begins in the glands on each side of the throat behind the lower jaw and may extend as far down as the sternum; it is painful and much difficulty is experienced in swallowing. High fever, catarrh, free flow of saliva are present, the patient takes even liquid nourishment with difficulty and so falls off very much in condition and not unfrequently dies exhausted, or bursting of the abscess gives relief. Strangles occurs most frequently in the hot weather, but cases come in for treatment at all times of the year, young animals especially are affected. Natives treat by poulticing the wound with medicated cataplasms, such as those of viola, vitex, margay root, or solanum nigrum with amaltus. If the abscess tends to recede or "hangs fire" they apply the actual cautery. The correct treatment is to support the strength and encourage suppuration as in horses. Gilchrist bleeds, purges, and foments the whole head. He attributes the disorder to the animal drinking or being washed when heated with exertion. We should bear in mind that it is possibly contagious.

Rabies.—Baron Larrey when in Egypt noticed with regard to Hydrophobia that camels suffer from a form of madness during the time of rut, and bites from them in this state are dangerous, but the disease is not contagious. The symptoms are the escape of an abundant thick saliva, constant bellowing, horror of water, wasting, fever, falling off of the hair, and bad temper which showed itself by their pursuing men and other animals. If excited the symptoms increased and often ended fatally *(Lancet)*. There seems to have been in the mind of the learned French Surgeon a considerable amount of confusion in this matter, some of the symptoms described are simply those of genetic phrensy, others seem imaginary (such as horror of water), others again seem not unlike those of true Rabies which undoubtedly affects the camel, as was long ago observed and reported in India, the disease being familiar to natives as Dewanah Kootha ka murz, and as such described by Gilchrist who records a case which he saw. The patient was bitten on the lip and two days after went off feed, became restless, got loose, and ran away. He was secured and tied up but kept trying to get loose and in doing so frequently fell down, and frequently started convulsively as from fear, frothing at the mouth, wild aspect, terror when approached. On the fourth day after the bite he became insensible, and then died. The natives treat with opium and jingili oil, but ineffectually.

TUBERCULOSIS has been described as affecting the camel, especially the pulmonary form of the disorder.

RHEUMATISM is almost universally considered of frequent occurrence in the camel. It is known under various names *Ghurrum* (Hodgson), Jakar Jana in Shahpur, Tak or Akrá, "stiff," in Montgomery (Nunn), Aker or Bhai (Leach), Vahee ka durudh (Gilchrist). This disease especially affects the joints; it occurs in the cold season when the animals are not sheltered at nights or are exposed to vicissitudes of climate. Probably it is the disease described by Yaldwin as "cold struck." Errors in diet are considered by the natives a fruitful source of this disorder thus Nunn speaks of the opinion that it results from eating dry tálli leaves (Dalbergia) and Leach that it follows feeding entirely on Mulberry or Shisham leaves. It is most frequent in old animals or those out of condition (Gilchrist). The symptoms are lameness, swelling and pain of the affected joints, generally those of the limbs—difficulty in rising (sometimes necessitating assistance in the act) or lying down, occasionally rolling in pain. Sometimes there is muscular rheumatism, according to Gilchrist, but he does not tell us how to diagnose it. Treatment comprises rest, good feeding, cordials, and laxatives; hand rubbing to the affected parts. In protracted cases the natives fire. They sometimes give the urine of another camel for three or four days or a mixture of coarse sugar, ashes of burnt horse skull, and putrid water, than either of which a much more clean and satisfactory alkaline solution might be administered. It is probable that as we learn more about the diseases of camels we shall find rheumatism much less frequent than hitherto supposed.

ZÉRBÁD is a term applied to debility with dropsy, especially when the limbs are the seat of œdema. It is a frequent disorder and well known to all camel men; probably some forms of it are specific others simple. Hodgson speaks of it under the name Bisova, Nunn considers that the English equivalent of Zérbád is Lymphangitis, Gilchrist mentions that it is sometimes known as Kussooree. There can be no doubt that many cases of anthrax, surra, and perhaps also purpura have been described under this heading as well as simple lymphangitis and simple anasarca. Charles Steel remarks that Zérbad was infrequent in his experience during the South Afghanistan Campaign (1878) but Oliphant noted it as frequent in the Kuram Valley. The order of frequency in which the several parts of the body are invaded is legs, belly, below chest, neck, head, thus it extends from below upwards. Some fever may be present but the bowels generally remain normal. Gilchrist describes under the name Sooka Zaarbahd extreme and often incurable cases the result of frequent attacks or neglect of the disease; these are always tedious. Zérbád is of frequent occurrence during convalescence from other disorders, it is not generally fatal, but seriously reduces the animal's condition. It is most prevalent in. cold weather and during the rains. Gilchrist advises after bleeding, physicking, and reducing with antimonials and mercurials for a week to give tonic mussauls, in Sooka cases after a purgative he gives tonics alternated with alteratives. The natives fire (in a most barbarous manner, Nunn), and adopt the judicious treatment of stimulant aromatics from the first with salt. Kalaziri, Gur, and Ajwain are given in balls "of about the size of a cricket ball rammed down with a stick" (Oliphant). Autopsy shows a sodden, dropsical condition of the tissues, pale heart, often much gelatinous lymph with serum in the peritoneal, pleural, pericardial, and arachnoid sacs. Cysts are generally found in considerable numbers in the lungs, liver, and spleen and they must be considered as a very serious factor in production of the debility. Experience shows that these Hydatid Cysts are of very frequent occurrence in the camel, and one writer of authority has not hesitated to term them "a very common cause of loss in camels." They are commonly by nonprofessional observers considered to be abscesses and described as such, an error which should be most carefully avoided, as complicating statistics. Abscess does not occur in the lungs, liver, or spleen without inflammation of those organs to a considerable extent but these hydatids (which are the larval form of Tænia echinococcus, a tapeworm of the dog) increase in size very gradually and cause only such irritation as suffices to condense the connective tissue in their immediate proximity whereby is formed the white cyst of fibrous substance in which they are contained. This cyst is generally so elastic as to squirt the watery fluid which it contains to a considerable distance when it is punctured and on slitting open the cyst we may give exit to a number of bladder-like masses, the larval tæniæ, or may find the contents, if the cyst be old, gritty and dried up from calcareous degeneration of the larvæ—thus gritty nodules are found in the lungs and other viscera which must not be mistaken for tubercular deposits. The cysts vary in size from that of a pea to that of a cricket ball; they cause anæmia solely by replacing the useful substance of the organ in which they are situated and so can prove the cause of death only when extremely numerous. Very occasionally, however, they prove fatal when ruptured by falls or other accidents in man and perhaps also do so in the camel. All parts containing these parasites should be destroyed after autopsy by fire. It is probable that the immature Tæniæ gain their situations for development into Hydatids by direct boring through the tissues, one of the earlier stages of development being a minute larva with six chitinous or silicious hooks. The only hæmatozoon (if the surra organism be not an animal) hitherto described is Filaria Evansi, discovered by Dr. Evans in blood clots from the camel and described by Dr. Lewis.

POISONING may here be noticed. It presents but few special features as concerns camels. We have no evidence that like cattle and horses in India they are apt to be poisoned for the sake of their hides, but this may be so. The men in charge when collecting fodder for their camels are careful to avoid certain plants some of which are unsuited to the time of year while others are known to be poisonous; Charles Steel remarked the care with which in South Afghanistan the plant called ateri was avoided. Yaldwin has known many hundreds of animals die from eating the Oleander-bush, the Leghumai, and the Gungao in Afghanistan. Outbreaks of communicable disorders, such as Rinderpest, and especially Anthrax, are apt to be mistaken by nonprofessionals, for poisoning, an error to be specially avoided during advance of an expedition into a new country, whether for hostile purposes or exploration, thus poisoning is described as frequent at first starting into the Australian desert.

We must rely on future research to solve the following problems among many others with regard to blood diseases :—

(*a*) Does the camel suffer from true glanders and farcy obtainable from the horse?

(*b*) Or from Pleuro-pneumonia Contagiosa and Rinderpest pathologically identical with those diseases in the ox?

(*c*) Does the camel recover from Surra and what is the natural history of this disorder and its spirilloid in camelidæ?

(*d*) Is Rheumatism so frequent in the camel as is generally supposed?

(*e*) Is Strangles of the camel the same disease as Strangles of the horse?

(*f*) Is Zérbád of camels ever a distinct specific disorder and if such be the case how may we distinguish between true Zérbád and Anthrax, Surra, and other disorders liable to be confounded with it?

Chapter V.—THE DIGESTIVE SYSTEM AND ITS DISORDERS.

The alimentary canal of the camel presents some extremely interesting peculiarities of anatomical conformation. The arrangement of the teeth, the peculiar appendage to the soft palate, the water cells of the stomach, also the lengths and capacities of the several parts of the intestines are worthy of note. The teeth are 36 to 38 in number, the anterior ones, incisors and tushes, being essentially cutting and puncturing organs, the posterior or molars being rough on their edges and sharp, having Crusta Petrosa of a black colour and generally five in number on each side of the jaw, the three anterior of each set being more or less rudimentary. The Pálu or Uvula did not fail to attract the attention of the older anatomists and most varied ideas have been expressed as to its physiological value. My researches show that it is a loose sac of highly glandular mucous membrane depending from the antero-inferior surface of the fixed and pendulous portions of the enormously developed soft palate.

The stomach presents the ordinary ruminant arrangement in that it consists of more than one compartment, but it is much more simple than that of the ox and sheep. It varies in detail of structure in the Camel, Dromedary, and Llama; but in all consists, in the main, of two compartments more or less subdivided, the first into Rumen and Reticulum, the latter into Abomasum and, sometimes, an extremely rudimentary Omasum. The following summary of the description by the late Professor Garrod from Nature, 3rd June 1875, will be found accurate and interesting:—

Rumen globose: muscular band from right of cardia runs along ventral surface, and opposite the middle of this a long and narrow aggregation of water-cells starts to run transversely to the left side of the organ. On the right side of this band a much larger collection of deeper cells embraces the right posterior part of the rumen in its crescentic mass. *Reticulum* in usual position, deeply honeycombed, with villi and slight muscular walls. Mucous membrane of rumen thin and smooth. The water-cells are formed on a frame-work of many intersecting muscular sheets arranged in layers with intervals of less than an inch between them one-half being at right-angles to the other so as to form rows of quadrilateral cavities. These are again incompletely divided up by secondary septa; diaphragm-like membranes partly close the orifices of the cells. *One* muscular fold represents the two of the œsophageal grove. A single cavity follows the Reticulum and represents the third and fourth compartments (but the *psalterium* is really absent). In the Bactrian Camel there is a small constriction serving to indicate the boundary line of it.

The measurements made by Colin have shown that the intestine of the Camel is about fifteen times the length of the body, that is one-fifth as long again as in the horse and three quarters the relative length of that of the ox. The small intestine is about two-thirds of the intestinal canal (63·37); which is relatively *short*, for that of the horse, ox, and sheep is about four-fifths. The cæcum, too, is (like that of the sheep) small. With regard to the capacity of the alimentary canal and its parts, the total capacity is put at 302½ litres (ox, 356½ litres; horse 211⅓ litres). Of this the stomach contents constitutes 810 parts in a thousand, small intestine 131, cæcum 11, colon and rectum 48. Thus the stomach is ten times as capacious as that of the horse, the small intestine not half as large, the cæcum about one-fourteenth the size, and the remainder of the large intestine about one-tenth, these proportions being relative. Thus, if we may judge from size, digestion in the camel as compared with that of the horse must be much more gastric, and, as far as intestinal digestion goes, mainly in the small intestine. As compared with the ox and sheep gastric digestion predominates in the camel by about one-eighth, but this about corresponds to the capacity of the water sacs, which compensates for the extraordinary smallness of the cæcum.

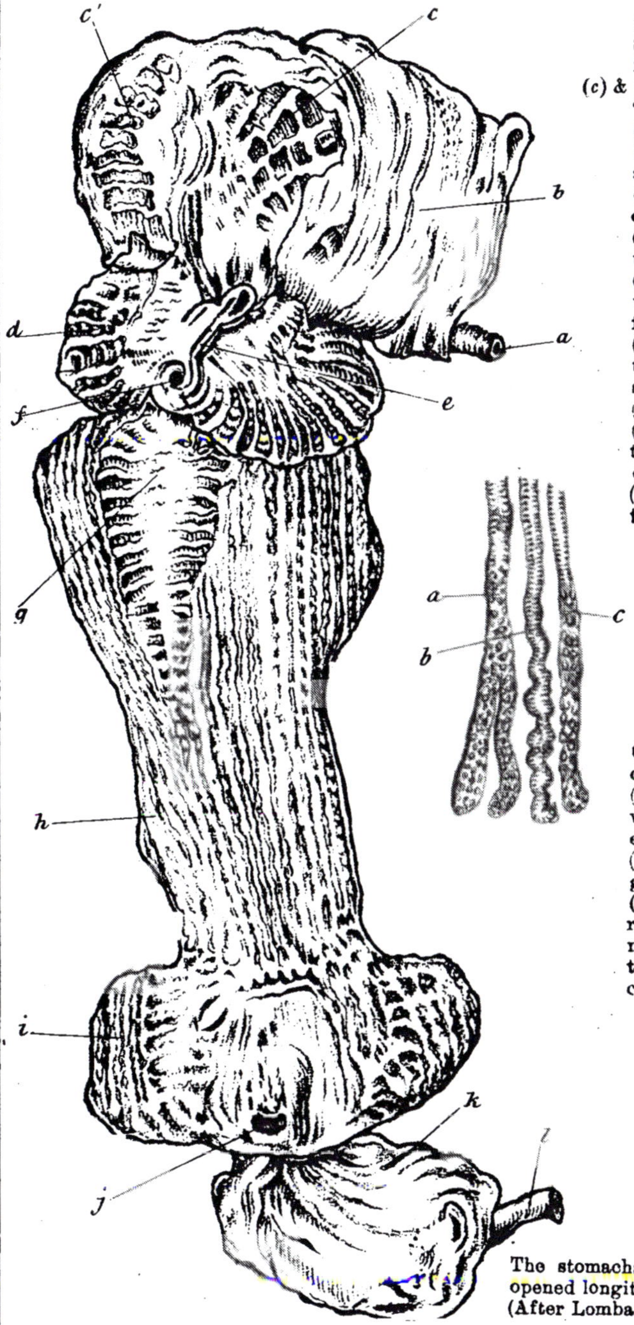

(*a*) Œsophagus.
(*b*) Smooth lining of Rumen.
(*c*) & (*c*) Sacculi or "water pouches."
(*d*) Reticulum.
(*e*) Single œsophagus pillar.
(*f*) Opening into omasum.
(*g*) Omasum with transverse plicæ.
(*h*) Abomasum with longitudinal folds.
(*i*) Terminal dilation of fourth stomach.
(*j*) Pylorus.
(*k*) Pyloric dilatations of duodenum.
(*l*) Duodenum, tubular part.

Glands of the sacculi of the Rumen.
(*a*) double peptic with spheroidal epithelium.
(*c*) Simple peptic gland with ditto.
(*b*) Single and spiral with columnar epithelium throughout (mucous)

The stomachs of a camel opened longitudinally.
(After Lombardini).

LITHOG: FOR LAWRENCE ASYLUM PRESS; MADRAS, 1890

BY ALEX: BARREN.

Making allowance for these anatomical peculiarities the relative capacities of stomach and intestine differ but little from those of other ruminants. Colin's estimates are worth insertion here for reference.*

The disorders of the alimentary canal and abdominal organs have not in most cases been adequately diagnosed; so that for the present we have to fall back on the old form of classification of cases as Indigestion, Colic, Diarrhœa, Dysentery, Constipation. These conditions are really only indications of disorder; they are useful for practical purposes to an extent, but in order to treat cases rationally the practitioner must go into their nature much more thoroughly. Thus, it is certain that almost all cases of Indigestion in the camel have their seat in the stomach rather than in the bowels and we have reason to believe that many cases of colic, *i.e.*, abdominal pain without inflammation, are either flatulence or spasm of the stomach. Theory informs us that, as the camel is a ruminant his stomach is more liable to disorder than his bowels, and that as his intestines are proportionally small so will they have but little tendency to disease as compared with the stomach. Yet we know that the camel is extremely liable to Diarrhœa and dysenteric complications of disorders undoubtedly intestinal.

The pendulous portion of the soft palate has hanging from its anterior surface a loose bag of mucous membrane which contains in its substance a number of glands. This is termed the PÁLU and it is, in someway or other, distensible with fluid to an enormous size and capable of protrusion through the mouth from which it projects in the form of a mucous, white or pigmented, bladder of very remarkable appearance. This extraordinary phenome-

---

* I. Length in relation to body:—

Body: Intestine		Sm. Int.	Cæcum	Colon	Total
1 : 15,	in Dromedary	·63	·01	·36	1.
20,	Ox	·81	·02	·17	...
27,	Sheep	·80	·01	·19	...
12,	Horses	·75	·04	·21	...
4,	Cat	·83	·17 (Cæcum and Colon)		...

II. Capacity.	Total Contents of Canal.	St.	Sm. Int.	Cæcum.	Colon and Rectum	Total.
Horse	211·34 litres	·085	·302	·159	·384 × ·070	1
Ass ...	104·50 ,,	·097	·229	·201	·397 × ·076	1
Ox ...	356·40 ,,	·708	·185	·028	·079	1
Dromedary	302·50 ,,	·810	·131	·011	·048	1
Sheep ...	44·20 ,,	·689	·204	·023	·104	1
Cat ...	·58 ,,	·695	·146	·159 (Cæcum, Colon and Rectum)		1

non is associated with a peculiar gurgling sound and is especially seen when the animal is in the condition known as Must. The physiological value of the Pálu is obscure. It has been currently accepted as a means of moistening the throat and mouth when the animal is "dry" through a feverish state of the system or as a result of work in dry hot air. Gilchrist alludes to INFLAMMATION OF THE PÁLU as *Gahasha,* the result of accidentally wounding the part by biting the "uvula and loose skin about the top of the throat which he can protrude at will," but, occasionally, this state is seen as a result of constitutional condition. The patient is off feed on account of pain in swallowing, and the upper part of the neck is painful on pressure, as shown by a distinctive grunt of pain, which may occur even without pressure being made. The disorder yields to astringent emollient gargles, fomentation externally, and antiphlogistics.

Three forms of SORE THROAT are described in addition to that just referred to, *i.e., Sulfa ka murz or Zillay Baaz* and *Choodee ka murz,* catarrhal affections which occur in cold or rainy weather. The former seems to have its seat in the mouth and larynx the tongue being pale and rough, there being some difficulty in breathing, and the patient frequently grinding the teeth. The latter resides in both larynx and pharynx there being swelling of the throat, no cough, lachrymation. It results from sudden cooling of the animal when heated.

The third form of sore throat is a peculiar swelling of the larynx said to result from the animal overstretching the neck when reaching to a high branch to obtain food, or otherwise overstraining the parts at the top of the wind-pipe. These disorders must be treated by good nursing, stimulant mussauls, and fomentations. The natives use sternutative powders (errhines) largely for them. A case of sore throat may, it must be remembered, prove either strangles or nonspecific inflammation of the throat glands, PAROTIDITIS, exhibiting the symptoms and requiring the treatment for that disorder when seen in the horse, as in the case described by V. S. (1st Cl.) Thos. J. Symonds in the *Quarterly Journal of Veterinary Science* for October 1885.

A simple GLOSSITIS has been described under the name *Kookra;* it readily yields to emollients and, therefore, can only in the earliest stages be confounded with Gloss-anthrax.

VOMITION, Joogál, is described by Gilchrist as due to inflammation and distension of the stomach especially during the hot weather. It also results from consumption of the leaves of a Dekhan plant known as gumchí. In such cases Nature must be assisted in relieving the distended or inflamed stomach.

Two principal disorders of the Rumen are described. HOVEN or FLATULENT COLIC. *Bissel* (Leach) is probably the disorder here referred to, but the seat is sometimes the intestines. The disease most frequently occurs in cold weather and is associated with a certain amount of fever which indicates that there is more mischief going on than simple gaseous accumulation, indeed there seems to be in these cases a subacute inflammation of the mucous lining of the alimentary canal; the urine is generally scanty and always high coloured; the bowels are torpid or loose, and in slighter cases it is noticed that the dung-balls are not properly formed. The patient suddenly goes off his feed, becomes restless, moving from one hind leg to the other, uneasy when touched, and irritable in the extreme, as denoted by a tendency to bite his neighbours; the belly becomes swollen and he sometimes lies down and rolls violently or simply presses the belly against the ground, champs his jaws and shows other signs of pain. Occasionally a little wind may be passed per anum. Dietetic errors of various kinds, excess of green food, especially with dew on it, bad food, and, sometimes, poisonous plants give rise to this disorder. It must be treated on the ordinary lines, namely by active fomentation, administration of agents suited to disperse the accumulated gases, and endeavours to allay pain by hand-rubbing or stimulants to the belly; warm ghí or til—or taramera oil in half seer doses may be given followed by active purgation and great care in selection of food. The natives fire in two lines from shoulder up the neck to the ear and with the palm leaf brand on each shoulder. They give, daily, beef, sarson oil, salt, and aromatics (Leach.) Severe cases are termed by the natives *Soale,* milder ones *Malole* (Gilchrist). A very severe form (termed also *Sül*) is mentioned by Nunn as attacking animals of about two months old and carrying off large numbers annually. It is considered quite incurable. Another form of colic is spoken of by Hodgson in the *Veterinarian* for 1852 under the name of *Rus,* as attacking animals under a month old.

Impaction of the Rumen has recently been observed as a fatal disorder among camels used in warfare in the Soudan, due to long periods of dry fodder feeding without supply of water for drinking purposes. The symptoms are those of not-very-urgent colic, some benefit results from pouring numerous bottles-full of water down the throat and from frequent doses of oil, combined with the ordinary treatment for colic.

Enteritis is disease insidious in its approach and most dangerous in its results. It seems to generally have its seat in the small intestines in the camel and to assume a subacute character. It is one of the numerous disorders known to the Serwans as *Bhao.* There is fever, as denoted by warmth of the surface of the body and panting, exhaustion indicated by a pendulous state of lower lip, staggering gait, and the patient resting on its side stretched out; twitching of the ears, firm closure of the jaws, and nasal breathing are also given as symptoms. This state generally results from impaction of the intestines and leads to Ascites, when the belly, at first tucked up, becomes round and full and may contain as much as six gallons of fluid (Gilchrist). The best treatment seems to be opium or bhang in considerable doses combined with calomel and hot water applications or blisters to the belly. Gilchrist mentions "tapping the belly" for ascites but does not state if he ever performed the operation.

By most authors Costiveness or Constipation is considered a disease *per se.* Leach describes it under the name *Sukhbund,* Hodgson *Guptul Hudha,* and Gilchrist *Guttud ka Murz.* The animal with bowels persistently confined becomes dull, weak, off feed, restless, and drowsy, and a certain amount of tympany may set in, or severe abdominal pain supervene. When a seer of warm ghí or two ounces of aloes in a pint of milk has opened the bowels the evacuations will be found hard and scanty, often coated with slime, and of a dark colour and fetid odour. The urine is scanty and high coloured. Enemata, laxatives frequently repeated, and fomentations to the belly and, subsequently, calomel in drachm doses will be of benefit. *Post-mortem* examination, for this state not rarely proves fatal, shows the liver in a pale flabby condition and the bowels ulcerated. Indeed Chronic Constipation must be considered a form of Enteritis.

Diarrhœa, Purging, Dysentery have long been noted as frequent and severe in the camel especially during the exigencies of active service. Even in private camels constant care is needed to guard against these very fatal conditions, changes of weather or diet, exposure when heated, a severe day's work, leaving the animal without a covering on a cold night, in fact almost any chill or change, may bring on an attack of diarrhœa. Tassy speaks of purging on service from eating acrid plants especially one described as Bonnafao *var.* Alpha. Gilchrist alludes to the disease as arising "spontaneously during rainy and cold weather or the result at the commencement of the rainy season of the animal eating of the young and tender growth of the plant called Kaatamoal, of which the animal is very fond and which at a greater age is a very nutritious diet." The plant is also called Junglee Erundee or Wild Castor Plant. Feeding on gram only, or on too much grain, have been found to produce this disorder, as also have irritants of any kind in the bowels, such as coarse indigestible fodder; neglect and hard work, cold, and continuous non-supply of green fodder are active factors in the production of dysentery on service. Young camels suffer most, and, as Nunn has shown, it causes great fatality among them in the Punjab where it is known as Rik and treated by giving rice and bhang with the milk of a drying-up cow. It is not unfrequently associated with liver disorder. Both diarrhœa and dysentery prove very fatal by exhausting the patient, generally a severe case of skin disease results in fatal diarrhœa. I have recorded, in the *Quarterly Journal of Veterinary Science in India,* Vol. II., p. 136, a case of fatal diarrhœa in which the lining membrane of certain parts of the alimentary canal was studded with round nodules either the results of tubercular deposit or of parasites, and I have on record a case of fatal diarrhœa due to the presence of whip-worm (Trichocephalus Cameli) in the intestine. This latter case is the more important to remember because Gilchrist did not succeed in finding *parasites in the alimentary canal of the camel.*

Symptoms; the fæcal evacuations vary in liquidity and colour, and they generally smell most offensive; the skin dry and coat staring, the eyes look dull and heavy, the urine is scanty and high coloured, the patient dull or showing slight signs of abdominal pain, some flatulence may be present, appetite is capricious, and the patient falls away in flesh very rapidly. Simple purging is termed by the natives *Dust Júláb* or *Soolee;* dysentery, in which blood is present in the evacuations, is *Penchees.* Dysentery may assume a chronic character in old animals and keep them in a weak and emaciated state with unthrifty, hide-bound skin. *Treatment;* the routine administration of stimulant mussauls during cold weather is beneficial for the alimentary canal as well as for the skin. On an attack of diarrhœa setting in all grain should be promptly stopped, the bowels cleared out by doses of ghee, stimulant aromatic substances administered and, if pain is present, doses of opium or bhang. The strength must subsequently be supported with tonics, and the liver occasionally acted on by doses of calomel, for it generally after death is found pale. Rice congee is the best vehicle for medicines in this disorder but milk of the cow may occasionally be substituted for it with benefit. If acute pain sets in the belly may be fomented or even blistered.

Having thus reviewed our knowledge of the diseases of the alimentary canal, we must confess its utter insufficiency from a modern pathological point of view, and must see what anatomical and physiological facts have been ascertained concerning the stomach and intestines of the camel with a view to improved pathology in the future. We have described the more striking features, but must look in the pages of Lombardini's erudite work for details in anatomy and refer to Colin for information (scanty though it be) on physiology. The cloven condition of the upper lip and the communication of its groove by a short canal with each nostril, the enormous size of the upper lip, the length of gape of the mouth, and the pendent lower lip are familiar to all observers. The duct of the parotid passes obliquely over the masseter to pierce the cheek as usual. Müller and Wede first studied the peculiar structure of the buccal papillæ of tylopods; these organs are remarkable as having the ducts of small glands (salivary) piercing their bases and opening on their surfaces a little below the points, there may be more than one gland to each papilla and several ducts may unite for a common opening: Richardi avers that he has found fibres of the red muscle of the cheek entering into formation of these papillæ. The molar glands pour their secretion through a number of openings against the molars

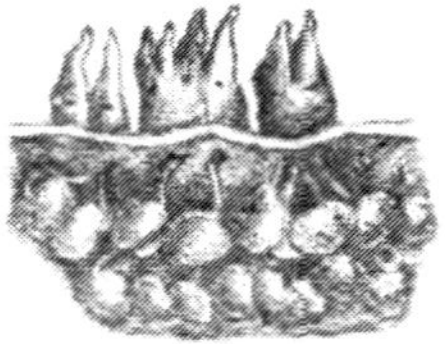

M M MOUTH, VERT.

M M MOUTH, LONG.

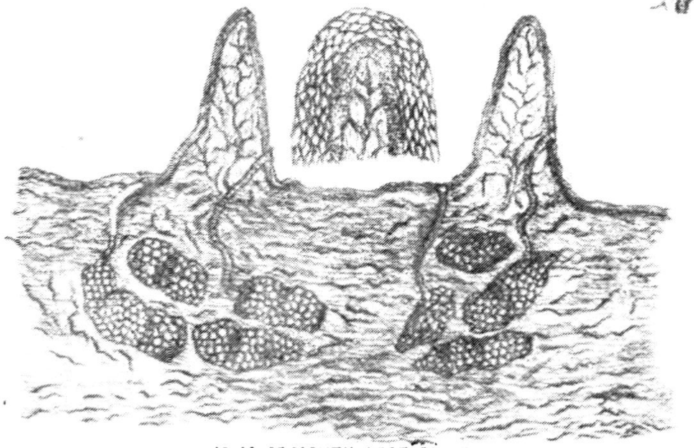

M. M. OF MOUTH, VERTICAL, ENLARGED

STRUCTURE OF PALU

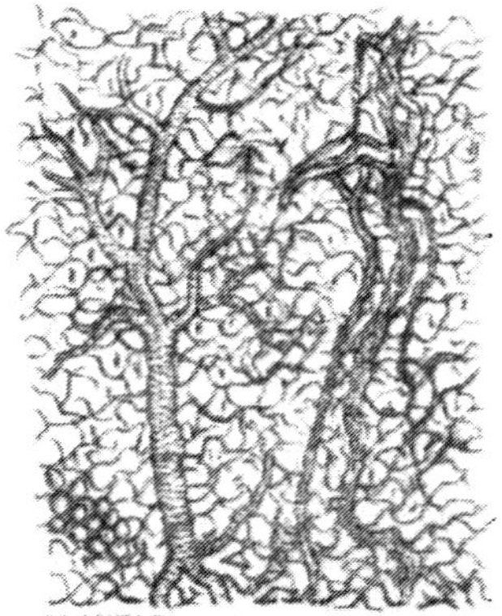

PLANTAR CUSHION STRUCTURE.

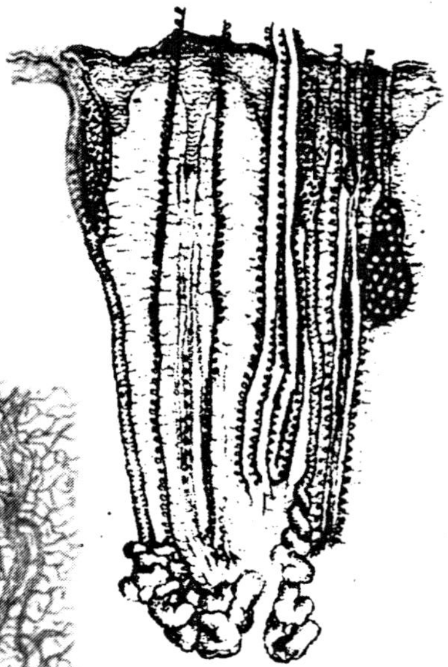

SECTION OF SKIN

HISTOLOGICAL DIAGRAMS
OF VARIOUS STRUCTURES.
(FROM LOMBARDINI).

LITHOG: FOR LAWRENCE ASYLUM PRESS, MADRAS 1890.

BY ALEX: BARREN.

in linear series: the large horny papillæ cover the inner surface of the cheek leaving that of the lips free, these papillæ look mainly backwards and downwards. The palate, tongue, and salivary glands do not differ materially in arrangement from those of the ox.

In consideration of the teeth, a number of questions arise. Firstly, the exact nature of the two upper incisors; secondly, the exact number of teeth in a full mouth; thirdly, the sexual variations in the number and form; fourthly, the periods of development or variation with age. These questions cannot as yet be considered satisfactorily solved. Lombardini "considers as incisors, teeth implanted in the anterior maxillary bone, and below in the anterior free margin of the inferior maxilla; as canines those which have the alveolus hollowed out of the anterior terminal angle of the superior maxillary bone above and opposite the maxillary foramen below; as premolar, the teeth situated in the region of the jaw which is called the bar." He then fixes the dental formula at *i.* $\frac{2}{6}$; *c.* $\frac{2}{2}$; *pm.* $\frac{2}{2}$; *m.* $\frac{10}{8}$.

An important point to be remembered is that the embryo camel distinctly presents the rudimentary tooth capsules of the upper incisors, as may be seen by dissection of a four months' fœtus.

Research seems to show:—That in the female the upper incisors are frequently absent, the premolars in the lower jaw are imperfectly developed, often one is absent, and the right is most frequently the deficient one. In the male the number of lower molars is somewhat irregular.

In male or female the total number (18) of molars may be differently distributed, the ten being either in the upper or lower jaw.

Tonsilar Concretions.—Lombardini records a case of accumulation of calculous material in the tonsils. This occupied the glandular orifices, being rather blue in colour near the surface and squamous but yellow and granular in the deeper parts. Analysis showed that the principal bases were calcium and magesium, there being traces of iron and sodium. Carbonates and phosphates abounded, but sulphates and chlorides were in very small quantity. There was organic substance both azotised and non-azotised. Density 2·2147.

Lombardini describes small guttural pouches as present in Pisan camels. He mentions occurrence of follicles of Lieberkühn in the rumen and reticulum; also that careful examination of the microscopical structure of the third gastric compartment proves it to be the analogue of the omasum throughout the greater part of its extent, but its posterior dilatation to correspond to the abomasum. The commencement of the duodenum is a dilated pouch. The spleen is large and adheres anteriorly to the diaphragm, posteriorly to the rumen.

Lombardini in discussing the functions of the so called water sacs of the rumen concludes (1) that the function of the sacs of the rumen is not really to collect and retain water, but rather to secrete the moisture necessary to enable the alimentary mass to become sufficiently soft to return into the mouth; (2) that the great secretory activity of the stomach on the one hand and the hardness of the normal diet on the other fully suffice to account for the presence of liquid matter in the rumen even two days after the ingestion of drink; (3) that slaughter of a camel to utilize his stores of liquid can only be practised effectually within forty-eight hours after drinking, *i.e.*, when it is hardly likely a caravan will have exhausted its other sources of water-supply. Home and Daubenton wrote that the muscular fibres of the cells of the second stomach of the camel closed that cavity when the food passed from the rumen into the third stomach, but permitted the fluid to pass when solid matters were going towards the œsophageal canal to be returned into the mouth. Otto, later, seeing in these sacs many muciparous cysts, considered they had some other office than simply retaining water, but he could not establish his position by proofs. Lombardini argues that if the stomachal sacs of the camel had for their principal duty only the preservation for a longer or shorter time of water ingested against its admixture with food in the rumen, then water perfectly pure ought to be drawn off on puncture of these sacs. As a matter of fact the material drawn off (from an animal bled to death) differed but little from that obtained from other parts of the rumen. This might, however, have been from *post-mortem* relaxation of orifices of the sacs. Again the position of these sacs at

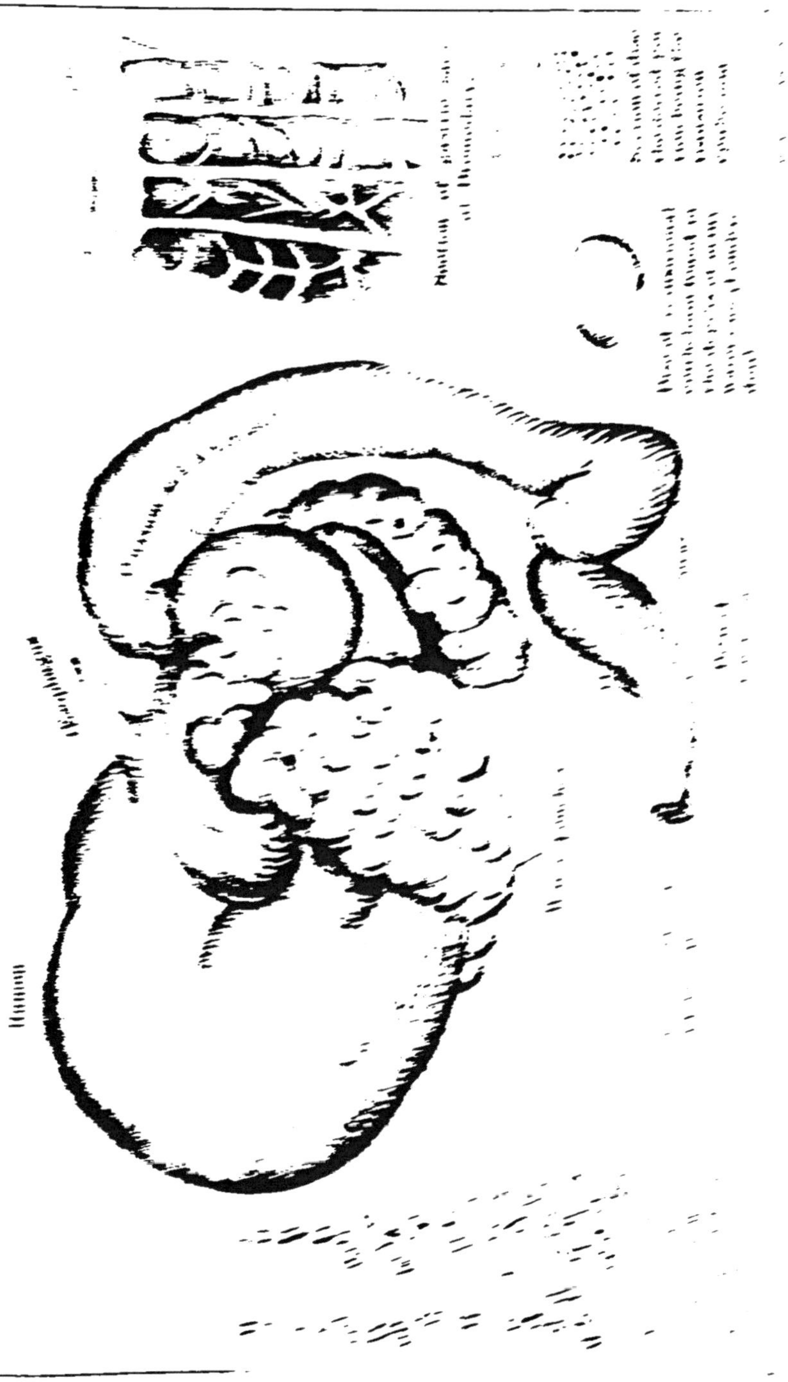

the upper and posterior part of the rumen is not suited for direct entry of water from the œsophagean canal; therefore it is probable that solid and liquid ingesta mix in the rumen of the camel as in that of the ox or sheep. Chemical analysis of the liquid drawn off from the sacs shows that it must have undergone admixture with the contents of the rumen, and moreover, that it must have been added to by the secretory activity of the follicules of Lieberkühn of the rumen. Thus the old idea of the water when consumed passing into the sacs and remaining stored up there is no longer tenable and the suspicions entertained by Messrs. S. Smith and Bennett as to its correctness are justified by Lombardini's experiments, but the view that the gastric arrangement of the camel is such as to enable him to retain in the rumen a considerable store of moisture still remains uncontroverted and in the absence of further proof to the contrary we must hold that the water sacs are the agency in this remarkable and beneficent process. Whether the water enters them directly from the œsophagus, as seems improbable, or simply diffuses into them from the rumen, or is secreted into them, or accumulates as the result of a combination of those processes is as yet doubtful, but two practical *facts* remain, that the camel above all domesticated quadrupeds is capable of enduring drought and that he may artificially be adapted for greater endurance by free and somewhat enforced ingestion of water prior to starting on a journey over arid tracts.

Fogliata has placed on record a case of Umbilical Hernia in an aged camel, the protruded organ being part of the small intestine; the surgical condition was not diagnosed during life of the animal. The same observer records the occurrence of Indigestion in Pisan camels, most prevalent during the winter among animals fed on hay. They go off feed and off the cud, the visible mucous membranes become red or yellowish, the belly swells, the nostrils are dry, and colicky pains may be present. The disease is not severe but readily yields to the treatment adopted by Fogliata, which consists in the ordinary Italian method of treating indigestion, *viz.*, in administration of a little senna infusion combined with manna and English (Epsom ?) Salts. Solid purgatives are considered not to give good results. In impaction or distension of the belly with solid matter sulphate of soda with tartrate of antimony is advocated, and in dyspepsia table salt and green food (Fogliata). The Native treatment for indigestion is to fire on the stifle three times on each side, each line being three or four inches long. Gilchrist, under the Native name of VAHEE GOLAH describes a form of *indigestion* which is sometimes associated with hydatids in the liver. It is denoted by weakness and a mangy condition of the surface of the body, often with obstinate eruption. He recommends well washing the surface of the body, giving grooming, and an occasional purgative, and putting the animal through a course of alteratives.

INTESTINAL PARASITES in the camel are considered to be rare, but certainly they sometimes cause mischief, as in cases referred to above under the heading diarrhœa. The Trichocephalus mentioned as Trich. cameli may have been either Trich. affinis of Rudolphi, which occurs both in the Bactrian Camel and the Dromedary, or it may have been Tricho. echinophylus described by Nitzsch in the Zeit. f. ges. Naturwiss; 1886, xxviii, p. 271.

Appendix: THE LIVER AND PANCREAS.—The Liver in the camel is discoid in form and principally remarkable for the amount of division it undergoes at its free margin, whereby it is broken up into lobes numbering over two hundred. In addition to these minor fissures there are the ordinary larger furrows extending on to the anterior and posterior surfaces. The whole organ is small for the size of the animal. Its duct is small, *devoid of gall bladder*, and unites with that of the pancreas before terminating in the intestine, which it does at some 58 mm. from the pylorus. The pancreas is elongated in the direction of the spine and bifid posteriorly. It occupies the usual position and sometimes has a small supplementary duct which opens into the bowel apart from the bile duct. CONGESTION OF THE LIVER has been described by Veterinary Surgeon (1st Class) Symonds in the Quarterly Journal of Veterinary Science in India, Volume III., page 368.*

* Symptoms: dull, off feed, lying down, very uneasy, twitching of ears, respirations nasal but normal in number, mucous membrane of a deep yellow, lower lip pendulous, bowels constipated; fæces small, dirty white,

Hepatitis, both acute and chronic, is recorded by Gilchrist as rare. It is denoted by unusual paleness of the dung, by irregularity of the bowels, and indigestion; chronic disease must be diagnosed by negative symptoms. Hodgson mentioned acute Hepatitis as known to the Natives under the name Heca Belau and treated by purging and firing, Gilchrist substitutes fomentation and bleeding for the firing and in chronic cases he gives alteratives, especially calomel, and tonics. There can be no doubt that at *post-mortem* examinations frequently the liver has been considered diseased because of ignorance as to its much divided condition normally. Hydatid invasion of the liver is extremely common, but is probably seldom a cause of death directly, although on active service it exaggerates the debility caused by the fatigues of campaigning. It must be remembered in making a *post-mortem* examination of a camel in which these larvæ are found that they are only to be considered the cause of death if they have burst or if there are manifest signs of inflammation of the liver traceable to their presence or if there is practical complete loss of functional liver substance. The latter is sometimes the case, the organ assuming an enormous size in consequence of the presence of cysts, but whether or no actual excess in bulk of the liver may so disturb intrathoracic or intra-abdominal pressure as to cause death has not been established. Unfortunately in so far as we know at present hydatid disease of liver admits neither of exact diagnosis nor cure. The ordinary liver Fluke (Distomum hepaticum) has been found in the liver and gall passages of the Bactrian camel, but no record is to hand of it giving rise to pathological conditions.

Chapter VI.—THE CIRCULATORY SYSTEM.

The heart of the camel is small and sometimes undergoes fatty degeneration, but the condition most familiar in *post-mortem* examination is a sort of semigelatinous change due to effusion between the fibres and the fat in the furrows being entirely replaced by yellow jelly-like substance. This appearance has given

and slimy; abdomen distended, body surface warm, temperature 103°F; Later purging set in. Sal ammoniac and decoction of neem leaves cured the case in eight days.

rise to the impression of frequent occurence of death from heart-disease, an idea which seems to be often quite erroneous, though the following observations would seem to lend it support. Burke described sudden death of camels with dyspnœa, tossing of the head, restlessness, more or less pain on pressure of the left side, and, generally, rolling over to the left side before death. Young animals suffered most; *post-mortem* examination showed changes in the walls of the heart of the same nature as "rapid cirrhosis" in man. These were general and gave rise to a swollen flaccid state of the walls, sometimes with extensive rupture and extravasation into the pericardium [Q. J. V. S., Vol. V., p. 179.]*

As a matter of fact the circulatory system of the camel is not highly developed and is little liable to disorder. No artery gives a distinct and easily recognisable pulse; but, taken at the heart, the average number of beats per minute is found to be 54. There is a cartilage in the ventricular wall which becomes ossified in the adult. The venous system is described as capacious, the jugular being 2-2½ inches in diameter and commonly used as the place for VENESECTION, which is performed by making the animal sit down, tying his fore-legs, and then fixing a ligature round the neck to raise the veins, as is the custom in bleeding the ox.

CHAPTER VII.—THE RESPIRATORY APPARATUS.

Neither lungs nor air passages present anatomical features worthy of special comment. These organs are larger and more capacious than those of the ox and yet not so developed as those of the horse. Respiratory diseases are of frequent occurrence but difficult to detect, or rather have proved so hitherto in the absence of full auscultation. The sides of the poor brutes are so covered with filth and parasites as a rule, their necks are so long and their teeth so threatening, and their bite so well known to be severe that placing the ear against the chest is apt to seem anything but pleasant even when the report of the Serwan or other symptoms have led us to a suspicion of respiratory disease. Hence our present ignorance, which may be summed up as follows.

* Since the above appeared in type Mr. Burke has informed me by letter that he only saw lesions of "rapid cirrhosis" in *one* case.

NASAL CATARRH, (Koodkay or Surdee), called by Leach Khoorka, is denoted by fever, indifferent appetite, watery discharge from mouth and nostrils succeeded by flow of mucous or muco-purulent matter, coat dull and dry, evacuations slimy and fœtid, mouth sometimes full of frothy saliva. The disorder varies much in severity, at times the bowels are a good deal out of order, cough is generally present. The patient must be clothed and sheltered, also rested in some place free from draughts, or, if in the open, native blankets must be piled on him. Then he must be given stimulant-tonic medicine and draughts of conjee of cholum, raggy, or cumboo, as Gilchrist suggests; further the chest may be fomented freely, as recommended by the same authority, but we would hesitate before adopting his further advice to purge, the utmost means we would suggest to be adopted for opening the bowels being febrifuge doses of the salines and enemata.

LARYNGITIS was one of the diseases reported as frequent among camels on the Nile Expedition, the great extent of the mucous membrane of the larynx of the camel being supposed to make him very liable to this disorder.

COUGH (Karachna v. Dansna) is mentioned by Gilchrist under Catarrh and he advises bleeding. Leach, however, and other authorities suggest very different treatment, of which the following are examples: give hot sheep and bullock head broth; take of the Philiaria thowar cactus half a seer, cut it up into pieces eight inches long, tie in a cloth, cover with mud and place for an hour in hot ashes, after taking it out break it up and give with gur, one seer, daily for three days; or soak four chitaks of Kaliziri in a seer of tobacco water or hooka pani for twelve hours and give the mixture daily for a week; or take of Kattheli, cut into small pieces and of ak leaves, each half a seer, and give it with two chitaks of huldi in water daily for three days. It will be observed that mysterious as these three native methods seem they really amount to taking care of the animal for three days and giving him aromatic stimulant and narcotic medicines which could be represented by the following dose, nitrous ether, one ounce; extract of belladonna, one drachm; tincture of ginger, four ounces, in water one quart.

We have already noticed the different forms of inflammation of the throat found in the camel, perhaps we may best here deal with one of the mysteries of cameline practice known as KAPAULEE. In all unusual cases the Serwan or Salootri informs us the animal is suffering from "Kapaulee," even though he be showing the most varied symptoms. Gilchrist considers the term is applied to inflammation of some part of the head, generally the soft parts of the orbits, and that if uncontrolled it will extend to the brain and cause death, but if properly treated the inflammation may be confined to the orbit and simply destroy its contents. It not uncommonly appears to be an inflammation of the areolar tissue of the upper part of the head which if uncontrolled speedily runs on to sloughy suppuration. It usually shows itself when the animal has come off the march and has drunk plentifully and, therefore, seems due to suppressed perspiration. Tremors first occur, on the second day the neck becomes stiff, and on the third day a hard and prodominant tumour about the size of a small hen's egg appears on the top of the head, or if the eyelids and the eyeball be the seat of disease these swell and there is much watery discharge, later the eyeball is destroyed by sloughy ulceration and a foul ulcer results which heals slowly. There is a discharge of unhealthy mucus from the nose and this discharge is specially profuse when, as is sometimes the case, the tumour is in the nostrils. If the tumour is protracted in appearance the case will probably prove fatal, therefore treatment must be prompt. So much for Kapaulee as seen by Gilchrist, Nunn saw it in Shahpur and termed it Catarrh or Influenza. The symptoms he observed were drooping head, off feed and cud, mucus coming from the nose, and hard swelling in both ears. The natives gave aromatics and fired in circles and round the roots of the ears. Cases of Kapaulee pointed out to us as such have been either ordinary cases of Catarrh in which swelling of some part or other had been caused by the cautery or obscure cases of internal disorder in which the animal had for days until death occurred been sitting with neck upright watchful of all that was going on but taking no notice of food and never chewing the cud. We have not had any opportunity of making *post-mortem* examination in these cases and regret that we must

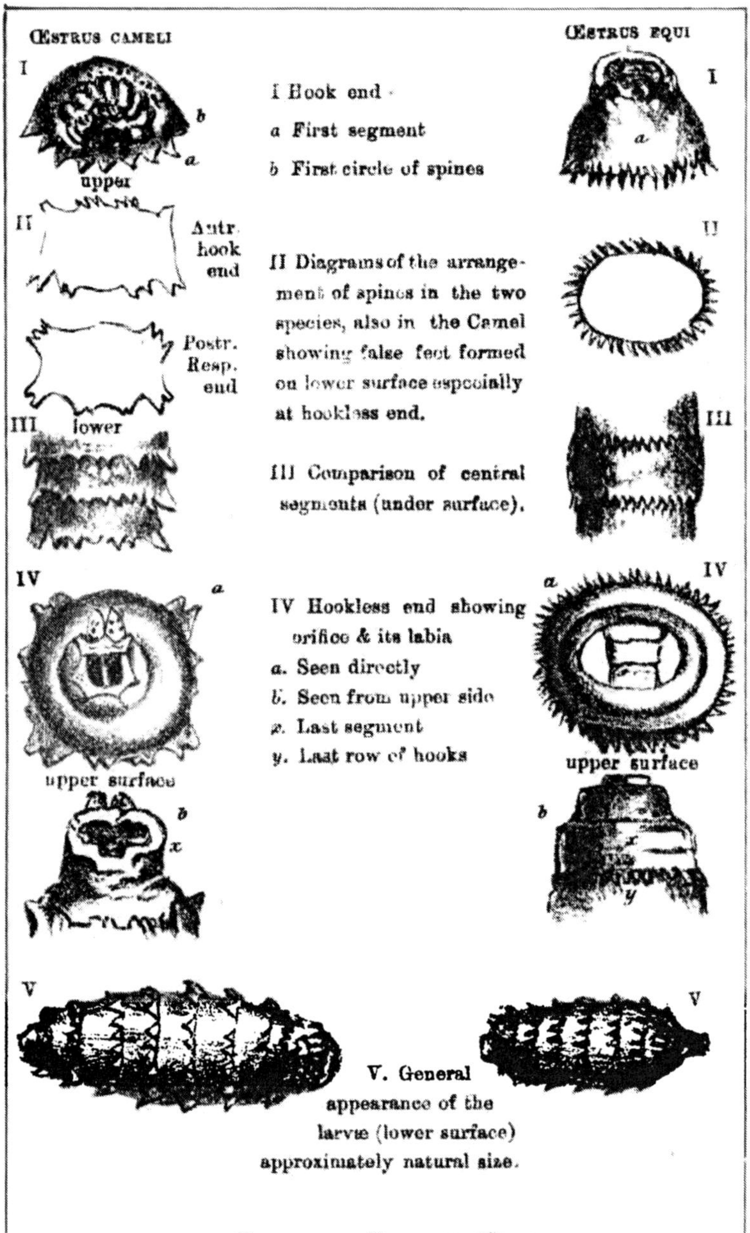

Bots of the Horse and Camel.

LITHOG: FOR LAWRENCE ASYLUM PRESS, MADRAS, BY ALEX: BARREN.

leave the question of pathology of Kapaulee for solution hereafter. The only observation bearing on this subject which has at all a solid basis is a *post-mortem* made by Queriple in Egypt where he found that in a case of fever with abscess of the head, absorption of the cranial walls had occurred and death from Encephalitis. Gilchrist suggests as treatment prompt and free bleeding (half a gallon to a gallon), purging freely with four ounces of aloes in milk or with half an ounce of croton seeds, and free fomenting of the affected part. He tells us the natives fire on the head, give stimulating mussauls and blow acrid substances into the nostrils, but he considers this latter practice calculated to do harm in the earlier stages though beneficial later, after suppuration has set in, as clearing the nasal passages.

Ulceration of the Nostrils.—We have already seen that this condition occurs in the camel and may possibly be associated with glanders. Nasty sores are caused by *dragging out of the nose peg* and invasion of the resulting wounds by maggots or their taking on unhealthy action from various causes. The most frequent cause of this is in baggage camels tying the stronger and more swift animal in front of the weaker, the latter begins to lag behind through exhaustion and the peg is dragged out; another cause is brutal violence in use of the nose rope as a guiding rein. The best dressing on service is simple camphorated oil.

Such maggots as occur in wounds must not be confused with what have been constantly seen on service and described as "*maggot in the nostrils.*" These in the Nile Expedition caused great inconvenience, an offensive sanguineous discharge from the nostrils, continual shaking of the head, dullness of the animal, and loss of appetite. They are the Œstrus Cameli *v.* Pharyngobalus. We have elsewhere written about them the following information:—

Inspecting Veterinary Surgeon Oliphant recorded their frequent occurrence in Afghanistan during the 1878-79 Campaign and Veterinary Surgeon (1st Class) Rayment noted their frequency in the Soudan. Veterinary Surgeon Fenton brought me some specimens when he returned from Suakim this year with the Madras Troops, from these specimens I derive the following conclusions.

The camel bot is half as big again as that of the horse, is much softer and more tapering towards the hookless extremity, whereas it is blunter and much more compressed towards the hooked end; while the section of the horse bot is evenly oval, that of the camel bot is flattened on the lower surface. In both, the body-rings *bearing spines* are nine in number and the spines point from the hook end. The following contrasted list of characters may best be given in the tabulated form :—

Horse Bot.	Camel Bot.
Spines.—Small, hard, sharp, very numerous on each ring, and largest on the central rings. Small extra spines alternate with the main ones and are situated behind and in the intervals between them, forming as it were, two rows in each circle. The bulging parts between the rings are smooth.	*Spines.*—Fleshy and in single row, very large, teat-like, and blunt. The largest are in the central rings but not markedly so. The main spines vary in size and tend to collect into groups with spaces between them. Those on the lateral parts of the lower surface tend to develop into temporary feet. On the most projecting parts of the segments between the rings of spines are small spinelets which below are very numerous and form continuous bands. In the different parts of the body the teat-like spines vary in relative position.
Hooked-end. — Hooks brownish-black and sharply divergent, short and much curved, situated inferiorly near the extremity of a long narrow hook-end. A central organ of chitine is midway between the bases of the hooks, and there are a few spinelets above and on either side of two well marked sense organs (situated above the hooks). These sense organs are all but sessile. The first row of spines is complete.	*Hooked-end.*-Hooks black, diverge at an acute angle and are slender, long, and little curved, situated below the anterior extremity and beneath a 6-lobed mass surrounded above and on each side by irregular circlets of spinelets which communicate at each extremity with the first zone of hooklets above and below. This first zone is a very irregular one. There is no chitinous organ between the hooks. The pigmented sense organs are on long peduncles the bases of which are connected by a band. There is another transverse band

below the hooks. The first row of spines is deficient inferiorly.

Hookless or orifice end.—Opening oblong. Its cavity black throughout. Its lips transversely bifid and the lower one much larger than the upper. The upper one continuous laterally with the side lobes. The last segments are arranged telescopically and bear no appreciable spinelets.

Hookless or orifice end.—Opening an almost circular cavity, black only in two lateral spots, upper lip semicircular and with four well marked angles, lower bifid, consisting of a tuberous part elongated transversely and also of two bifid protuberances each bearing a mammillary process. There are spinelets on the two latter and on the lower lip. The general aspect of the opening is upward. Last segment irregularly telescopic.

The characters amply prove that the camel bot serves as a connecting link between the peculiar tough horse bot and ordinary maggots. They show that the strange leathery spines of the horse bot are not chitinous or horny nails but true papillæ, they show that these papillæ tend to arrange themselves in groups and some develop into foot-like organs while the others lose their importance. By contrast of these organisms with common maggots we may infer what features of structure are necessary for a grub that lives in the stomach (as the horse bot does) and what for a resident in the pharynx (as the camel bot). The latter, it will be noticed, is softer and less irritant than the former and probably, as having rudimentary false legs, a much better traveller. He makes his exit from the body through the nose, whereas the stomach bot of the horse passes through the anus. The difference in position of the hooks is interesting; the camel parasite has them arranged like a pair of delicate anchors, which he can throw down when he wishes to ob tain a grip sufficing to prevent his being swallowed with food, whereas the horse parasite has much stronger grappling hooks arranged like the horns of a stag beetle and suited to enable him to hold tight in whatever direction the churning motion of the stomach may drag him.

The posterior orifice-like cavity is considered a respiratory sac, but what the black material in it is I am not prepared to state. Why does the camel parasite have stalked eyes and the horse parasite stalkless ones? Why has the latter only the chitinous organ between the hooks? And why should the lips of the orifice of the camel parasite develop into artistically arranged lobes while those of the horse bot are severely devoid of ornament? All these and many other problems suggest themselves in the study of these peculiar creatures.

The continuous irritation produced in the nostrils and pharynges of our poor camels exiled to the shores of the Red Sea, the probability that a certain amount of their now historic exhaustion depended on these bots, and the certainty that in future campaigns where camel transport is used these parasites must be remembered and got rid of, give the *Œstrus cameli* a considerable practical veterinary interest.

The escape of these larvæ through the nostrils is their natural migration prior to their assuming the chrysalis form and doubtless occurs at special times of year, whether special agents such as carbolic or terebinthinate gargles would or would not hasten removal we have no evidence, but they are worth trial. It would be interesting to know whether any one of the several forms of sore throat described owes its origin to the presence of these parasites.

DISEASES OF THE CHEST, both acute and chronic, are frequent on service, especially owing to the animals being exposed to extreme cold and atmospheric vicissitudes. Want of protection by means of jhools or by keeping the saddles on at nights is a frequent cause. Some of these diseases are epizootic and very fatal; Hodgson speaks of one Pakdar as infectious and not invariably fatal, we have already noticed it in detail. Acute pulmonary disease was not frequent up the Nile; C. Steel reported it as of common occurrence on the road to Candahar in 1878 and he remarked on the fact that in no one instance did he find the pleura involved, though Gilchrist almost always found hydrothorax present in lung cases; he describes the symptoms of the disorder and considered it largely due to want of proper food, to neglect, and hard work. Tassy has recorded the frequent occurrence of pneumonia of acute type in Algeria. Oliphant records PNEUMONIA in the Kuram valley, the symptoms being cough, quick and laboured breathing, and profuse rust-coloured discharge from the nostrils. To these Gilchrist adds as signs of Pæprah, Pupday, or *Papesa ka murz* considerable distress, discharge from the eyes, and cold extremities and body surface in the *bronchitic form;* still greater distress and disturbance of breathing in the *pneumonic form* in which the heaving of the flanks is very marked. When the pleura is involved the symptoms are obscure, but painful cough is present. A case of pleuropneumonia was recorded in the *Quarterly Journal of Veterinary Science,* Vol. III., p. 245, in which the animal died immediately after doing a long march and advanced lung disease was found. The pluck with which a camel keeps at his work without giving way even though suffering from most serious disorder should, we submit, be rather to the credit of the camel than, as it generally is, put down to his general "cussedness and contrariness of nature." Professor Lombardini records *pleuro-pericarditis* as frequent in very young camels under two months old. They first are off feed and sluggish in movement, they suck little and half-heartedly, and lie with head turned towards the belly and cry out when disturbed. Costiveness, injection of visible membranes, and urine red and scanty are also symptoms. The respiration next becomes disturbed and the heart's beats violent, auscultation and percussion at first give little result, later we can determine loss of resonance of the thoracic cavity, absence of respiratory murnur in the lower part of the chest, and supplementary respiration in the upper. Dyspnœa sets in and the symptoms increase in severity and end fatally. No cough is present, but towards the later stages there may be a mucous discharge from the nostrils. In addition to ordinary causes Fogliata considers that there must be present a blood derangement, he found peritoneal lesions present in some cases and marked hydræmia. Autopsy also showed abundant serous effusion into the thorax and some fibrin intermingled with it in suspension as flakes and recent deposits (false membranes) on the parietal and visceral pleura and on the pericardium and exocardium; lungs atalectic and sometimes exhibiting the lesions of caseous pneumonia. Animals up to two years of age may be affected by this disorder which seems little amenable to curative measures. As regards ordinary pneumonia, its treatment comprises protection from inclemencies of weather, especially from wind and rain; hand-feeding with ghee, flour, and other strengthening substances, and a mixture of garlic, methee, and salt, as recommended by Leach, to be thrown down the throat every morning. This is similar to the stimulant treatment mentioned by Gilchrist and doubtless is superior to his recommendation to bleed energetically, physic, and give calomel ℨj, tartar emetic ℨss., made up into a ball with soap twice or thrice daily for five days. He recommends tonics during convalescence. Oliphant gives opium in half tolah doses and bhang in two ounce doses, and supports the strength; and, further, applies oil of Turpentine with friction to the throat and chest.

Pulmonary Apoplexy, described by Gilchrist as Budda Bhao, is a sudden death after the animal has all at once commenced to breathe laboriously. In autopsy the lungs are found gorged with black blood and with bloody serous effusion in the air passages. Whether this is true pulmonary apoplexy as induced by excessive work especially when the animal is out of condition and the weather trying or whether it is but a pulmonary form of anthrax must be determined in each case. Prompt and full bleeding affords the only chance of saving the animal. This is but one of the forms of severe disease terminating speedily in death termed Bhao by Natives, they have apparently no idea whatever as to its true pathology but Gilchrist tells us that they are under the impression that in inflammation of the lungs those organs become over-distended within which becomes forced into the lower part of the neck.

Strongylus filaria (Rud.) has been found in the lungs of both species of camel but there is no evidence to hand as to occurrence of Verminous Bronchitis in this animal.

Chronic Disease of Lungs [*Soolfay ka murz* (Gil.)] is of three kinds, which must be carefully distinguished from one another in records of cases. The first is Chronic Bronchitis and Pneumonia in which abscesses may be found in the lungs and some fluid in the chest. Lombardini notices this disorder and thinks it may be considered as generally supervening on previous acute disease, although he has not yet sufficient evidence to settle the point. He finds that affected animals may frequently work until the disease has become much advanced but probably many cases of chronic cough are due to such lung changes. Gilchrist considers it may result from neglect in treatment of acute cases. The second form of chronic lung disease is that due to HYDATIDS, frequently found in this organ, they vary much in number and size and generally contain opalescent grumous fluid. Occasionally they have calcified, or have lost their watery contents and contain simply the membranous cyst. Piot of Cairo considers them a cause of considerable mortality among Government camels and reckons on an annual death-rate of 30% on the Government Domains from this and phthisis. TUBERCULAR PHTHISIS is the third form of chronic pulmonary disease; its occurrence is acknowledged by Bennett, Tassy, Vallon, Piot, and other writers, who have found tubercles in the lungs. These chronic disorders are generally quite undiagnosed, but in some cases persistent cough, debility, loss of condition, some deficiency in breathing, indifferent appetite, and pale visible membranes cause us to suspect the state of the animal. The effect of tonics and alteratives may be tried, housing and good diet also may prolong the life of the animal. Gilchrist considers it generally advisable to destroy the patient and suggests that, where this course is not adopted, husks of chenna or coolthee or of ooddodh will be found the best fodder and that ooddodh (ured) grain should be given instead of gram.

CHAPTER VIII.—URINARY DISORDERS.

Since the kidneys and urinary passages present nothing special as regards their anatomy, being constructed on the equine type, and as the chemical composition of the urine remains yet to be investigated, we have but little to say upon the subject of urinary derangements. There can be no doubt as to the occurrence of RETENTION OF URINE giving rise to considerable inconvenience in animals kept too long on the march without the halts necessary for urination at intervals, some camels are known to be liable to this and they are given a mixture of kattera, 2 chitaks, with nitre and borax, of each ½ chitak, in water, two seers, three times a day. Gilchrist mentions DYSURIA *(Phudmooth)*; the urine is scanty and high coloured, the animal loses flesh, and becomes weak. The disorder is protracted though not fatal, and must be treated by making the patient drink conjee and tyre infusion freely. To Gilchrist was described by Serwans *Roosne ka murz* or *Soozark*, which he considered to be HÆMATURIA, the principal symptoms being scantiness and the presence of blood in the urine which is passed *guttatim* and with difficulty. Liberal supplies of demulcent fluids with nitre, bleeding, purging, and fomentations are recommended.

The Museum of the Army Veterinary School, Poona, contains specimens of RENAL and URETHRAL CALCULI from a camel. Two large ones were taken from the kidney and a small one, the cause of death, from the urethra. A case of this disorder was recently recorded in the American Veterinary Review.

CHAPTER IX.—GENERATIVE DISORDERS.

Charles Steel has noticed an oozing of red-coloured fluid from an opening two inches below the ear during trying marches. This is, doubtless, from the temporal gland figured by Lombardini and found by him to be absent or rudimentary in females. These glands consist on each temple of two greyish lobes with several orifices of ducts, they are specially active in the rutting male and resemble the ched gland of the elephant. Baron Larrey observed that camels in Egypt at the time of rut sometimes suffer from a kind of madness and that bites from them when in this state are severe but not contagious. The symptoms exhibited by the camel under these circumstances are flow of an abundant thick saliva, constant bellowing, horror of water (?), wasting-fever, depilation, and bad temper shown by their pursuing men and other animals. If the animal were excited the symptoms increased and often ended fatally. Doubtless the learned French surgeon in these records has somewhat confused phrenitis, true rabies, and genetic furor, but we record his views in order that they may be verified or controverted hereafter among the mass of uncertain and superstitious matter which cumbers Cameline Pathology.

Temporal Glands (after Lombardini) × ½

Exposed by dissection (internal surface).

As indicated when hair is shaved from the temple.

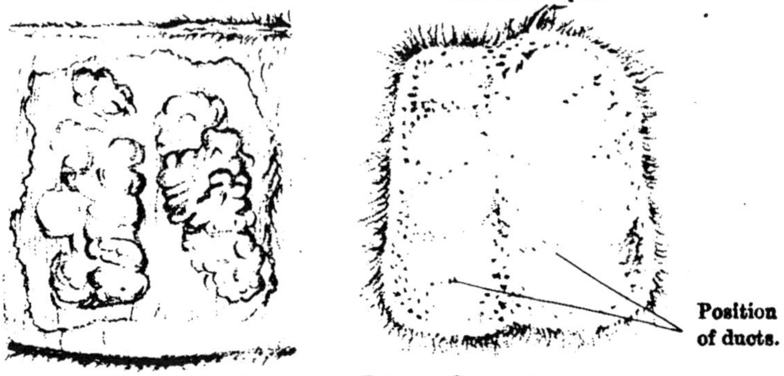

Internal Generative Organs of Female Camel (after Lombardini)

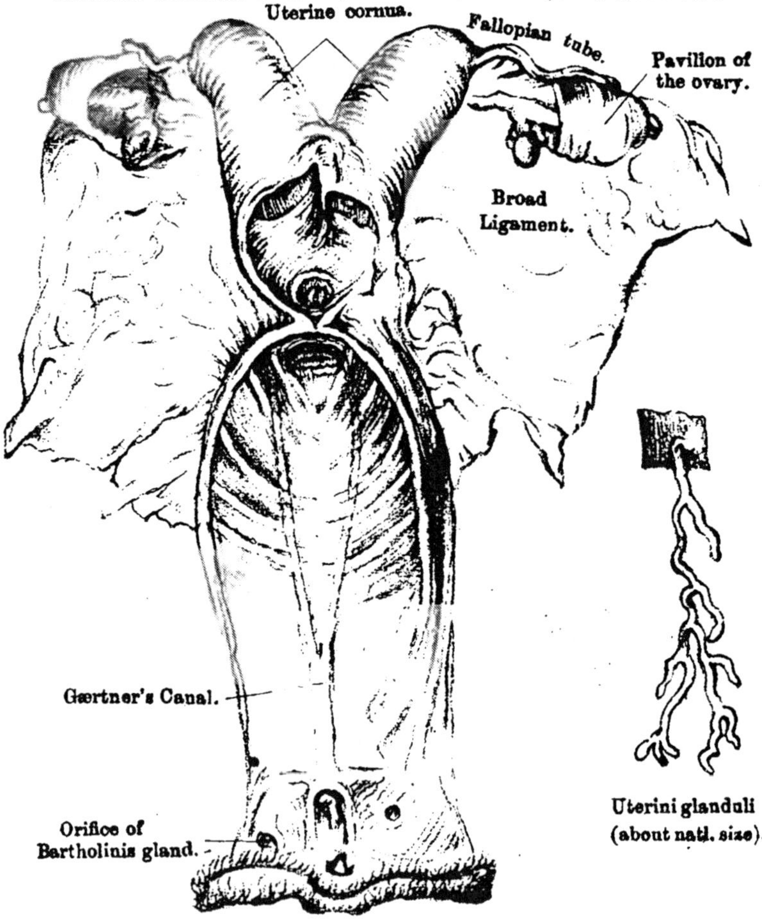

Uterini glanduli (about natl. size).

LITHOG: FOR LAWRENCE ASYLUM PRESS, MADRAS
BY ALEX: BARREN

PENDULOUS PENIS (*Dhundee ka murz*) is described by Gilchrist as affecting young and robust animals only and resulting from frequent seminal discharge, the patient becoming so weak as to be unable to rise and at length dying exhausted. The natives treat with cooling mussauls and firing over the loins, but bleeding and saline purgatives are said to be better, probably castration would prove most efficient in this emergency, and, as we have already urged, it ought to be carried out as routine practice for animals not required as sires. The advantages would be:—Being able to work male and females together in caravans, they would not be temporarily incapacitated by musthee, they would be more cleanly, and less liable to the disorder under consideration. The operation would be easy to perform and the experience of the Central Asian tribes is in favour of it. Thus everything suggests general adoption of castration and Government ought to consider the matter for its Transport establishments. A minor consideration is that the musthee camel is a very objectional object in camp on account of the noise he makes, his ugly appearance when protruding the pâlu, and his having to be picketed apart in more violent cases.

The female camel resembles the mare in having a diffused placenta involving the whole chorion, Sani has pointed out some minor differences but is inclined to attribute great zoological importance to this fact. Copulation is prolonged and effected while the animals are in the couchant position. The period of uterogestation is twelve to twelve and a half months. The internal generative organs of the female are very similar to those of the mare and the canal of Gœrtner and Bartholini's glands are well marked. Lactation lasts 12-15 months and the male will generally be received a month after birth, so that a female camel will breed every two years (Lombardini). Cameline obstetrics is entirely a study for the future.

APPENDIX 1: Of the DISEASES OF YOUNG CAMELS, the ULCERATIVE STOMATITIS recorded by Lombardini seems one of the most important. It is a very fatal affection in which lesions are found on the uvula, velum palati, and the neighbouring parts. This prevents sucking and causes death from starvation. These ulcers resemble those found in the aphtha of bovine animals, they are small and circular or larger and eliptical with irregular margins and of variable depth. They may be seen also on the internal surface of the lips and gums. Lombardini from careful investigation of the meconium and *post-mortem* conditions concludes that this disease is one of the blood which probably comes on some days before birth and is of a typhoid nature; attempts at cure should therefore be made through the medium of the mother in the latter stages of pregnancy.

APPENDIX 2: A valuable series of analyses from the Records of the Royal University of Pisa Chemical Laboratory gives the following results, compared with those of French and Russian observers:

Constituents.	Milk of			
	Cow.	Camel.		
	C. Marchetti.	Carlo Marchetti.	Chatin	Dragendorf.
Density (distilled water at 0° C = 1).	1·03557	1·04042	1·042	1·035
Casein	Grammes 2·8837	3·9596	} 40	3·67
Albumen ...	— 0·3227	0·3842		
Fatty matter ...	— 2·6603	3·2328	—	2·90
Lactose	— 4·6614	5·0311	5·8	5·78
Salts	— 0·7339	0·9114	—	0·66
Fixed residue by direct estimation... ...	11·4915	13·7965	—	13·01
Total solids ...	— 11·2620	13·5191	—	93·01
Water	— 88·7380	86·4809	—	86·94

Marchetti and Dragendorf thus agree as to the greater richness of camels' than cows' milk as regards all classes of nutritive solids. We have no reason however to consider that this would be found true as regards the improved and high class milking breeds of cattle.

Chapter X.—THE NERVOUS APPARATUS.

The nervous system is said to be more highly developed in the camel than in the ox, and to closely resemble that of the horse. The brain is remarkably long, and the basal ganglia are heavy; in these respects the camel predominates over the horse, in other respects he generally occupies a median position between equines and bovines. All the evidence tends to show that derangements of the central nervous system are frequent in the camel; how far this depends on the length of the neck as an anatomical feature is uncertain.

We have already commented on the peculiar genetic furor of the male. Oliphant has described as *Megrims* a kind of stomach staggers denoted by a state of semi-coma succeeding a period of excitement. The animal falls and remains struggling about on the ground, salivating profusely, and having his mucous membranes of a dark blue colour. This condition yields to purgation and extraction of blood either from the jugular or the palate. Wallon noted that *vertigo* was frequent, and was preceded by the animal becoming furious and rushing about recklessly. Tassy records that cerebral congestion results in the camel from isolation. The above-mentioned conditions are probably the same as that described by Leach as *Tup Surga,* which the camelmen attribute to the influence of a certain wind. This is denoted by the animal shivering all over, falling to the ground, and dying very soon, or else reviving after two or three hours and recovering thoroughly in a few days. Camels liable to this are branded with three lines on each flank and on the head, jaiful or gur is considered good for medicinal treatment. Gilchrist describes as due to exposure to severe weather, either cold or excessively hot, the state which is known to the natives as *Moorghee ka murz,* because the camel shows symptoms supposed to be like those of a fowl similarly affected. Not uncommonly an animal apparently healthy commences to give an occasional guttural roar and to walk restlessly round its picket; it then falls, the neck is bent round on itself and drawn backwards, the limbs move convulsively, the animal rolls from side to side, and roars almost continuously. Several of these fits may occur at indefinite and irregular periods in twenty-four hours, each fit lasts from four to eight minutes, and when it is completed the animal rises and commences feeding as though nothing had happened. Gilchrist goes on to say that always a morbid sanguineous fluid is found in the spinal canal on *post-mortem* examination, and the disease is considered uniformly fatal, though the natives give stimulant mussauls and errhines. He advises us to bleed with a view to protracting recurrence and lessening the number of the fits, to fire the head or blister the neck, to purge with aloes and give alterative doses of Sulphide of Antimony (℥ss) with Calomel (ʒss) for a week and then follow them up with tonic mussauls. As a preventive the camels should be kept in a shed and sheltered.

A very similar affection is spasm of the neck described by Gilchrist as *Cumaun ka murz.* The animal is suddenly attached with convulsions, its neck gets twisted, its limbs and lips quiver, and it grinds its teeth. This occurs in cold weather, and the usual firing along the back of the neck, and if fits persist, bleeding, purging, alteratives, and tonics are recommended; recovery is slow.

The condition well known in India as "*cold struck*" is described by Queriple as a form of megrims. The animal suddenly falls, with conjunctivæ injected, pupils dilated, pulse slow and bounding. These symptoms are followed by apparently complete recovery, but shortly afterwards fits set in, recurring at intervals of ten minutes to half an hour, and during them the patient is apparently quite mad for about five minutes; sometimes recovery takes place.

Cerebritis or true inflammation of the encephalon is considered to occur, but probably the majority of the cases recorded under this heading are merely congestive. The treatment recommended is to bleed the patient, tie his feet, heap clothing over his body, and gave him stimulants.

Gilchrist describes that form of the Bhao ka murz, Dhudkay, or Ahren Bhao, which affects the brain as either cephalitis or apoplexy. The inflammatory form is *Ahren Bhao,* similar to the disease of that name which affects horses, and is denoted by symptoms of great urgency. The camel attempts to bite his keeper or other persons, becomes unable to stand, rolls on its back bellowing loudly, is constantly restless, and has convulsions of its limbs. Ears and body surface cold, tongue protruded, frothing at mouth, conjunctivæ congested, eyes protruded, and aspect wild. This may be a cerebral form of anthrax, but it is generally due to such common causes as exposure for a long period to an ardent sun or check of perspiration by washing directly the animal comes off the march. It is seen at all periods of the year. The natives treat by stimulants, acrid substances put under the eyelids, and application of the hot iron along the sides of the body and round the navel. Gilchrist prefers free bleeding (to 1½ gallons) repeated if necessary, cold lotion to the head and warm applications to the body and, with subsidence of active symptoms, the administration of alteratives (such as sulphide of antimony and calomel), followed by tonics.

Cœnurus cerebralis, the Gid hydatid, has been observed in the brain (cerebellum) of the dromedary (von Linstow).

Of nervous diseases not generally seated in the brain the most frequent is *Paraplegia,* described by Gilchrist as jolay ka murz and jenuk; the latter he tells us is loss of power, partial or complete ; in mild cases amounting simply to a dragging of the limbs but in more severe instances being a complete inability to walk. It is treated by purging with croton beans, firing over the lumbar region of the spine, applying friction to the hind legs and fomenting the loins. This is probably the condition described by Hodgson as Kumree or Hurva. Jolay is described as weak loins, generally with complete loss of power ; in some cases, it may be anthracoid or possibly due to Surra. The general health seems good, and there are no local signs of injury. It is incurable, though sometimes relieved to an extent by internal remedies and firing ; but these different form of paralysis (the distinction between which Gilchrist hardly makes clear) are very liable to recur on exposure to cold, and they are seldom paralysis pure and simple, being generally complicated with disease of lungs, liver, or bowels.

TETANUS, Chándni in Hazara (Nunn), Dhadbund ka Murz,

(Gilchrist) is attributed to exposure to cold nights, and appears to be associated with derangement of bowels, according to Gilchrist. Nunn mentions the idea of the Panjabis that it affects riding camels with galled or sore backs, which are left exposed to the rays of the moon, particularly of the full moon. There is a fixed state of the jaws, drooping of the under lip, pain on pressure of the temples, salivation, lachrymation, mucous discharge from the nostrils, torpid bowels, and a dull listless state of the animal. The disease is incurable, but Gilchrist recommends, as giving relief, a warm purgative with a tonic, fomenting the head, and firing over the temples and lower jaw.

Hewa or Heat Apoplexy is denoted by a preliminary stage in which the animal seems more or less foolish, then without cause he suddenly gets up and tries to bolt, his coat is staring, his ears quivering, and he refuses food and drink; the treatment is as for cerebritis. In ordinary apoplexy (Bhao or Dhudkay) the animal suddenly staggers, falls, and dies. Gilchrist suggests that cold applications to the head, hot applications to the limbs and body, free bleeding, and purging with 2½ drachms of croton seeds may be tried.

CHAPTER XI.—THE CUTANEOUS SYSTEM.

Of all the diseases of camels perhaps the most important as regards practical value of these animals in the field is Mange or Itch. It invariably turns up on service when camels are present in any number; it spreads rapidly, since the conditions of service are especially those which give rise to extensive outbreaks of the disorder; it obstinately resists such treatment as is practicable on active service; it is an important factor in production of that serious loss of condition, which camels on service invariably suffer from; and, from its very prevalence, it is apt to be so neglected as to get a serious hold on the camel transport before it receives attention from those in charge and proper veterinary treatment. This disease, termed Garab by the Arabs, Kharisk by the natives of India, and Pan on the Indus at Dhera Ismail Khan, is extremely common in all parts of the world where camels are used. The first difficulty we have to deal with, and one which was specially felt during the Nile expedition, is the fact that the natives distinguish, and camels certainly are liable to, two forms of skin-disease known as Kharisk. Of these the least important is *Eczema* which is non-parasitic; it occurs periodically due to ordinary causes, such as also prove predisposing and aggravating conditions of the true mange or parasitic form. Doubtless the latter exists, as Fleming asserts, *at all seasons* among Afghan, Scindh, Punjab, and Bikanir camels; but we may extend the geographical range to all camel-using countries, for which statement recent experiences on the Red Sea Litoral and along the Nile by British Veterinarians, and long experience by French Veterinary Officers in Algeria give us full warrant. Nunn speaks of the disease as occurring in the Montgomery District of the Punjab in August and September, and again in December and January. In Bikanir, Marwar, and Jessulmir the herds of camels are described as seldom free from the disorder in the cold season, and it disappears in the hot weather. Oliphant records that it is prevalent in the Kuram Valley in the later part of the year. The non-parasitic and non-contagious eruption is considered to be due to dry indigestible nature of the food, also to insufficient diet, for it is frequent in drought years and when green food is scarce, bad and scanty drinking water also may cause it; and, indeed, it seems to depend on any cause of indigestion, as well as exposure to hot sun, insufficient grooming, and the phenomenon of changing the coat. S. M. Smith considers that keeping the animals tied up aggravates this condition on service. Nunn tells us that the natives of Montgomery consider it specially due to deficient supply of lánâ (*Caroxylon fœtidum*) for feeding purposes. The sypmtoms of this form of disease are not unlike those of the contagious form, and a great deal of confusion between the two exists in this as well as in other points as regards them. Oliphant in this Eczema finds the inner sides of the thighs and on the sheath favourite seats of primary eruption, a scab forming on a round white spot of smooth skin. Clayton is apparently writing of non-contagious Eczema, when he tells us that "at this part of the year (July) the skin is smooth to the touch and the axillary, scrotal, perineal and sub-coccygeal regions are covered with a layer of hard, dry, brittle cakes of a lightish brown color, easily detached by friction;" elsewhere the sides, flanks, neck, and tail are said to be specially affected, but it is evident that in severe cases the seat of eruption is no guide in distinguishing between the contagious and non-contagious enzootic skin-disease. Burt describes the disorder as follows "The indications of the disease in the early stage resemble those of eczema, and in the latter those described as ichthyosis. Symptoms: in the early stage the first symptoms observed were small bare patches about the size of a pea, with altered condition of the cuticle, consequent on eczematous eruption. This eruption was noticed in all parts of the body excepting the top of the neck and back, where the hair is thickest. This did not appear to be accompanied by any marked irritation. It was followed by an apparently thickened state of the skin and increased irritation, and the patches running together; the parts now most affected were between the fore limbs, under the chest, the flanks and inside the thighs, where the skin is thinnest and least covered with hair. It was also observed that the muzzle and the parts just above the foot-pads became affected. There was a peculiar papillated appearance of the skin immediately above the feet. Later on, the skin assumes a very thickened and corrugated appearance, more especially between the fore legs, flanks, and inner side of thighs. About this stage, the camel, if previously in condition, begins to fall away; eventually the lymphatics of the part become involved, being noticed to be enlarged, and œdema of the extremities follows, accompanied by great loss of condition and general febrile symptoms rendering the animal quite unfit for work. At the same time the top of the neck and back remained perfectly free, the rest of the body being denuded of hair. At this stage, also, many camels thus affected would be seen standing in the lines perfectly quiet, apparently showing no symptoms of irritation. It was also observed towards the close of the Expedition, that several camels, the private property of Officers, having received better treatment, as regards feeding and work, than other camels, were no worse than when first seen at the commencement of the operations, the small bare patches, however, still remaining. Again, it has also been noticed that when camels affected with this disease have been standing close to others, the latter have not become affected. It was, however, observed that the large, coarse bred camels suffered far more than the others. I do not consider the condition of skin thus described to be due to the mange insect. No microscope could be obtained to ascertain if the acarus existed, but as far as natural vision assisted it could not be detected." Differential diagnosis must depend on observations as to actual communication by contagion. on the obstinacy in resistance to treatment, and on detection of the mange parasite. The latter is the sole absolute distinctive, and as the ectozoon is detectible by use of a hand lens or even by means of the naked eye there is no reason for reservation of diagnosis in ordinary cases.

The natives of all camel countries have learned by experience the necessity for adopting prophylactic measures against the non-parasitic skin-disease. Vallon (Mem. de la Comm. de hygiéne hippique, Paris, 1856,) tells us the Arabs of North Africa tar their dromedaries. The natives of India annually adopt a course of preventive treatment (tel karna), which varies somewhat in different localities as to time of year when adopted and the substances used. The Panjabis and inhabitants of Beloochistan in spring (March and April) rest their camels, give them doses of nutritive oil (about 1 seer daily from 3 to 12 days), and apply Taramera oil or mustard oil to the skin. The Egyptian camel corps was the only part of the Nile Force in which eczema was not prevalent. This seemed due to the camels having been clipped in September and smeared with ghi, sulphur, and salt, also each camel having a man in charge of him and being properly and regularly groomed. Mr. Oliphant found simple administration of Taramera oil internally, and its external application caused the disease to yield readily, in marked contrast to the true parasitic form, which is proverbially obstinate. Liberal diet and general attention to hygiene of the patients is a matter of some importance. Whether or no this form of disorder is related to scurvy has been debated; it probably is non-specific and simply due to the congestion or inflammation of the skin when exciting causes act on the organ rendered predisposed to disorder by the physiological process of shedding the coat. Although the disease is at first purely local in extent, it may involve so extensive a cutaneous area as to cause considerable interference with the camel's health, and the amount of irritation present may be almost as considerable as in TRUE MANGE. The mange insect, Sarcoptes dromedarii (Vallon), Sarcoptes cameli (Lomb.), Sarcoptes scabiei cameli (Megnin), Acarus cameli (Haslam) of the camel was discovered (to science) on a dromedary by Professor Paulo Gervais in 1841 (Annales, Sc. Nat. II., Series XV., p. 6—10). Probably it was known by painful experience to camelmen in the time of the Patriachs or earlier. Vallon made some observations on it in 1856; Megnin has noticed in his work on the Sarcoptidæ; Haslam described it in a communication to the Veterinary Journal; and Lombardini has recently given us a special detailed account of its zoological characters. As regards habits this acarus is a true sarcoptes in its method of burrowing in the true skin; hence it is rather inaccessible by remedial agents and difficult to eradicate, as we shall shortly see. There can be no doubt that this parasite can be transmitted to mankind; all the evidence tends to this view, and further to the belief that though the acarus burrows in the human skin it neither lives long nor propagates on man, but causes only temporary inconvenience. "Constantly on service camelmen are admitted with skin-disease probably taken from their camels" (Clayton); but it must be remembered that these camelmen are generally subject to such predisposing causes as affect their camels and herd together in a state of filth and want of sanitation, such as would be specially favorable to spread among them of human itch. Experiment, however, has decided the question of transmission of Sarcoptes cameli to man, and that it takes place somewhat readily on account of the similarity in form and characters of the species of the man and that of the camel. The question of intercommunicability of scabies in camels and other animals is manifestly one of the greatest importance, and on which we much need careful experiment. The French

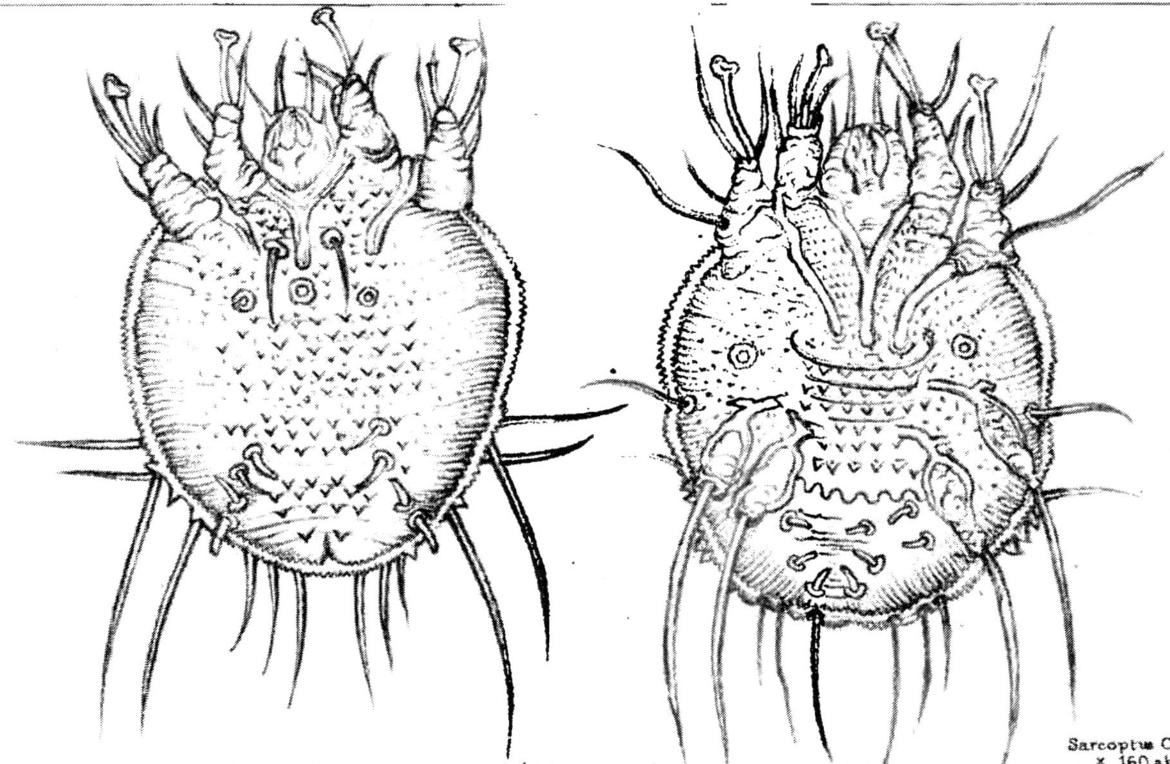

Dorsal View (Adult female.) Ventral View.

Sarcoptus Cameli
× 160 about
(after Lombardini)

LITHOG: FOR LAWRENCE ASYLUM PRESS, MADRAS, BY ALEX: BARREN

Veterinarians have noticed in Algeria that a disease similar to mange in camels breaks out among mules used for pack purposes and working with camels; as it especially manifests itself under the pack saddle, the probability is that it is ordinary equine scabies, but we are cautioned that it is as well to keep mules apart from scabby camels. The llama and giraffe are invaded by the same acarus as are the two species of camel (Megnin). The readiness of passage from one animal to another and with which are produced morbid conditions is well illustrated by the fact that mange has been seen in camels two or three days old (three or four days according to Lombardini's observations); middle-aged camels are said to be less liable to become affected than the young or the old.

Causes.—The only absolute cause of the disorder is the acarus or its ova, which may be conveyed mediately or immediately. Mediate contagion results from imperfect isolation of the sick, such as use of pack-gear by sound animals after it has been put aside without thorough cleansing on account of its original wearers suffering from mange and dying or being put into hospital; temporary interchanges of gear; rubbing of animals against trees or other fixed objects, which have been used for the same purpose by the mangey; use of contaminated serais and camping grounds; finally, care of the affected and non-affected by the same drivers. Want of early attention, neglect of veterinary advice, and injudicious system in working are causes of isolated cases developing into enzootic outbreaks of this disorder, a fact to which Mr. Oliphant has drawn attention. We may add to these want of promptitude in diagnosis and of attention to the good practical rule in such cases to always suspect and provide against the more severe disease when the diagnosis is at all doubtful.

Symptoms.—The disease commences as spontaneous loss of hair, followed by somewhat profuse serous weeping, and then pustulation with scanty discharge. The signs first appear at some point or points of the surface of the body, and from them they spread rapidly. Stress is laid by different writers on the order of invasion of the several parts, thus Yaldwin mentions that it commences under the thighs; Haslam, that it attacks the parts in the following order :—groin, sheath, axillæ, below the belly, below the neck and throat, sides of neck and shoulders, between the toes, legs, face, sides of chest, back. Another writer says it generally begins in the axillary or inguinal region and thence extends to the neck, head, shoulder, arm, forearm, and anterior costal region, thence passing to the flanks, back, coccyx, and so on. The parasites cause severe pruritus, the itching being greatest at sunset (Haslam). The animal nibbles, scratches, and bites the seat of irritation, and rubs himself against trees whenever possible, enjoying the friction as giving him temporary relief, but perhaps in scratching conveying parasites to fresh parts which thus become secondarily affected, "again, much like a dog with chorea, throwing first one foreleg and then the other in a spasmodic manner to the front," as Clayton informs us and goes on to point out that others as they progress rub one thigh against the other. In the parts which have longest been affected the hair is lost and the skin becomes irregularly furrowed, and in that condition known as Psoriasis; it is coriaceous, squamous, and chronically altered throughout its thickness, often covered with crusts of an offensive odour; some affected parts of the skin become black, but this is considered, by Martin, an indication that the disease is being conquered. The gradual spread of the disorder and the regular series of changes through which the several affected parts pass is rather diagnostic of this disease. The acari travel about, and may be seen among the debris, crusts, and dirt on the skin. The affected parts become torn and ulcerated by the teeth and hoof nails of the animal; sometimes the acari are found in the subcutaneous areolar and muscular tissues of the abdominal walls, and in neglected cases peritonitis may be caused by the great inflammation in the neighbourhood, as Haslam has pointed out, and he enumerates Septicæmia and Pyæmia among the results of this disorder. The most serious result in relation to working power is the debility and loss of condition entailed by the continuous irritation of the unfortunate animals; this, in some cases, culminates in diarrhœa, a precursor of death. In this way a force may become crippled as regards Transport, and its expense enormously increased by the prevalence of mange among its camels.

Treatment.—Primarily comprises preventive and curative measures; these are of equal importance, but the former naturally takes precedence. It comprises avoidance of introduction of the disease, and prevention of its spread when it has been unfortunately introduced. Camels at place of shipment and at the base of operations should have all showing signs of skin-disease weeded out from among them; but when the operations are in a camel country it is almost impossible to avoid some cases occurring from contagion in halting places, by animals captured, and in numerous other ways. Thus constant inspection and prompt isolation of skin-disease cases, purification of gear and infected standings, destruction of old polluted gear, and non-interchange of pulans should be strictly enforced from the first, not when the emaciated and mangey condition of the camels begins to become conspicuous. The influences of bad feeding and watering and defective grooming in generating mange should not be forgotten either in case of the healthy or in treatment of the sick, and the latter should earn their keep and improve their chances of cure by working where they are not likely to come in contact with the healthy,—a method which has, on several occasions, been found to answer well. Every writer on this important subject has his special method of treatment; we may enumerate the principal which have come under our notice:—

Leach's method.—Cut off all the hair, apply tara mera oil or sulphur 10 tolas with 4 lbs. kurwa oil over the whole of the body. Allow to stand for three days in the sun, permitting to lie down only at nights, and then only if a clean grassy spot can be found. Again apply the oil and allow the animal to stand two more days in the sun, then take him to a pond and cover him from head to foot with adhesive mud, which leave on for three days in the sun. Then well scrape the animal with a curry-comb or pieces of stick, wash perfectly clean with soap and warm water in warm weather, but in cold rub thoroughly clean by means of a piece of tût. On any signs of recurrence, (for the animal must after all this be carefully watched) the spots which looks suspicious must be promptly rubbed with oil, and if this course of treatment is not effectual, repeat it! Internal treatment also is necessary.

Haslam's method, under which "in three or four weeks' time the severest cases should be convalescent," consists in keeping the patient on dry, soft, sandy soil; for dryness alone will kill the acarus. Then scrape the animal over, dress with sea-water, and walk him about in the sun until thoroughly dry. Apply sparingly, but thoroughly, every third hour the following mixture:—Stockholm tar lb. ij, sulph. lb. j, fish oil lb. jx, crude carbolic acid oz. iij. This method proved practicable and efficacious at Suez in 1885.

Clayton's method consisted in applying oil of mustard, phenic acid, and sulphur, and subsequently removing each dressing with soap and water. Three or four such dressings generally sufficed.

Yaldwin's method.—Shave the animal, isolate him, and give internally gandak and sarson oil or tara mera oil and chek; we presume also apply it externally.

Gilchrist's method.—A mussaul of sulphur, marking nut, and milk-hedge juice to be applied daily at noon.

Bennett, on the Nile Expedition, found that skin-disease did not exist to any great degree, for it always could to an extent be kept under control. He treated the contagious form by isolation, clipping the hair, and cleansing with soap and water. MacDougall's dressing, when dissolved in water, caused chapping of the skin, so it was used dissolved in ghee, some three or four dressings often being required.

Queriple shows that in Egypt Ketran, an oil obtained by expression from Kharouat is used in treatment of skin disease. He found that a mixture of ghi and sulphur answered well. Of Ketran some 5 lbs. would be required per camel, a formidable practical difficiency as regards its use.

The Montgomery method, described by Nunn.—Give internally a mixture of gur, oil, and onions daily for a fortnight and dress the body with oil and sulphur. This seems rather adapted to simple eczema than to the parasitic form of skin disease.

Carbuccia tells us that the best tar dressing is in North Africa obtainable readily in the desert in 5½ gallon skins at a cost of

$5\frac{1}{2}$ francs French. That made with Tágá is preferable to that with Aárare and the Arabs are liable to sell it bad or adulterated. That obtained from Ouled Auteur, Ouled Ibrahim, and Sahan in the neighbourhood of Bersuagnia is preferred (Byrne).

Lombardini tried the "*traditional method*" of Africa and Asia, *i.e.*, inunction with butter, tar, and sulphur every third day after preliminary shaving of the affected parts, without success in a severe outbreak. He found in the crusts of parts thus treated actively-moving parasites in the several stages of development, also undamaged ova. Hence he was compelled to resort to agents which experiment shows suffice to kill the parasites, thus oil of turpentine, aqua regia, decoction of tobacco, and creosote with olive oil, proved useful in different cases, the aqua regia being particularly efficacious. These measures were supplemented by good feeding and attention to correct hygiene in other respects.

A letter received by the Editors of the *Quarterly Journal of Veterinary Science in India* in December 1886, from Major Elliot, Assistant Commissary-General of Transport at Quetta, puts the main bearings of this question of best treatment practicable in the emergency of service so forcibly that we cannot do better than extract the queries and suggestions contained in it for the benefit of our readers :—"To state the problem briefly, all the dressings adopted by Veterinary Surgeons *demand oil* as their basis, as their chief component part. Oil is the vehicle commonly used either with sulphur or carbolic acid, &c. But on field service oil on a large scale is simply not procurable. At Suakim common oil cost 10 shillings per gallon, and then was only procurable in small quantities. What was the consequence? Not one-half the scabied camels were ever dressed. I can state this from my personal experience of the Punjab Camel Corps, 1,500 camels strong, which I commanded. It was the same thing at Kabul* and Kandahar, where I also served as a Transport

* Veterinary Surgeon Clayton, Royal Horse Artillery, writing to the Veterinary Journal from Zurgundshade, North Afghanistan (July 1880), says: "One form of mange is giving me a great deal of trouble at present, affecting every camel in the Transport of this Division (3,200)." Oliphant found mange prevalent from November 1879 to March 1880 in Kuram Valley, but it was stamped out in April; almost every camel in the force was affected (Eds. Q. J.)

Officer. If mange appeared on a large scale, oil at once became unprocurable. If many camels have to be dressed the problem becomes more difficult, as each camel takes a very large quantity of oil. Veterinary Surgeon Meredith, who was at Quetta during the war preparations last year, experienced the difficulty I point out above. Oil in sufficient quantity for cure of mange on a large scale he never succeeded in obtaining, *and this at a cantonment station.* What it would be on field service you can imagine! The question now is—knowing from past sad experience this difficulty about getting oil on a large scale—*can or cannot the Veterinary Profession adopt an efficient dressing for scabies which will have water and not oil for the basis,* for the administering vehicle? I have heard it stated they positively cannot dispense with oil for the reason that the parasite, which is the cause of true mange, can breathe through water but not through oil. Is this a fact or only popular error?* Does oil suffocate the mange insect and so cause its death?

"I confess the out-look is most gloomy *if oil is an absolute necessity.* The Transport Department in this case will never be able to cope with scabies, for tons of oil they cannot, and will not, get on field service * * * *

"This difficulty has cost Government enormous sums of money in the past, and will do so again, unless, in the mean time, science interferes and invents a cure for scabies which will not demand oil for its chief component part. For my part I look to phenyle, but, on the other hand, it is stated phenyle is only suitable for mild cases. If you will refer to No. 15 of the Journal you will see that Veterinary Surgeon Rayment at Suakim used for scabies a mixture of Sulphur Sublimatus and Ol. Picis with Ol. Comm. as a vehicle.

"You can imagine for yourself how much Ol. Comm. would be expended in dressing a thousand camels, to make no mention of ponies, bullocks, &c., and yet on field service we have to face the problem I bring forward for your examination. The general belief seems to be that without oil, scabies is incurable. Is this a fact or not?

* The oil plugs the pores of the skin through which air for respiration enters; it also is thought to clog up the mouths of the burrows of the parasites (Eds. Q. J.)

"I am, of course, aware that in itch the acarus scabiei is safely ensconced at the end of a long gallery which it has burrowed for itself in the skin, and that unless the remedy be so applied as to enter the air-holes of the gallery it is comparatively safe, for this reason all greasy or oily remedies, by obstructing their spiracles or breathing holes, are rapidly destructive. It has been suggested to suffocate the animalcules *with chloroform.** Have you ever seen this remedy tried for scabies? Would it be possible to use chloroform on a large scale in Transport operations and so dispense with oil, tar, grease, &c. Camphor and musk rubbed together with olive oil has been used successfully as a cure for itch. So also sulphur, which by formation of sulphuretted hydrogen within the skin destroys the parasite. It is known that acarus scabiei has a distaste for scents, as *iodoform,* which has a very strong offensive odour, has this agent ever been tried in scabies?†

"To give you some idea of the quantity of oil necessary for Transport sick lines when scabies appears on a large scale, I explain as follows:—It takes at the very least four gallons of mange dressing to cure a camel of bad scabies; this is only an ordinary bucket full. There are 10 lb. in a gallon, hence 40 lb. equals four gallons. In other words, *each camel requires about half a maund of oil* before the scabies can be eradicated.

"For 1,000 camels this will be 500 maunds. Where on field service can you calculate on getting oil by the 500 maunds? At Suakim oil costs 10 shillings per gallon; to dress a camel properly, took four gallons or £2 worth of oil alone, to make no mention of sulphur, &c. For 1,000 camels the expenditure would be £2,000! This is why, as above stated, not one-half of the scabied camels were ever dressed. Sheep dip was issued in lieu, but did not prove a success. It seems to be a good preventive as a disinfectant, but was in some way defective as a cure in bad cases.

* We have had no experience of use of chloroform as suggested in mange; we fear its cost, volatility, and the consequent difficulty of carriage and supply would militate against its use on field service. However, theoretically we doubt its efficiency (Eds. Q. J.)

†We are not aware of its having been resorted to for this purpose (Eds. Q.J.)

Probably suitable for sheep it was not strong enough for camels." By the Anglo-Indian Contingent and along the Nile, it was said to prove too astringent in effects causing the skin to dry up wherever it was applied and rendering it liable to crack and gall. Having fairly stated the problem which Major Elliot propounds for solution by the Veterinary profession, we must leave it for future experiment to solve, for we do not think either of the methods enumerated above quite meets the necessity of the case. Some readers of this article may help us out of the difficulty, the most hopeful indications of solution being Haslam's observations as to the benefit derived from sea-water and from dryness, also Lombardini's results with tobacco decoction and aqua regia. This matter might well be made the subject of Government enquiry with a view to the devising of means practicable in future emergencies of war service. No single Veterinary Surgeon, under present circumstances, has the opportunity of making the necessary researches, and on a campagin, though opportunities are not wanting time and appliances are deficient. We may point out that the question is not "can we cure?" but "can we cure by means practicable on Field Service?" We believe some method may be devised, but pending it being made known to the world, must point out that outbreaks are thoroughly repressible by isolation of the sick and precautions against contagion.

Another form of ECZEMA, AGEEN BHAO, is a vesication of the skin of various parts of the body supposed to be generally due to over-exposure to a hot sun. The blistering is apt to be followed by suppuration, and the parts must be cleansed and dressed with Ol. Camphoratum, an occasional purge being given.

In all cases of cutaneous or subcutaneous suppuration tonics are useful, because the animal is generally in low condition and anæmic; when practicable the patient should be given exercise or light work, hand-fed with coarse wheaten flour (gehun ka dalia) or Jouari flour (Bajri ka atta) and given such fodder as he will take; a good serwan will easily so tempt the appetite as to get the animal to eat with enjoyment a fair amount of nutriment.

The skin is frequently covered with offensive ECTOZOA. JEHUN (LICE) are well known to camel men and are constantly spoken of as a great source of annoyance. They can be dislodged by use of tobacco water infusions (Oliphant); or the camel should be allowed to roll in ashes of a brick kiln or pottery work and dressed with maline and tobacco water, of each 20 tolas, with red pepper 10 tolas, powdered and mixed in a gurra of water, heated and well rubbed in. Repeat daily for three days (Leach). An enormous arachnidan, described even by Cobbold as "most horrible," is often seen on camels and may assist in producing loss of condition and debility. He is a legitimate object of shikar by the men in charge and when caught should meet the fate of all vermin. "Snipe" tells us that "In Persia the bite of the camel tick (Galeodes araneoides) is said to cause intense suffering to human beings, even producing irritative fever."

The *temporary parasitic ectozoa* of the camel are interesting. Byrne writes of blotches as supposed to be due to the bite of a poisonous fly and that they may be treated by giving internally olive oil mixed with tobacco. Colonel Colborn ("With Hicks Pasha in the Soudan") mentions the SEROOT FLY, which was first seen between Abu zed and Ghebel ain (its northern limit). He considers it as probably not the Tsetze fly, for it attacks men. Horses and even camels are driven simply mad when these flies are found in large numbers. Sir Samuel Baker mentions them as occurring on the Abbara river during the rains. Lombardini refers to the *Debab fly* as it is termed in Algeria. Carbaccia considers this to be the Tabanus bovinus or gad fly of the Ox, which prevails from the beginning of June near water. So serious are its effects that the Arabs are accustomed at this time of year to march their camels southwards into the desert, far from stagnant water and thick undergrowth of marsh plants. In Cantonments the camels are crowded together as much as possible and the outer ones only suffer; and on the march the camels are halted by eight in the morning, camped as close together as possible, and then surrounded with a fire of straw and damp brushwood. Tar dressing suffices to keep off the fly for a few days (Carbuccia), the Debab fly bites also horses and mules. Camels attacked become in a short time literally covered with the maggots, which especially occur on the belly and thighs in abscesses. In different parts of Africa the tribes of Arabs give different names to the parasite. The larva at the end of July is termed narrah. It seems that the British traveller Bruce was the first to notice this parasite. What relation, if any, it bears to œstrus cameli of the pharynx is uncertain, as also is whether the Seroot and Debab flies are the same or of altogether different species.

Chapter XII.—MINOR SURGICAL CONDITIONS.

WOUNDS IN GENERAL.—It has been stated by writers on diseases of the camel that his wounds heal slowly, but this is by no means in accord with universal experience. In the warm dry climate of the Bayuda Desert they were noticed to heal very rapidly, and we have in the Deccan observed the same fact. The real difficulty in dealing with wounds of camels is to keep them clean and untampered with by Serwans. They are generally in the first place due to ill-treatment by attendants, and they are apt to be aggravated by mal-treatment or neglect, in the latter case becoming invaded by maggots, in the former much aggravated in intensity so that sinuses, lymphangitis, and chronic ulcer are of special frequency in cameline practice. Smoothly cut strips of raw hide may in emergency be used for sewing up wounds. The various forms of galls are frequent and severe, needing much care and attention especially on active service. Camels often bite each other when out grazing (Byrne).

Bullet wounds present no special features, but the stolid manner in which even very severe injuries of this nature are received by camels has been a matter of comment. One common method of desert fighting consists in using camels as a breastwork, another is to huddle the camels together in a couchant position in the hollow of a square; either of these methods exposes the animal to numerous and varied injuries from fire-arms, cutting and thrusting weapons. Rayment found at Suakin that only a moderate amount of success resulted from treatment of gunshot wounds.

Branding sores result from too deep sloughing and lead to the

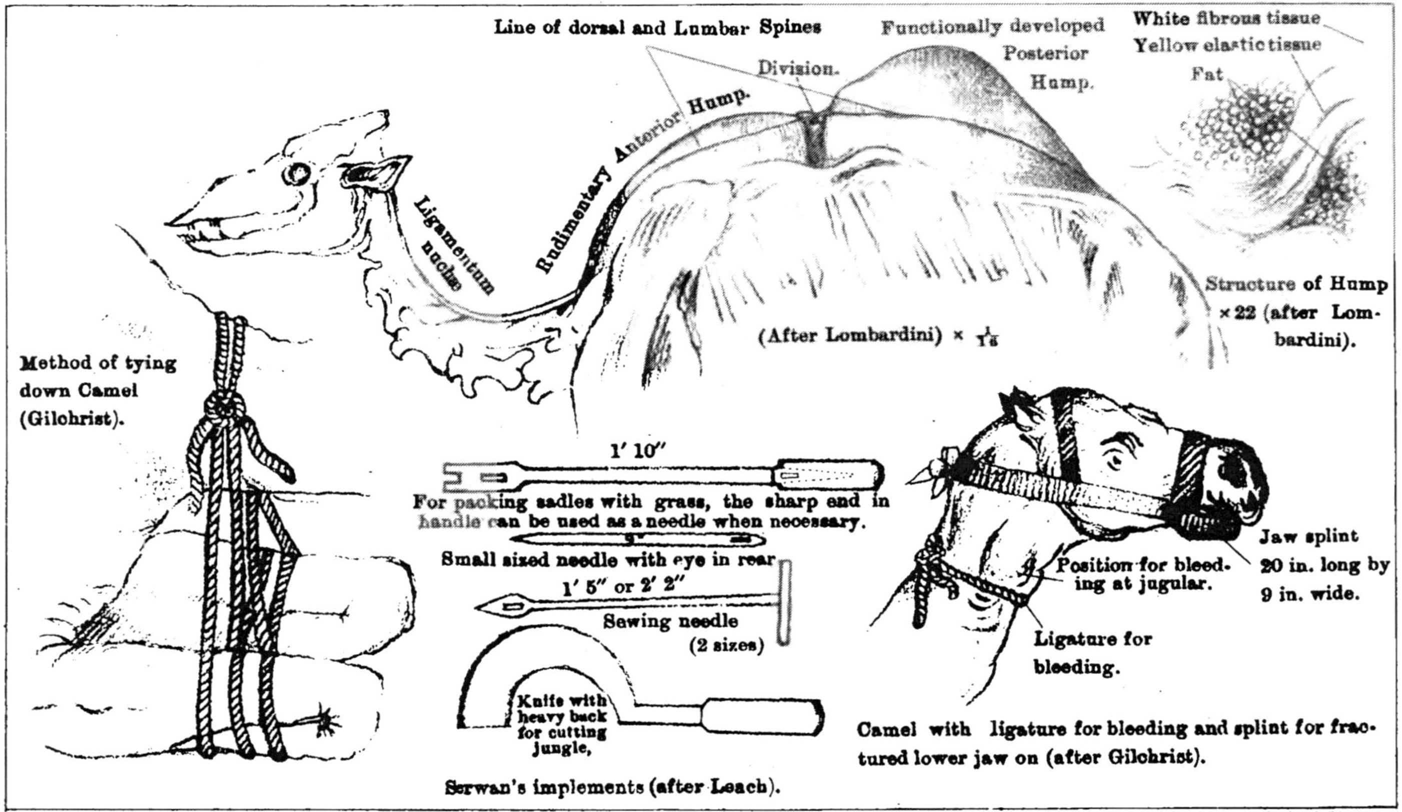

LITHOG: FOR LAWRENCE ASYLUM PRESS, MADRAS.
BY ALEX: BARREN.

mark becoming undecipherable. Branding irons should be cut out clear and not simply in relief on block, also they should have iron handles or they will in use be too hot to ensure niceity of manipulation (Bennett).

Government Branding is on the near side of neck with last two figures of years of purchase; contract hired camels are branded G. on near side of neck (if only engaged for short time hair merely singed). Figures and letters should be made three inches long. Throw the camel, form the letters with ordinary branding iron, then deepen the lines with thin small iron; afterwards dress with Ol. Carbolici (Byrne).

In positions which can be sprinkled with urine wounds are apt to be aggravated by the acridity of that fluid and the tail must be tied to prevent splashing. Treatment of camel wounds in no respects differs from the methods adopted for other animals, although the Serwans have made it out to be mysterious. Leach gives some simple and practicable measures for such severe bruises, *contusions*, as result from an animal falling down the khud with its load on, for instance. These comprise fomentations with infusions of neem leaves and poppy heads, and internal administration of alum (4 chtks.) in a pint of sarson-oil in hot weather or til oil in cold; or 2 chtks. of alum with two seers of milk daily for three days. Another method is to pour through the nostrils karil wood charcoal powder (1 chitk.) in 12 chitaks of mitha tel, daily for two or three days. If maggots be in the wound, cotton dipped in spirits of turpentine may be stuffed in the wound and the whole plastered over with mud. In emergency and when ordinary medicaments are deficient these rough expedients may be resorted to, usually traumatic methods as adopted in veterinary practice in general are best. A poultice of Bilawa, Ak leaves, and Taramera oil together is said to cure wounds extensively invaded by maggots in a few days and in Central Asia the same purpose is accomplished by smearing the wounds with snuff; there the nomads operate with wooden lancets, or having lanced the whole of the affected part they apply a poultice of mutton fat or chii grass (Byrne).

Of Galls we meet a considerable variety. At ordinary work

and under experienced management they do not occur to any serious degree and native camel drivers take care to at once throw out of work any of their animals showing the slightest signs of gall; on service the conditions are such as to render the occurrence of galls a certainty, but it is possible to limit their prevalence and severity, and thus to prevent their being such a serious cause of inefficiency of camels in a force as they have sometimes proved. We may first notice the less serious forms and then come to those of most practical import. The *nose becomes lacerated* by dragging out of the nose peg, and may be seriously invaded by maggots and look as though "eaten up by worms." Bilawa, Akh leaves, Tara meera tel, and Tootia mixed are applied to sore-nose and cure such cases in a few days if applied twice daily (Byrne).

The tail is liable to injuries of various kinds. Sometimes it has been required that the ears and tail of fallen camels be produced as evidence that the animals are dead and of validity of claim for compensation for loss; under these circumstances some cases occur in which these organs are removed from the *living* animal and serviceable animals are subsequently seen devoid of the appendages, hence this form of proof is alluded to here merely for the purpose of pointing out that it is apt to mislead and to give rise to cruelty.

Ulceration of the tail has been described as a constitutional disorder under the name of Bumnee (Gilchrist). First papules form, then pustules, and finally large phagedænic ulcers producing a specially fœtid pus. The organ is lost joint by joint. In some cases the disease is noticed to extend to the skin of the croup in the form of a scaly eruption and the animal to become distinctly out of sorts. This condition is curable in some cases by internal use of cathartics and alteratives, and local application of stimulants, especially the camphorated oil. More frequently the ulceration is due to purely local causes, such as the string by which the tail is tied up when the animal is in "musth" being too tight or never loosened, or a string may be tied round the organ to prevent the head rope of the camel behind slipping off the tail to which it has been tied and if this be left on it may strangulate the tip and cause sloughing (Burt). It is quite practicable in many cases to let the camels go free from each other and not tied together. Often a broad front for convoy is better, as regards defence, than a long string extending over several miles. The common practice of tying camels together by head rope passing to the tail acts in another way. If the camel in front be stronger than the one behind the latter cannot keep up on a long march and drags at the tail, hanging on the head rope in a way which may result in serious injury to the tail. This is especially liable to occur when the pace of a camel train is forced, when the camels are overloaded, or when they are weakened by the emergencies of service.

As regards *crupper galls* proper; they may result from the load shifting forwards or from the crupper rope being too much shortened, but experience has shown that the crupper can almost always be dispensed with, and the cause being thus removed little subsequent attention will be needed for the abrasions. Wrapping the crupper rope round with rag, washed daily to keep it clean and occasionally oiled and greased, is recommended by Byrne. *Injuries of the inferior maxilla, mouth, and chin* occur where mouth gag and head collar are used or where the rope of the headstall is twisted into the mouth; cases of fracture of the lower jaw have been found to result from brutal jerking by an attendant at the head rope. *Elbow gall:* is a scraping of the sides of the chest which results from the elbow pads being very large or from ill shape of the camel, *i.e.*, narrow chest, toes turned out and elbows in. Oliphant is particular in cautioning us to look carefully for this conformation with a view to avoidance of it in purchasing, for it renders an animal almost useless. *Boss or Pad galls* are peculiarly obstinate and apt to result in quittor, effects of the horny nature of their epidermis and of the large amount of fibrous tissue in their structure. Any of the callosities may be thus affected, but the Rahafay or chest pad is the most frequent seat of aggravated disorder. It is supposed that these pads are the result of development in adaptation to the severe pressure put on the parts where they occur and that they have in course of time become hereditary. The largest of them is the Rahafay below the sternum, those on the stifles and elbows are considerable in size, and the knees are also callous. The latter point has given rise to one of the familiar service jokes of India, about camels being rejected by a griff on a purchasing board because they were all broken kneed! These callosities are considered specially beneficial to the animal as enabling him to rest on hot sand without discomfort in the couchant position. Traces of them are present in newly born camels. An over-laden or fatigued animal may bruise them in lying down, and this is especially liable to occur to weak animals whose legs give way under them; also when the ground on which the animal has been rested was not previously freed of sharp stones. Thus these injuries are to an extent preventable by care; and this is the more important because bruise or puncture of the pads is very apt to result in sub-acute inflammation and tardy sloughing often incurable and so rendering the animal useless; in case of the Rahafay, the abscess even has been known to penetrate the chest cavity and cause pleurisy and death, the sternum becoming absorbed (Gilchrist). These injuries become aggravated every time the animal sits down, owing to pressure and the entry of foreign matters, and an important point in treatment is to keep the patient on his legs as much as possible, although it involves serious loss of necessary rest. Cases must be treated by antiphlogistic measures and surgery, underrun horn must be removed, sinuses slit up, and all accumulated pus (which will be found very fœtid) evacuated. Camphorated oil or other fly dressing and stimulating substances will prove very useful to promote healing. The Arab method of firing around the diseased part proves beneficial in chronic cases. Above all things the wounds must be kept clean and regularly dressed thoroughly. All the pads must be carefully examined in purchase.

Sore Back or Saddle Gall demands detailed notice on account of its immense practical importance and constant occurrence on active service. Although it agrees in all essentials with the lesions of the same name seen in other pack and riding animals, a number of differences in detail deserve mention here and attention from the practitioner. In every war where the camel is used too much experience of these cases is gained, practically all the animals become affected, fatal sequelæ such as tetanus, pyæmia, debility, paralysis, and exhaustion lessen the number of transport animals, and many are found utterly inefficient through severity of their galls. The withers, hump, sides of chest, loins, and hips are the seats of most frequent galls, as also are the points where the four lower corners of the pad touch. These are parts which require to be specially examined at purchase for traces of previous lesion, great judgment is required from the Veterinary Officer as to which will "stand" and which cannot be passed. If all with traces of galls were rejected the number of camels would as a rule, prove quite inadequate.

The *causes of saddle galls* may be enumerated as follows :—

(1). Camel's skin under the saddle being dirty and matted, or soft and unaccustomed to pressure ;*
shape altered by emaciation from service exigencies.

(2). Saddle ill-fitted, so long as to gall the points of the hips ;
belonging to another camel (dead or transferred) and not properly altered owing to want of time or carelessness, too deep in the pannels, or with side sticks too long ;
badly constructed, its back is apt to become too flexible and to need re-stiffening ;
of bad materials, its stuffing being bad (full of stones, thorns, &c.), or liable to shift as not tight enough ;
out of repair, owing to want of leisure during continuous marching, want of materials, or carelessness ;
kept on too long, as for days together.

(3). Load too considerable, absolutely or for the particular animal under its particular circumstances ;

* In June camels begin to sweat on the neck and under the saddle and then gall readily unless undressed sheep skin with the wool turned inwards be used to supply the place of the hair the animal is then shedding. Hence camels should not remain long in camp without work and at first the loads should be light and the marches short (Byrne).

kept on too long, not removed when possible or kept on necessarily through long and tedious marches;

badly put on or mal-adjusted, tilting to front or rear, top heavy or unevenly balanced so that it twists and squeezes the sides;

put on carelessly or badly, owing to ignorance and want of training of loaders. It should not press on the backbone;

tilted backwards by head rope of camel behind being attached to the back of the saddle;

shifted, owing to original loose tying or to too long marches over bad roads;

difficult and unsuitable. Sacks are much better than cases as camel loads, and long articles, such as ladders and tent poles, are particularly trying.

(4). Mismanagement or emergency, such as use of riding camels for baggage purposes;

If more than nine or ten hours continuous marching daily (Davidson).

Treatment of saddle galls is preventive or curative. The former comprises all such points in Camel Hygiéne as concern the adjustment of loads, methods and kinds of work, care of saddlery, and so on. Bennett's recommendation that a sacking saddle cloth be part of the equipment of each camel for use under the saddle by day and as a protecting jhool at night might beneficially be generally adopted. Good condition of the animals must be attained and kept up as much as possible, for not only will it lessen liability to injury but also it will tend to thoroughness of repair and to lessen any defects in vital activity. Care should be taken that each camel man has repairing tools which he should know how to use and should not neglect; the lining of the saddle should be dusted and dried daily and chambered where it tends to abrade. By cutting off any ill-fitting parts, re-adjustment of stuffing, and other expedients, pressure on special spots may be avoided. The skin must be kept in good order by regular grooming, animals should be brought gradually into work whenever it is practicable to do so, and it must be the object of the Veterinary Officer to keep every animal at work as long as possible by expedients such as experience suggests; work is good for the general health of galled animals whenever it can be enforced without severe pain, as, for example, when the injured parts can be relieved from pressure. In war inefficiency of baggage animals cannot be tolerated and what would be inhumanity from working galled camels in peace becomes necessity on service. The Veterinary Officer must not shirk responsibility in this matter, however much he may pity his patients he must never forget the necessities of service. The most important means of prevention lies in original selection of sound and well-formed animals, in training of the transport before operations, in vigilance of executive officers to prevent slight galls and to spare galled individuals or injured parts in the course of work. Nevertheless cases *will* occur and get worse so as to present conditions of great severity, and will prove tardy in healing, sometimes quite incurable. We have to contend with fractured summits of spinous and transverse processes, loose portions of bone, and carious surfaces, sloughing cartilage and fibrous tissue, extensive infiltrations of pus, and sinuses, abscesses, sitfasts of enormous size, and masses of bruised skin. Often very rough and ready methods have to be resorted to, the Arabs explode powder on the ulcer surfaces or they apply tar dressing mixed with grease without salt, or apply the desert plant "Dugust." Lord and Baines find leather burnt to a black crisp mass and then finely powdered and strewn over the wound useful, frequently the actual cautery is used freely, a method which practical scientific surgery will often not disdain. Gilchrist recommended poulticing with Kataymaht or Pahnee Cumar ka puttha, two handfulls with half an ounce of common salt pounded together and heated for ten minutes, applied every morning, as good for severe sore backs, and when the animal has to be worked he suggests putting a piece of waxed cloth over the ulcer and beneath the saddle, but insists that whenever practicable, the animal should be kept at rest.* Applications of blue

* In the Soudan McDougall's sheep dip 1 lb. in water, 1 quart, allowed

vitriol are favourite treatment among the natives, but reprehensible because they simply dry up the surface and produce a false appearance of healing. This surface healing is specially to be avoided, all dead tissue must be carefully removed, depending orifices for escape of pus made, the ulcerated surfaces aroused to activity in various ways as by scraping or dissecting off their surfaces, application of the hot iron, or other stimulant. Tonics will be found beneficial in promoting the healing process. The notes from the Nile Expedition Report concerning saddles for camels are of considerable practical value.

The HUMP is specially tedious in healing; it is also liable to slough and to become the seat of fistula. This part of the body is mainly composed of fat in the meshes of fibrous tissue and careful examination has shown that it contains some muscular structure. Its firmness is considered a guide to condition of the animal and a large full hump is a good point in a dromedary. The camel man before an expedition feels the hump critically to determine whether his animal is "fit" and aims at keeping the hump in good order. This part must be carefully examined in purchase of camels both as an index of fitness for work and also because it is liable to *hump gall* from the saddle, and as Vallon discovered, even when there is no outward sign of disease, *cancerous disorder* may be going on centrally in the part. Vallon describes this state as true encephaloid, but there is reason to believe from experience in India that such a state is very rare and that the apparently cancerous ulceration is generally only ordinary traumatic lesion aggravated by neglect or maltreatment. An interesting observation by Lombardini is that even in the dromedary there is a rudiment of the second hump, the two fatty masses being separated by a well-marked septum. A diagram published by the latter observer well illustrates this point and also the relations which the humps bear to the spines of the dorsal and lumbar bones. A glance at the skeleton of the camel

to cool until partly solidified, and then applied with a paint brush was found good for galls. Applied night and morning it served well to keep off flies (Byrne). Martin found a mixture of salt, flour, and burnt felt a useful application.

at once suggests liability to severe galls in consequence of the considerable length of the various vertebral processes.

ABSCESS, *phora,* is a surgical condition of special frequency in camels and which has been much misunderstood, if we may judge from the literature of the subject. Experience tends to show that it is almost invariably lymphangitis due to maltreatment of wounds and assuming a farcy-like form, the lymph vessels or glands being the seat of pus accumulation. Both Gilchrist and Leach give valuable information on the subject of abscesses. The following local abscesses have been described and receive special names from native camel men :—

(1) *Tumours of the neck glands,* two in number, which are normally visible at the root of the neck. This is by Gilchrist termed Gooroosh.

(2) *Chest abscess.* When the prescapular glands are affected it is called Yahcud (Gilchrist) ; Leach applies the names Ghariz and Hekar to chest abscesses. It is said to occur independently of condition of the animal and of the season, to affect an animal only once, and not before it is ten years of age ; whether or no it is ever specific seems not yet to be settled. The animal is feverish, off feed, and walks with difficulty ; shortly local swelling occurs, then suppuration is evident, and sloughing takes place leaving a foul deep ulcer. Leach gives in detail the treatment adopted by natives in these cases. They fire with the palm leaf pattern (Kajuria Dagh) to cause dispersion or bursting of the abscess, and, commencing from the third day after firing, apply for seven days paste of wood ash or cowdung with camel's urine ; by the time this is completed it will be found that the abscess if it has not burst will be ready to be lanced ! This is done, all pus removed and the sore dressed daily with camel's urine to keep it healthy and keep off flies. When it becomes quite clean the following wound ointment is applied. Marking nut and pure turpentine of each a chittak, garlic 2 chittaks, sweet flag ½ chittak, and sandur (red lead) 2 chittaks, boiled in 8 chittaks of kurwa, sarson, mustard, or taramera oil, or else red pepper boiled in kurwa oil (whereby its irritant properties are removed) may be applied. These details are alluded to as

curious; less filthy, complex, and more scientific methods should be resorted to in such cases.

(3) *Abscess in the groin:* Randuk (Leach and Gilchrist), Gathar (Nunn) has been observed especially in the hot season in animals of all ages. It generally results from injury and probably also from ulceration and offensive accumulations in the sheath. It seriously disables the patient, but is curable; Nunn mentions the native treatment as application of the cautery and drenching the patient with camel's milk and turmeric every evening for a fortnight. Leach describes how the abscess is allowed to ripen, then lanced and the pus removed, after which the parts are washed with nim leaf infusion or camel's urine, and then the complex ointment recently described is applied. The disease, termed by the Arabs *El magoub,* is seen in the Sahara. Byrne describes it as a tumour of the sheath and to be treated by slitting up the sheath, pulling it back, and constantly applying vinegar and water.*

(4) *Abscess outside the thigh,* anteriorly, (Godi, Gadik, or Rusoli) is considered to be especially benefited by firing with a circle surrounding a cross (Choufulli Dagh) and subsequent treatment similar to that of the other forms (Leach).

(5) *Abscess over the eye* giving rise to extensive infiltration of pus into the upper eyelid is evidently a result of inflammation of the temporal gland (*quod vide*).

(6) Gomri or Kapali was mentioned long ago by Hodgson as *abscess of the neck* and treated by firing first and then opening. Leach also writes of it as denoted by pain in depressing the head, and states that the firing is performed in a single line three inches long. We have elsewhere entered at length into the question of the true nature of the disease known as "Kapaulee."

(7) Gilchrist writes of *subcutaneous abscesses* which occur, though rarely, several simultaneously and on any part of the body and prove very troublesome. This condition he terms Bale-ka-murz or Joluk-ka-gudday. If on the trunk these abscesses are called Nurbale, if on the legs Mahdeebale and

* Soft swelling preventing the animal from staling may result from gall by the hind girth (Byrne).

are larger than those of the trunk, which generally are about two inches in diameter. These tumours are recurrent, and at length may render the animal unfit for further service, especially when they become fistulous and cause permanent leg swelling. *Boils* are termed Rusoli, they affect all sorts of animals in all seasons, although not frequent and seldom serious enough to materially affect the health of the animal. They average about two inches in diameter and contain liquid or caseous matter. They ulcerate, burst, and the cyst sloughs out or slowly refills. Treatment comprises opening them early, dissecting out or cauterising the interior, dressing with stimulant anti-fly dressing, such as Ol. Camph., and giving a cathartic followed by alteratives. A general eruption of boils is termed *chandri* or *chhahliyan.*

CHAPTER XIII.—THE LOCOMOTORY SYSTEM.

The following points concerning the skeleton of the camel must be remembered. The skull is very like that of a carnivore in the prominence of the parietal and occipital crests, the temporal fossæ are very deep and the postero-superior part of the skull is triangular. The cervical vertebræ are remarkably long and the vertebral foramina in each are so deep that they seem to be in the spinal canal. The spinal formula is C. 7, D. 12, L. 7, S. 4-5, Cocc. 12-17. The ribs are arranged in twelve pairs. The sternal bones are numerous. The superior spines of the dorsal and lumbar regions are long, as also are the lumbar transverse processes. The sacrum is short and consists of four or five bones. The shoulder girdle consists of a simple scapula with moderate-sized coracoid process, the limb bones are long and stout, there is a double humeral groove, the ulna extends to the knee. The knee bones are seven. There are no splint bones, no traces of rudimentary digits, except inside the hind limb where in the very young animal is a small splint. The lower extremity of the cannon bone is divided, and each part bears two sesamoids. The terminal phalanges are rudimentary, the others are long and narrow. The bones of the hind limb are proportionally small. The femur has a marked neck and no distinct small trochanters. The patella is rudimentary. Os calcis has a long narrow process, astragulus has the usual ruminant form. The small tarsal bones are six in number. Ligamentum nuchæ has a very long rope-like portion but only a small membraniform expansion. The Diaphragm has remarkably long and strong fleshy pillars and contains a bone in its central tendon. The muscular system in general is simple in arrangement.

FRACTURES.—Vallon considered the bones of the camel fragile and very apt to become fractured on service, and it is found that when the bones of the extremities have given way mechanical difficulties exist in the way of setting the fragments and keeping them in position, so that it is generally necessary to have the animal destroyed. The non-repair in such cases is not due to any inherent defect in healing power, for when the lower jaw has been broken by violence (as from jerking at the head collar gag) union occurs rapidly if the parts be set in an iron splint. This accident is denoted by the part being depressed and the animal being unable to approximate the lips. Gilchrist had a successful case which extended over only six weeks' treatment.

DISLOCATIONS were found by Tassy to be frequent among baggage camels in Algeria; Gilchrist refers to thigh dislocation and luxation of the shoulder. The latter is the most frequent and necessitates rejection of the animal as unfit for further service, because the lesion is not thoroughly curable. In traversing slippery places it is the custom of camel men to tie the two hind legs together in such a way as to prevent their slipping apart and the camel "splitting up." In which latter accident there may be extensive muscle laceration and dislocation according to the severity of the case. In the Quarterly Journal of Veterinary Science in India, Vol. III., p. 244, is detailed a case of *dislocation of the neck.*

ANCHYLOSIS: *Bone Spavin* is not rare in the camel, it causes lameness, dragging of the toe, and other characteristic symptoms; and may be treated as in the horse. There is a good specimen of *Anchylosis of Vertebræ,* the result of overloading probably and perhaps of previous fracture, complicated by exostosis, in the Museum of the Poona Army Veterinary School. It was from a Bangalore Transport camel which was not known

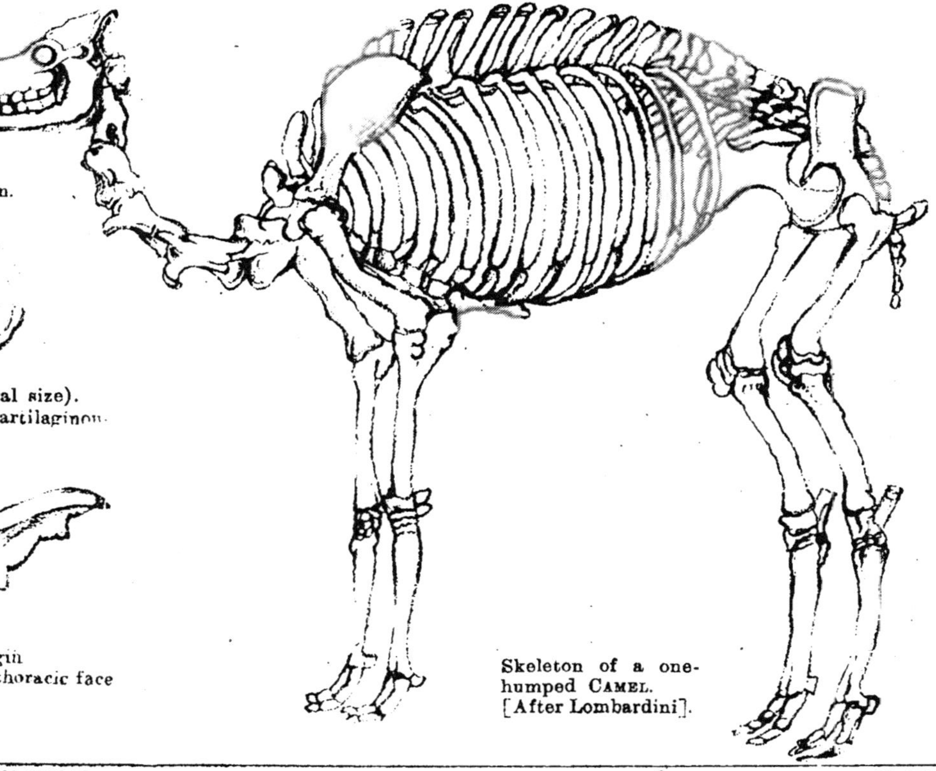

Ant. internal Prolongation.

Os Cordis (natural size).
This is often only cartilaginou[s].

Inf. external Margin
Diaphragm bone, thoracic face
(natural size)

Skeleton of a one-humped CAMEL.
[After Lombardini].

LITHOG. FOR LAWRENCE ASYLUM PRESS, MADRAS.

BY ALEX: BARREN.

to have, during its service, suffered from spinal injury. Doubtless overload and accidents give rise to such conditions much more frequently than is generally supposed.

SPRAINS (Lutchuk) of various kinds are frequent in old and overworked camels, they are indicated by *levelled legs* (baed), *swollen joints,* and stale action or actual lameness. Gilchrist writes of *sprained shoulder* as Kutchwah, and Hodgson of *atrophy of limb muscles* as Seemuck. These conditions are generally treated by firing. They result from false steps, work on slippery ground, over-work and over-weighting, premature work, and so on; they are tedious in treatment and necessitate prolonged rest. *Laceration of the ham muscles* inside the thigh is especially frequent on service, the hind limbs being painfully and sharply diverged. Sprains in general are most frequent in the hind limbs.

TUMOURS: *Fibroma* is perhaps the most common form of hypertrophic growth. Tumours, however, seem to be rare in camel.

CHAPTER XIV.—THE ORGANS OF SPECIAL SENSE.

We have little to record under this heading. We have seen how the ears are sometimes cut off as proof of death. The conchial cartilage is small and short, which has been considered to be a special provision against the entry of sand in desert marches. *Ear Canker* is described by Byrne as rare but presenting the usual symptoms.

The EYE is large and prominent and so is very apt to be injured, especially by the end of tent poles as carried by the camel in front. Rayment mentions *Ophthalmia* as one of the principal disorders treated by him among camels at Suakim in 1886. Bennett describes blindness as frequent in old camels.

The Pedal Apparatus; The standing posture is pluckily maintained by sick camels. The animal rests freely in the position of decubitus, and is then described as couchant, camping, or sitting. From this posture he rises, sometimes in the case of good riding camels more sharply than the inexperienced rider anticipates, with two consecutive and opposite upbearings. When the camel is sitting he rests on the chest pad and belly, the trunk being vertical. The limbs are folded evenly, the hind ones below the belly and fully flexed with somewhat of an inward twist at hock and stifle, the fore fully flexed at the knees. The stifle and elbow pads thus assist the Rahafay in supporting the body; in rising the knee pads prove useful to support the weight for a short time.

As regards the paces of the camel, Colin informs us that the amble of the dromedary resembles that of the giraffe (the two limbs of each side being not quite contemporaneous in action). It replaces the walk as progression becomes more rapid; the so-called walk is a kind of half run, a little like the ordinary walk and the amble without being absolutely like either of them. Captain Peel found the stride of a camel to be 38 per minute, and each 6 ft. 6 in. to 7 ft., *i.e.*, the pace is 2·62 geographical (or 3 English) miles. The foot is considerably less cloven than that of most ruminants for the division is distinct only in its anterior part, there is one wide horny sole or hoof-slipper reminding us of that of the elephant, but as a rule, bearing only two claws or hoof walls anteriorly. Colin says—"The dromedary is very extraordinary (in the structure of his feet). The two digits instead of being distinct and separable to their free extremity are united inferiorly by a horny, extremely supple disc, which carries at its anterior part two small caps (capuchons) serving to envelop the points of the ungual phalanges. Above the flexible sole and slightly convex are two very thick ovoid cushions on which lie horizontally the two terminal phalanges of each digit. These cushions, enveloped in many layers of yellow elastic tissue and fixed to the phalanges by very strong bands, are composed of a special tissue, pale red in colour, slightly fibrous, markedly elastic, but in many respects differing from the tissue of the ligamentum nuchae and the superficial abdominal fascia. This peculiar conformation gives the foot of the camel extreme flexibility. When the weight falls on it the sole flattens, the cushions diminish in size, approach one another internally and fill to an extent the interphalangeal space, as may be plainly seen from in front. When the pressure ceases the horny disc again becomes slightly convex and the two cushions resume their original form."

The tread of the camel, like that of the elephant, has been noted as very silent.

Diseases of the foot. These are mostly due to injuries and are specially frequent in hilly countries. They were often seen in the Kuram Valley and in Algeria, but are recorded as not frequent in the Bolan Pass in 1878 (C. Steel). The Algerian Arabs, it seems, in traversing rocky and rough ground cover the foot with rough hide boots (Vallon). Lameness is infrequent in the camel as compared with other baggage animals. The following causes of lameness owing to foot injuries or disorders have been noted :—

(a) *Overgrown toe nails,* sometimes not noticed, must be pared carefully and the hoof slipper reduced to its proper shape.

(b) *Inflammation of the elastic pad,* causing the feet to swell enormously.

(c) *Whitlow, quittor,* or *guzmah* seems to be distinguished by Gilchrist from *Tahkne,* fistula, but the grounds of distinction are not quite clear. The latter, he tells us, results from journeys over stony ground or from puncture, and proves very tedious in treatment. The former generally is due to injury, but often its cause is obscure; sometimes it causes the toe nails to fall off. The Turkestanis speak of a disease under the name *Sarpo* as sometimes causing the animal's feet to fall off, but preventible by rest and good food. There is evidently confusion as to pedal lesions of a local character and those due to constitutional causes such as foot and mouth disease. Byrne recommends in treatment of *Sarpo* to wash the entire leg of the camel from the knee downwards with camel's milk, next sew a leather cover filled with hot mutton fat round the leg, which thus is in a closely fitting mould, and that the animal be rested while the healing takes place, which is a very gradual process. *Thullee* is the name given to puncture of the foot caused by thorns or sharp stones. In all these cases the feet must be kept clean especially by a loose leather boot over the foot, the patient should be kept recumbent as much as possible, and in neglected cases anti-maggot dressings, as Ol. Camph., may be needed. We need not specially detail methods of treatment for quittor.

(*e*) *Mooroos* is sore feet, overworn sole, due to too long marches, especially from travelling along bad roads. This is the condition that Tassy describes as a kind of founder and which Hodgson long ago recorded as treated by rest and putting the feet in wet clay. Some of the chobes recommended for elephants, or plain tar dressing, should prove useful here. Byrne considers EL MOOROOS as sandcrack, *i.e.* fissure of the sole extending from front to rear. Caused by long marches over stony ground, or by continued contact with dung or irritant mud. Remove from such ground, rest, and keep the parts clean.

(*f*) *Pedal fibroma* seems rather frequent in the camel and may attain a large size without causing lameness and apparently without proving fatal. This condition does not seem amenable to treatment although we have no evidence of malignancy in it. Early operative removal must be tried, otherwise as in a case recorded in the Q. J. V. Sc. in I., Vol. III., p. 246, traumatic lymphangitis is apt to result from the surface of the tumour cracking or becoming injured and the ulcers irritated in various ways.

APPENDIX I.—NOTES ON CAMEL CORPS.

A recent War Office publication, by Major D. B. Burn, 18th Hussars, (Intelligence Branch, War Office), deals in an interesting manner with the subject of use of camels in war for purposes other than Transport of baggage and supplies. An epitome of the opinions expressed and the information given on this most important matter will doubtless prove of interest to our readers. From very ancient times camels have been used in warfare by combatants, and actually at one time were brought to the front to take part in the fight, their riders being armed with bows and arrows to greet the enemy from a distance, and with 6 or 7 feet long swords to enable them to reach a foot soldier on the ground. Antiochus the Great, we are informed, used such soldiers against the Romans in the battle of Magueria (190 B.C.); Cyrus gained his great victory over Crœsus through the cavalry of the latter, taking to flight at sight of camel-archers of the former. Thebes, in 420 A.D., was garrisoned by a Camel Corps, which rendered distinguished service in the time of the Emperor Diocletian.

The French have used Camel Corps for their operations in Africa. Napoleon organised a Dromedary Regiment (that of Cavalier), which did good work until it surrendered to Major Wilson in 1801; Desaix, in September 1799, used running dromedaries for his troops, which caught up with Mourad Beg's cavalry after a vigorous pursuit and defeated them. Abdel Kadir used camels to carry men in raids and surprises, as, when in 1837, he marched for 36 hours and captured Medesh. In Algeria Carbuccia organised Camel Corps, which, in 1844, took part in an expedition to Djebel Sahri with not good results, but later it seems to have done very well.

British experience comprises—Napier's Scinde Camel Corps (1843) used in operations against Beloochi horsemen; corps organised by Vesey (72nd Highlanders) and Bethune (Gordon Highlanders) for pursuit of Tantia Topee after the mutiny in Central India; Major James' Suakim Camel Corps in 1885; and the following regiments in the Nile Expedition, 1884-85:—Guards, Heavy, Light, and Mounted Infantry, also I-1 Battery of the Southern Division, Royal Artillery. The details of these several corps are interesting to contrast.

Chevalier had at first 100, subsequently 700, riding camels with the necessary complement of baggage animals. Each camel carried two men (Europeans) at first facing back to back like the old archers used, in order that one man might fight while advancing, the other while retiring, later both were placed in the modern position of facing forwards.

Carbuccia's regiment was about 300 camels strong, two Frenchmen being carried on each, of these seven became available for fighting, one man being left in charge of four camels. Napier's Corps consisted of 500 to 600 camels, each carrying an armed driver and a Light Infantry man, also ammunition, blankets, ten days' rations, and entrenching tools. Vesey's Corps consisted of 100 camels, each carrying a Native and a Highlander; its baggage was carried on seven elephants; there were also camels for spare ammunition and officers' baggage; it only marched with other troops, so that its special value as a Camel Corps was never properly shown; we may, therefore, dismiss it with the record that it was on the move for some 17 weeks, passed all over Central India at a walk of 3 to 3½ miles per hour, averaging 20 miles per diem. On one occasion it did 36 miles in 13 hours; in all it covered 1,496 miles, and always had 95 per cent. of its camels serviceable, the animals being well taken care of, for it is noted that the men were always dismounted at wet slippery nullahs. The Commanding Officer rode on horseback. Bethune's Corps consisted of 155 camels, of which 150 each carried a driver (Native) and a Highlander. The Nile Corps had a European per camel, no Native driver. Each gun of the Artillery Battery had six Natives for its 18 camels, there being nine Europeans to work the gun.

The Suakim Corps was never fully put to the test, but it was organised so that five European soldiers and one driver were carried on every three camels, the former when necessary to look to the grooming and general care of the camels which in camp was carried out by the driver. Thus five fighting men became available for every three camels, and certain amounts of ammunition, rations, and water, besides blankets, were to be carried, each camel having a load of 418 to 430 lb., which, it is presumed, would be too considerable for a long and fatiguing service. It is concluded that *experience is in favour of one fighting man and one armed driver per camel,* other camels for water, food, and ammunition, and 10 per cent. camels spare.*

As to the DUTIES OF CAMEL CORPS, Napoleon's were infantry regiments, capable of rapid movements, and they proved useful in dealing with predatory tribesmen harassing the line of march. It was found that the dromedary would run nearly as fast as a horse could gallop, and could keep up the pace longer, and so could run the horsemen down; the camel-men proved useful as bearers of despatches, for keeping up communications, and as scouts, their height when mounted enabling them to see to great distances. Sir George Green shows that Camel Corps are specially useful for covering considerable distances in a night (60 or

* The hind seat is most comfortable and the rider is less shaken than in the front one, and therefore after a long march can sooner come steadily into action. Especially is this the case if he has learned to ride loosely in the saddle without knee-grip, or can sleep in the saddle.

70 miles), and thus striking a blow and inflicting panic on an enemy which was under the impression of being beyond striking distance. Also by means of camels small detachments may be conveyed for keeping open communications with distant posts, or for relieving far outlying pickets, for bringing up supplies rapidly in emergency, and for staff escort and reconnoitring. The camels are essentially a means of rapid carriage of infantry from place to place, and for the purpose of making long marches "the camel is a long traveller, but a slow mover" (Redvers Buller), so he is not to be used as a means of advance to or retreat from attack. *The camel soldier is to fight only on foot.* He can't mount his camel quick enough to retire in haste, so must fight for his camels. Either the drivers must be able to defend the camels, or else some or all of the fighting men have to do so. The best plan seems to be to make the corps consist really of two regiments, the Fighting and the Transport; the latter to carry the former and to be capable of defending itself; some consider it may at times prove auxiliary to the fighting body. Chevalier's Corps paraded with other troops, went through special manœuvres, and the men fought behind their couchant camels. The animals were trained for a week or longer—first to lead, next to follow; after this they were mounted and taught the use of the reins. The men learned the Arab "camel language," which is, doubtless, an accomplishment French troops would learn with more facility than British. Carbuccia calculated that in two years a soldier of the French Army would become as good a driver of camels as an Arab. A month's training suffices to make a man fairly useful with a camel. His camel corps manœuvred well, and fought in line of skirmishers of 7 men to every four camels (one man being left in charge of the latter. The difficulty in mounting was got over by use of a double stirrup as a ladder). Our soldiers up the Nile had to be cautioned against the danger of causing rupture by jumping off a standing camel. At Suakim it was apparently practicable to dismount the rear man without making the camel sit down. Napier's fighting men were light infantry carried by camels. The drivers of the latter were armed with carbine and tulwar; when attacked, they made the camels sit down in hollow

square, at each corner was a gun camel. This means of defence was very effectual against horsemen, for horses, it is said, although they may become accustomed to camels, as a rule, hate the sight of a number of them, and cannot face a square of recumbent camels. The camels are tied in the usual way to prevent them rising suddenly, but are notoriously stolid under attack. Bethune's Corps consisted of Highlanders as fighting men, independent and under their own officers, of whom the Commandant also controlled the movement of the Transport part. The latter was under an European officer mounted on an Arab horse and assisted by a Havildar-Major. Each driver was armed with spear and tulwar (it is suggested carbine and spear would be preferable in future). The Suakim Corps had rather elaborate drill, consisting in movements by fours, increasing and diminishing front as do cavalry in single line; each company or squadron formed two troops. The order of march where practicable was half column of troops, the baggage camels being in front of the rear squadron. For attack or defence the column closed up to the front, the camels were made to sit down, tied, and the men formed square around them in double rank, or else, leaving some with the camels and drivers, the remainder acted as ordinary infantry. It took 80 seconds to form square. The Nile Corps formed up its camels into square with the men around them to defend. Four hundred camels could be thus arranged to present a perimeter varying from 460 to 760 feet and from 28 to 46 running inches per file according to requirements. The orders were that in the event of small parties not able to form two deep round the square being attacked, the camels should be formed into a closely-packed square with the men formed into two small squares at the opposite ends of a diagonal, as one would place two bastions to a square redoubt. In other cases, and some consider this the best plan, the camels should form a hollow square with the men inside fighting under cover of the bodies of the camels. The Battery marched in four lines to each division, the gun and carriage in the first line, mounted gunners and drivers (Natives) in the second and third, spare and extra camels in the fourth.

Finally, to get the utmost out of a Camel Corps, it should be permitted and able to act independently of other troops, cavalry move too fast for it, infantry too slowly. The essence of such corps is to be able to strike blows unexpectedly at great distances and to perform long tedious marches in a small number of days. The camels must not be hurried; they must be groomed, well fed,* and *watered daily*. Ordinary marches of Camel Corps are 30 miles per diem, 6 miles per hour is said to be the best pace when there are only running camels to be dealt with. Grazing should be given when practicable, some grain daily is good for the animals, and should be flavoured with salt. The loads must not be too great; 260 lb. for camels doing severe continued work is sufficient; this has sometimes to be much exceeded, as in Artillery camels, of which the loads are arranged to vary from 551 lb. to 333 lb., and some of them, especially the Trail, are very awkward and prevent a driver being carried. Chevalier's Corps, on one occasion, marched 550 miles in eight days (nearly 70 miles per diem); Major Bethune's Corps was on the road 42 hours out of 48 hours before confronting the enemy; and lost only 2 out of 155 camels during five months' active service; rather a contrast to the Nile records! Carbuccia lost 5 by death and 16 became inefficient out of 277 on an expedition which lasted eighty days.

Sore backs are the greatest cause of inefficiency in camel corps, the saddlery needs experienced and constant attention. The Indian pattern saddle is the lightest and best. The men's blankets are tied over the saddle to make the seat comfortable. Napoleon's men used to carry the musket on the off side of the saddle, and some rations and ammunition in the saddle pockets. Cooking pots, intrenching tools, reserve ammunition, and water tins are generally carried by baggage camels.

Water has generally to be carried in the countries where camel corps are most serviceable. The common water-bottle may be used tied behind the saddle. Also at Suakim canvas hose water-bottles, 5 feet long by 2½ feet in diameter, proved very useful; they contained 5 quarts of water, were filled easily by means

* It is useful to carry some spices (masalah) for the camels.

of a funnel in a few minutes, and at first were carried looped round the camels neck, but as it was found this caused galls, they were later slung from the saddle between the two seats.

Of course, the success of all camel corps depends largely on the animals being managed by experienced men, hence the system adopted up the Nile was somewhat in error; further, camel corps have special uses, and are, therefore, capable of abuse; camels can no more than any other animals do without food, water, and rest, although they are remarkably tolerant of deficient supplies of each. Finally, with camel corps it is essential to have some such knowledge as can only be gained by actual practice in peace time as a preparation for war. A hastily improvised organisation is almost sure to break down, and failing the nucleus of such corps as a permanent field for study, some practice should be given and time for organisation before the corps is sent into the field. Properly managed camel corps should prove a useful addition to a nation's military resources.

Appendix II.

(*From the Records of the Suakim Field Force.*)

For the supply of water to troops at the Front, weighing three times the ration of each man, water tins each containing 12½ gallons were packed on camels, two tins to each, and these were started off before daybreak to join the convoy. The Camel Corps was under Capt. Gwatkin, 13th Bengal Lancers and Lieut. Watson, Central India Horse. It actually comprised 485 camels, 195 landed on 6th April and 290 on 17th idem. The camels were chiefly from the Hissar District, 100 were collected at Meean Meer, 50 at Ajmere, Jeypore, and Ulwar; the Hissar ones being the best. The Saddles were of two kinds: Government double seated with 4 stirrups irons, 2 girths, jurchee (saddle cloth), gudghee (under pad), gudru (upper pad), khaki cloth, and straps for securing the latter, weighed 73 lbs. 8 oz.; the Native saddle, purchased from the owners, weighed lbs. 65. Every three camels were to carry five British or Native soldiers and one Native driver who looked after the camels in the lines. The soldiers attended in the lines to saddle the camels and to unsaddle and groom them on return to camp, also to water and feed them. In camp the camels were picketed to long ropes by their head collars; but on an emergency could be securely tethered by the reins being fastened round the knee. Extra camels were used to facilitate a march on the "ride and tie" system, an operation practised once with fair success. Each camel was required (with 2 soldiers up) to carry 418½ lbs. plus saddle and saddle bags and 10 lbs. of grain for the day in bags. On 24th March, a forage and water convoy of 225 camels sent to Hasheen was attacked and over 100 camels with their loads lost. On 2nd April in the advance on Tamai out of 65 horses, 171 mules, and 1,639 camels which went out only 1 mule and 1 camel, which were killed in action, and 2 mules and 2 camels, which died, did not return. The force of 1,850 horses, 1,700 mules, and 7,000 camels required 110 tons of forage per diem beside reserves. That for the horses was chiefly from England as pressed hay, compressed forage, oats, hay cake, and grain cake. Enormous quantities of camel forage were received from Egypt and India.

The distribution of the Transport animals was as follows:—

1.	Indian Transport camels 2,500.			
2.	No. 7 Coy. Transport & Commissariat Corps	32 mules	900 camels.	
3.	„ 3 „ „ „ „ „	30 mules	1,100 camels &	90 horses.
4.	„ 5 „ „ „ „ „ ...		600 „	
5.	„ 12 „ „ „ „ „ ...		600 „	
6.	Hospital Transport „ „ „	220 „	330 „	
7.	No. 17 Coy. Transport & Commissariat Corps		unspecified.	
	Total...	1,050 „	6,800 „	250 „

Appendix III.

J. H. Steel contributes to the 6th volume of the Quarterly Journal of Veterinary Science in India, p. 39 *et seq.* his experiences at a Camp of Exercise, as follows:—

4. The Camels were arranged in lines on the southern portion of the ground occupied. All were males and very many of them "must." They were often very poor in condition, which was to an extent increased by the fact that those of them which were used to Jowari refused the indifferent Rhaggi straw supplied to them as fodder. They began to take a little when the fodder was improved in quality and on finding that nothing else as fodder

was supplied to them, but it seems as though the camel does not readily adopt change of diet, and will not easily yield to the pangs of hunger compelling him to consume food which he does not care for. It seemed to me that the gram ration of camels sent on service should be somewhat largely increased, 6 lbs. per diem does not go very far with such an animal as the camel, and the affinities of internal structure of this ruminant with the horse are such as lead us *à priori* to believe that he should be treated more as a granivore than the ox (which receives an equal allowance of gram). This idea is supported by the fact that in the dung of the camel not a grain of coolthee is to be found, all the pulse given being thoroughly digested; whereas the dung of Government bullocks (fed with soaked coolthee) contains a large amount of entire grains which are capable of growth into plants subsequently. Thus much of the coolthee given to these bullocks is absolutely thrown away, from a nutritive point of view, and on service, when supplies are limited, this should certainly be given to camels in exchange for an equivalent of straw, which is most useful to the ox being freely eaten by him and thoroughly digested in the complex gastric mechanism. The camel's stomach consisting practically of only two cavities, is less equal to the task of digesting dry woody culms. In fodder supply the camel has this advantage that he can and does eat all sorts of wayside plants while on the march even the most arid plains affording him something suited for consumption, no matter how prickly provided it be succulent. Thus I am opposed to the extensive use of dry non-succulent fodder for the camel and consider that any exchange within moderation of "dry fodder" for an equivalent of gram is an advantage to this animal, probably it is exactly the reverse in the case of the bullock in which animal it seems that almost all food must be ruminated, whereas in the camel much may pass through the stomach in the ordinary course of non-ruminant digestion (as it does in the horse). Whether the substitution of a smaller amount of coolthee *boiled,* would not be an advantage to *bullocks,* is a question for experimental and financial consideration. I am inclined to believe that it would be beneficial and am of opinion that the matter requires investigation. The common method of soaking gram in the chursah for *camels*, seems to answer well and is better for service, but boiled coolthee is a valuable article of diet for a sick camel.

The common method in this Presidency of Serwans and their families living in small tents among their animals is not apparently deleterious to the camels, whether or no it is so to the men I cannot say. It does not, appreciably, secure for the animals that care and attention from the men in charge of them which it ought. These individuals are apt to think that when a little fodder is constantly kept before their camels they are well tended and are under the impression that removal of the pulan (saddle) and proper grooming are quite unnecessary. There were a number of the camels in very poor condition and much rubbed (although not actually galled) by the saddle; consequently they looked better when saddled than stripped and the Serwans objected very much to daily inspection of the animals bare-backed.

Some of the camels were much tormented with lice and other forms, of Ectozoa, and thus required the more careful attention to grooming. Again, there is certainly much difficulty in keeping the hind legs and tail of a camel clean, especially when he is "must," one of the symptoms of which condition is irritability and frequent passage of urine which is generally expelled on to the tail. The organ thus dampened is flapped about, besprinkling the hind legs with urine and seriously retarding the healing of wounds. We had several cases of long-standing ulcer under treatment. I found that when kept clean and dressed with Ol. Acidi Carbol: (1-8) these did remarkably well, whether as a result of inherent tendency to cicatrization with great rapidity, or to the fact that now, for the first time in my experience I was using jingili oil as a vehicle, I cannot say. But it was very evident to me that the enormous ulcers cicatrized much more rapidly than in wounds of the horse of the same kind. Within a few days of the commencement of this dressing, extensive irregular granulating surfaces became covered with new skin. I mention this fact because either it draws attention to the value of jingili oil in animal surgery or it disposes of the idea, hitherto held, that there is something in the constitution of the camel which causes his wounds to take an unhealthy action. I am inclined to consider that both these ideas are true, and that the liability of wounds in the camel to take an unhealthy action is due to three causes—(*a*) contact with acid urine; (*b*) or other dirt (as from filthy standings); and (*c*) from the irritable state of the constitution during prolonged ungratified sexual desire. With regard to the first and second of these causes I may state that two cases of Traumatic Lymphangitis in the camel demanded my attention. I had treated both of these during the march from Secunderabad, and the histories of the cases are as follows :—

(*a*). Male camel with lymphangitis on the left side of the prepuce; three abscesses along the course of the lymphatic opened by incision and much pus evacuated. Continued to do well until the Transport pushed ahead of the Battery, 10th January 1884. Re-admitted to treatment in Base Transport Veterinary Hospital, with a bubo forming in the corresponding groin. Fomented freely, but not fit to be opened before I was ordered to a fresh charge.

(*b*). Male camel with enormous long-standing ulcer outside of thigh. Has evidently been constantly dressed with blue vitriol and other irritants. Treated with simple chalk paste as a placebo and protective; was healing rapidly when Transport left us. Re-admitted 8th January 1884 at Base Transport Veterinary Hospital with suppurative inflammation of the lymphatics running from the upper part of the wound, the result of dirt and acrid urine. Abscesses opened, carbolic dressings. Doing well when I was ordered away.

Case (*a*) was evidently due to accumulation of foul secretions in the sheath during Must. Now I would suggest for serious consideration that male camels for the public service ought to be castrated as a matter of service routine. The following arguments are in favour of this :—

(1). Must makes the animal troublesome to work, filthy, weak, and irritable for some time in the year.

(2). It prevents male and female camels being freely intermingled and sometimes causes serious trouble and insubordination when camels of opposite sexes come near one another.

(3). It probably materially assists other influences in keeping male animals poor and weak.

(4). It certainly makes surgical cases much more serious than they otherwise would be.

(5). Judging from the effects of this process on oxen and horses, castrated animals would be decidedly more useful for army purposes than uncut males and perhaps, if the operation were performed when the animals are young, their frames would become larger and they would be adapted to more work on less food.

(6). Camels for trade purposes are often castrated, as especially in Mongolia.

(7). There is every reason to believe that, owing to the position of the testicles, the operation could be performed with facility and without danger, and by ordinary salootris.

(8). Castration of males least suited as sires, would check indiscriminate breeding.

One camel was treated for obscure lung disorder, another for punctured and cracked foot-pad, and both were doing well. As out-patients in this section of the Hospital, we had cases of each of the following disorders:—Suppurating tumour of the elbow pad (1), of the rahafay or breast pad (1), sinuous ulcer of the temporal fossa (1), abscess in the cheek (1), gall of the thorax from inturned point of the elbow (1), chronic disorder of the eye with complete disorganization (1), ragged ulcerated tumour of the foot with thicking of its fibrous tissues (several chronic cases most unsightly but kept at work). A number of head collar galls and nose rope lacerations also came under my notice.

I might have treated a number of these animals for general debility, but they were required for work and so were allowed to go on the least exacting duties. During the march from Secunderabad a number of camels suffered from diarrhœa and two, after prolonged treatment succumbed to exhaustion, and there were no facilities for *post-mortem examination.* A third died, probably from an altogether different cause, and I had an opportunity of opening his body. His diarrhœa had been much better for some days and the bowels showed no signs of disease except what could be attributed to whip-worms, trichocephali, which were present in the large intestine in very considerable numbers. I had previously been unable to determine the exact cause of the diarrhœa in the camels under observation, but here I found apparently as the cause of the disease worms which are known to produce fatal diarrhœa in some other ruminants, notably in sheep; as no other cause was apparent I think we may conclude that whip-worms in the bowels may be the cause of enzootic diarrhœa in the camel, and even produce death, and further that the treatment I adopted in the last case (internal administration of common salt, iron, and chiretta) is that most likely to prevent a fatal result. I am not yet sure whether the whip-worm of the camel is a new species or the same as is found in other ruminants. With regard to the management of camels when sick, I found that although the Serwans thoroughly understand the methods of restraint, with side line, rope, or hobbles, as also the administration of solid or liquid remedies, they are very deficient in such matter as tending wounds and nursing the sick, and are generally rather frightened of the animals.

I am firmly of opinion that these (especially) and all other Transport animals require careful veterinary supervision to keep them in a state of efficiency for service and to protect them from the ignorance and maltreatment by Serwans. I do not believe that these latter dislike their charges but they give them as little attention as they possibly can and forget that they have to do with sentient beings. Probably the fact that the South of India is not a camel country has something to do with this and with the indubitable fact that the camels at the camp were the Transport animals in least satisfactory condition for work. Although not in a position to make an absolute statement in this matter I fear that the Transport animals told off as regimental carriage during the flying march and other operations during the latter half of the time of the camp fared rather badly as concerns supervision and diet. At the very time when animals especially require care and good feeding for Transport work they are apt to run short in both respects; and through inadvertence, indifference, or some other cause to be left entirely to the management of native subordinates. Only regiments experienced in service seem to properly care for their Transport animals. I allude to this as having been forced into my notice by numbers of minor observations which individually are not worth specifying, but collectively have made on my mind a very firm impression that here we have an influence at work which on a larger scale in war would prove seriously detrimental to the health and efficiency of animals of Transport. In this camp we had to deal with animals thoroughly trained, in most cases adults and hardened to work, and under trained attendants, but on service partially trained, impressed, or hastily purchased animals, of various ages, and, frequently, not thoroughly efficient for service have to be used and it cannot be wondered at that large numbers of such animals succumb to fatigues of the campaign when removed from the direct supervision of the Transport or veterinary officer. They require selection of work in adaptation to their capacities, which, at best, can only be partially carried out in the emergencies of service. The possibilities of these latter at any time render veterinary organization of Transport during peace imperative.

Appendix IV.—NOTES AND ADDITIONS.

Note 1.—Products of the Camel and uses of his various parts. Watt informs us the amount of the wool varies inversely to the warmth of the country in which the animal is found. The wild camel has most of all and this is much valued for its softness. In May or June in India the coat is shed, it averages 2 lbs. in India but in cold countries may attain to 12 lbs. Sacks, camlet, carpets, and paint-brushes are made out of camel hair. In Montgomery the skins are worth Rs. 2—3 (Nunn) each. They are made into oil and ghi vessels called Kuppas. There is little or no export trade in them, though trunks are made out of them both in Europe and India. Smaller vessels, kuppis, are made from the intestinal walls (Watt).

The bones are in Montgomery burned in fields as a cure for disease in gourds and melons (Nunn). In the desert they serve for various purposes as to mark the route, to line wells, and for tent pegs. Hulwa is camels' milk and honey.

Lions are said to be very fond of camel flesh. Carbuccia considers it hardly distinguishable from beef. The fat has a disagreeable taste but makes good candles.

From the *Recueil de Médecine Vétérinaire, 15th June 1889,* we *prêcis* the following:—

Boisse, Veterinary Surgeon of the 22nd Dragoons, has dealt with the subject of use of flesh of the Camel and Dromedary for butchers' purposes. This habit has been prevalent or rare from time to time mainly under the influence of religion. Moses forbade consumption of camels, which practice was in high favour among the Patriarchs before his time. For economic reasons the camel was classed as unclean (Leviticus, chap. xi). The Arabs continued to eat camels after destroying them with religious ceremony, and do so to this day. The Arabs drew blood from living camels and made "black puddings" (moconad) of it; also they held the camel in high honour, for Mahomed was originally a serwan and he wrote "speak ill neither of the camel nor the wind; the camel is a benefit to men, the wind is an emanation of the spirit of God." Two young camels were slain and eaten at his marriage with Kadijah. In North Africa there is some prejudice against camel flesh but further south it is taken freely, flesh of camels which succumb to disease even is eaten if pronounced fit. Among the Touregs the slaughter of a young fat camel is the acme of hospitality. The inhabitants of Fez and the Somalis are fond of camel. The meat is not so suited to the European palate as beef and mutton but is eatable. It is of bright red colour and, as being strongly fibrous, needs prolonged cooking. The savour is aromatic like plants and the broth not thick. The fillet and the heart are the tit-bits, next the leg. The Emperor Heliogabalus was very fond of the foot long cooked until it resembled carpenter's glue. The Soudanese are very appreciative of the liver specially cooked. The hump consisting of fat and elastic tissue is not good eating, though often placed as the dish of honour, but the Arabs find fat much to their taste. The Toubons, according to Nactigal, do not cook the flesh, simply beat it into a pulp with sticks. The Touregs powder up mumified fragments of camels, mix them with blood drawn from the working camels, and eat them. When these people drink blood they allow it to coagulate, and consume only the serum, otherwise it increases thirst. The flesh is eaten fresh, salted, or dried in the sun. The latter is termed Khéléâa. Only camels slaughtered with due form are supposed to be eaten but this regulation is evaded, and often where an animal gets down from injury or disease the ears are cut off as a sort of ceremony sufficient to warrant his being eaten in the event of his dying. The horses of the Touregs are reputed to be madly fond of camel flesh. The Mongols cut up the hump and use it in tea in lieu of milk, or else consume it as butter. Mangey and galled camels are frequently sold to the Chinese for sale in Pekin as butcher's meat.

Note 2.—Different kinds of Camels, their peculiarities and designations: Sources and distribution.—The Bactrian camel is less hardy but stronger than the dromedary and will travel freely over rocks and ice. One-humped camels are used by the Kerghiz of Oust Ourt, they are large and strong but can't stand cold, so migrate into Khiva during the winter and there have bred a red-haired variety which is remarkable as being able to stand the unhealthiness of the Delta of Amou Daria which depends on stagnant of water. Although the Kathiawar people sometimes graze their camels in Mangrove swamps, it must be remembered that the Tartars are very afraid of moist localities as causing cough and other diseases. The hybrid is said to be fertile but its progeny still more unmanageable than the male camel itself.

In Arabic Baa'reer is a male camel, Nôk a female; a running camel is Hejeen or Dolool; a two-humped animal, Bakhti or Baibiron (Palgrave). The running camel of Morocco and the Algerian Sahara is termed Mehari; the pilgrimage camel of Egypt is Agim; the indigenous camel or mule camel of Anatolia is a Maia.

Carbuccia considers the gelding the strongest camel. The process of urination is *said* to sometimes last 20 minutes.

Professor Palmer is responsible for much confusion concerning the term Dromedary. It properly means a running camel or sowari, but has now come to mean all one-humped camels as contrasted with those having two humps.

In Jerruch district in Scinde camels are scarce at the sea coast but in the upper part of Delta droves of 40—50 are frequently seen.

The Delta bred animal is smaller and lighter than the Arabian. The Kamati tribe breed a valuable camel considered to equal in pace and hardihood that of Thar and Parkar (Sind Gazetteer). The Bikanir breed is famous throughout India as the swiftest and best of riding camels. Oman in Arabia is for camels what Nejed is for horses (Palgrave). Of the Bombay Presidency camels those of Ahmedabad are less prized than those of Marwar. The Thal camel which can do its forty miles per day is much used by Sindis, the largest number is obtainable at Dhanduka and Viramgam. In Kathiawar excellent camels are bred in Okha, Navanagar, and Mália; some good ones are also obtainable in Mahi Kantha.

Note 3.—Byrne's notes on the Camels employed along the Nile are valuable, condensed they are as follows:—

Aden.—Light, clean-bred, fit for riding, of uniform dun colour, short fine coats (which lessened prevalence of skin affections and facilitated its treatment when it did occur), quick stepping, hardy, said to be good at hill work, unsuited to cold climates, falling rump. Price: Sowari, Rs. 150; Baggage, Rs. 100.

Soudani.—Different breeds distinguishable by brands.

1. Bishareen, the best but small; it is white in colour and used for fast riding work in the deserts; (*a*) Mekimmeh, with slash across the cheek; (*b*) line on either side of upper lip; (*c*) round blotch on neck; (*d*) line across quarters (behind the saddle), showing it came from Assiout; (*e*) short line across fore-arm; (*f*) circular mark on right cheek (each brand represents the house from which the camel comes).
2. Anafi (from Mesalamia on the Blue Nile south of Khartoum). Slanting line on either cheek. Larger camel than Bishareen.
3. Abâdi (Ababdeh tribe). Round mark (No'ala) under ear; large.
4. Kobashi (from Kababeesh tribe), hairy and large; (*a*) line (et bey) passing under chest or stomach; (*b*) three lines on hind legs.
5. Aboroof (from neighbourhood of Shendy), ears filled with hair, neck long. T along spine and down side behind saddle.

6. Sheikriya; (*a*) line from nose to eye; (from near Mesalamieh).
7. Darhami, two lines under either ear; (from Kababeesh tribe).
8. Binne Gerrar; (*a*) line from eye to eye under jaw; (*b*) four lines on either hind leg.
9. Es Dariyat (from Siwa); (*a*) "Gaim Saif" on any part of body; (*b*) under either ear; (*c*) "Malf" on any part of body; (*d*) El Midra on any part of body.
10. Schwam (from El Arish), very hairy and powerful.

No brand in the Soudan is suitable for Artillery.

The Kababeesh in and around Bayuda desert are larger and stronger than Bishareen; unaccustomed to grain; live on desert grass and mimosa and therefore useful where corn not procurable but require time to graze. Cross Moolaid; bigger and less fine than Bishareen; has coarser hair and head.

Dongola camels from Dongola and the South have peculiar heads, and hooked noses: camels obtained north of Assouan are superior to those south of that place but this breed is big, lumpy, and soft.

Ghizeh—from near Cairo is Delta × Desert, and, accordingly, is large and very powerful and useful for Transport, much esteemed by the Arabs and high priced.

Delta—large, powerful, slow-paced; useful for burdens; need much water; unsuited for desert; delicate.

Assiout is Ghizeh × Delta—most valuable for Transport of all breeds employed in Nile Expedition.

The Mehari or Algerian Sowari camel, *i.e.* TB × ordinary female, is very good; cost £20 in 1883 and in Mitidja 300 francs.

Byrne includes among the places to which the dromedary extends Senegal, Syria, Greece, and the Canary Islands.

In a recent novel "For Faith and Freedom" there is a notice of camels working on the West Indian plantations in the reign of James II., apparently a well authenticated piece of antiquarianism.

The European range of the camel comprises Constantinople, Pisa, and Spain. They were brought thus far by the Moors. In the U. S. of America they have been found to thrive on the sandy slopes of Nevada. Humbold found camels at Teneriffe and the Spaniards took some to Peru. In A.D. 1701 camels were taken to Jamaica and various parts of America, including Venezuela, Cuba, and Bolivia. In 1841 some were taken to Santiago and in 1856 some, for use by the Militia, were conveyed to Texas. Later some were sent to California and, still later, to Brazil and various parts of the States. The camels of Cyprus are small, and the southern limit of camel range seems to be the great equatorial forest of Central Africa, they extend freely into Lybia.

In 1860 some 24 camels were taken from India to Australia. In 1880 there were 600 camels in South Australia, there are now over 2,000. They cost £55—65. They have been used and harnessed eight in a dray (Byrne).

It is a common sight in Egypt to see camels working in the plough or drawing water from wells. In Rajputana they are sometimes yoked to the plough.

Note 4.—Camel losses on Service: In Skobeleff's Campaign of 1880, out of 12,596 camels but 350 remained. As contrasted with this enormous fatality we may quote the case of General Harlan who with 2,000 camels of mixed (Bactrian and Arabian) breed traversed 360 miles of the Indian Caucasus over snow and ice for seven months and lost only one, and that one by accident.

Grodekov considers escorts incompatible with camel convoys, except the escort be one of camel riders, also that Transport should be organised in small divisions.

Byrne insists that all camels required to go beyond the base should be bought outright, as it pays owners to maim their animals and obtain compensation, there are difficulties when batches have to be broken up and the drivers strike and desert. Compensation claims for 50,000 camels are reported to have been met after the 1878-9 Campaign in Afghanistan.

Note 5.—Procurability of Camels.—Numbers and cost: Oliphant, out of 1,895 camels examined in Peiwar kotal, found 566 unfit for service and one-third unsuited as too old or too young.

In Pishin Valley in 1878 good hill camels cost Rs. 60—70.

In Afghanistan in 1879, Rs. 89.

Baggage camels in Indian plains in peace, Rs. 60—70. In 1879, Rs. 80—100.

Price in Tashkand and Turkistan £6 to 10.

In the Government of Turkistan alone are 390,000 camels.

In South Australia camels range in value from £55 for a 3 years old through £60 for an animal broken in to draught and pack to £65 for the best.

For the Crimea, Consuls purchased camels in Syria.

For Abyssinia, contractors brought camels in countries round the Red Sea; Aden camels proved the worst; Egyptian and Berbera the best.

For Afghanistan were obtained 2,000 in Persia, 6,000 in Afghanistan and from Sept. 1880 to Sept. 1881, 25,000 in India, (7,000 of them from the Bengal Presidency).

For Suakim camels were brought from Lower Egypt, Berbera, and India.

Some thousands are procurable within 400 miles of Aden for liberal prices. Mocha, Aden, Maculla, Berbera, and Zaila are good purchasing places: at Berbera £15 per camel was paid for animals to be despatched to Suakim.

Algerian camels average £6; Mesopotamian, £7-8; Soudan in 1884, over £13; Egypt 1884-5, £9—15, baggage and £25 Sowari; Dongola Jan. 1885, £23.

Colonel Furse shows that often the owners will sell a whole batch of camels, old with young, or none at all and thus he accounts for the number of young ones sent up the Nile. Purchase or retention of young animals is false economy.

Note 6.—In the Soudan in 1885, Inspecting Veterinary Surgeon Walters found Delta camels in very large proportion inferior and unsound, unsuited to the requirements of a desert campaign. Camels of Berbera and Aden were lighter in build, smaller, and more active. Those of Berbera were fawn-coloured and specially suited for the desert. The Indian camels, both pack and sowari, were considered very fine. Of 1,872 camels admitted to Hospital, 465, died, *i.e.*, about 25 per cent. About 3,500 camels came from Suez and a similar number from India to Suakim; the average price of the former was over £16: of camels admitted to the Suez Depôt for diseases other than mange and injuries, all died. The average price of cast camels was three guineas.

Note 7.—An interesting record of difficulties as regards Military Camel Management is given by V. S. Fenton in Vol. VII of the Quarterly Journal of Veterinary Science in India, page 127. He took over Veterinary charge of the Suakim Expeditionary Force in October and found the camels in very poor condition, this he attributed largely to the absence of grazing. About one-third of the animals had died in the previous three months and *post-mortem* examination showed congestion of lungs, hydatids, degeneration of the heart, and a general anæmic state of the body. The fodder given was white bhoosa, which seems not to have answered so well in Afghanistan as mixed bhoosa; issue of compressed hay was advocated and an increased ration was given. In March the fatality ceased, but from October to April three-fifths of the camels died. Could Surra have been at the bottom of all this, or was it merely the absence of proper fodder?

Note 8.—Lord and Baines give CAMEL LOADS OF THE WORLD as follows:—

In Algeria, Morocco, Tunis, and Tripoli the load is	300—400 lbs.	
In Egypt ...	350—550 ,,	for country camels.
Syria, Asia Minor, Turkey in Asia, Persia, and Tartary.	550—600 ,,	large sized bull camels called "toks," are employed, also hybrids (booghdee).
Beluchistan, Kabul, Hindustan, Thibet, Burma, and Mongolia.	300—400 ,,	(ordinary breeds).
Crim Tartary, and the borders of Southern Russia.	300—500 ,,	(Bactrians).

Sir Charles Napier places the service load at 250 lbs. and says "we have 1,500 camels, with their confounded long necks, each occupying 15 feet. Fancy these long devils in a defile, 4½ miles of them"! Byrne insists that each camel on service should be labelled to show the weight he ought to carry and that in loading restive or vicious camels the fore legs may need to be tied to prevent the animal rising during the operation. If the camel be inclined to bite, a man with a stick must hold the nose rope and inflict chastisement when necessary.

Note 9.—CAMEL GUNS are light field-pieces on four animals:—

(1) Gun. (2) Carriage. (3) Wheels, loading rods, &c. (4) Ammunition boxes.

Note 10.—Camels have been used for TRANSPORT OF THE SICK in various ways, but are so rough in motion as to be avoided when other sick transport is practicable. The following methods have (among others) been adopted:—

(*a*) By Buonaparte in Syria, specially constructed boxes; and Larrey had a panier on each side with a mattrass.

(*b*) In Abyssinia, iron Kajawahs (119 lbs.) or cacolet Kajawahs (181 lbs.) for conveyance of two sick men per camel were tried but they gave no protection from sun or rain.

(*c*) The double-seated camel saddle (133 lbs.) was useful for fatigued, sprained, and foot-sore men.

(*d*) In the Punjab Frontier Force, the Kajawahs were small litters, 4 ft. × 2 ft., with sides a foot high, slung over the camel saddle by chains or hooks.

(*e*) A strong chain with sloping back and foot-rest.

(*f*) An extremely heavy chair on the suspenson-canvas-chair principle, almost a camel load when empty.

Note 11.—TRANSPORT OF CAMELS BY RAIL AND SEA: When camels are to be *conveyed by rail* four or five as a load are taken in open wagons with high sides. They can be made to sit down, tied, and hoisted in by means of a crane. Whenever possible they should be taken out to stretch their legs. *To embark camels* let them be rested after their railway journey, then bring them one by one to the crane, make each to sit down, let one man hold the nose rope, put on a head collar with rope (otherwise the man guiding the head will hang on to the nose rope and do mischief), blindfold the animal, and, if necessary, tie his mouth or put on a muzzle, stand a man on each fore-arm and on each thigh, then slip the sling beneath the body which is easily done if the camel sits square. Haul up and place the camels around the deck looking inwards and with fore legs tied. They can stand up if there be 8½ feet between decks, and may be allowed to do so if the sea is calm. Troublesome cracks form in the bend of the knee and of the hock of camels kept squatting too long, for the sand works into these parts. The party sent by the United States Government to bring camels over hauled camels into boats by means of a special tackle and sheer force. On board they were fitted with harness and other gear and conveniences. In rough weather they were carefully tied down fore and aft (*précis* from Byrne on Transport). The camels thus dealt with were evidently few and valuable but were cared for with great judgment and success.

Note 12.—Value, relative and absolute, of camels for Transport on Service: The camel is reported to be ill adapted for military purposes and difficult to deal with (Burt), of all campaigning animals the most delicate (Jones), very nervous, so that he often comes in for abuse and brutal treatment from attendants (Smith). His saddles are difficult to fit, loads to adjust, and his gait is rolling; he is slow, difficult to mount and dismount and also to control; he requires a long time for feeding and digestion (Burt). Queriple considers that although mules would have had to be imported they would have been better for use in the Soudan than camels, for the Military operations would not have been hampered as they were. That horses or mules would not live in the Soudan was amply proved to be an error. The reasons for preferring mule to camel transport are enumerated as follows:—

(1.) "That in proportion to the amount of food required by a mule he carries as much, if not more than, the camel.

(2.) That the mule would not have been subjected to the amount of cruelty that was practised. The ordinary Englishman looked upon the camel as, if I might use the term, an unknown beast, able to withstand any ill-treatment, and, consequently, but little attention was at times paid to saddlery.

(3.) That the mule galls much less quickly than the camel, although I must own that when once galled his wounds will not heal nearly so rapidly.

(4.) That the mule will fight against adverse circumstances much better than the camel; for undoubtedly the latter is devoid of spirit."

These arguments, it will be observed, bear mainly on the expedition in question and not on the general question of mule transport or camel transport.

The camel is a very delicate animal and requires a great deal of careful treatment. Camels in the hands of the average Transport driver, and looked after by experienced officers, will do as much work with as few casualties as the same camels will do in the hands of their owners and looked after by their own men. The Brahui or Pathan camel is the one required for frontier work. The camel cannot work with a force advancing rapidly, doing fairly long marches, say 14 miles, on consecutive days. In the Zhob Valley Expedition 89 camels were lost out of 1,722 (Pringle, Report on Zhob Valley Expedition, Quarterly Journal Veterinary Science in India, Vol. IV., p. 83).

Poyser urges the camel is difficult to feed in an enemy's country, for browsing encourages thefts and attacks. If properly managed there is no better beast of burden, he considers. Rivers too deep for laden ponies and mules may be readily crossed and re-crossed by camels, they are excellent for gentle slopes but unsuited for steep and winding ascents and descents (Quarterly Journal Veterinary Science in India, Vol. I., p. 544).

Queriple urges the impolicy of mixing baggage and running camels together in a convoy for transport work. The baggage camels keep the lighter animals back and the latter cannot carry so heavy loads as the former. The baggage camel is best for general service but some trotting camels should be attached to each column for conveyance of despatches, they can traverse 6—8 miles per hour for several hours continuously. Sometimes trotting camels were used for baggage purposes, an arrangement in many respects unsatisfactory, but it is considered that there was only half enough transport and it was most difficult to feed what there was (*Official Report ; Nile Expedition*).

The MARCHES in the Nile Expedition were too long (30—40 miles per diem) and often too fast (3 miles an hour, including halts). Often the animals were loaded up long before starting and long after arrival at the end of the march (Jones). The emergencies of the campaign often rendered these errors unavoidable, but it was made very evident that 20—25 miles per diem is quite sufficient for a camel force, that in a march of 20 miles the camels must be allowed two halts of 5 minutes each for staling, that the walking pace should not exceed 2½ miles per hour, including halts. Walking too fast interferes with rumination. Proper rest is absolutely necessary, but when a force halts long in one place exercise should be given and is especially good in the early morning (Queriple). Col. Furse in his Nile Report quite admits that, were it practicable, parking in circles or leaving free in corrals would be preferable to tying up in lines where camels feel the restraint and are restless.

The want of blankets at night was much felt. The temperature at Ambigol was at times 50°F. It was urged that the blanket might be used as a jhool at night and a saddle cloth in the day-time, but when it was desired to issue blankets for the camels the Commissariat Officer replied he had not enough for the men. It is noted as an exceptional fact that the gun camels were groomed; washing twice a week was considered good but great care was needed to avoid subsequent chill.

Sir Charles Wilson objects to *night marching*. He urges that "camels suffer enormously; they start on empty stomachs, get no proper food or rest, their loads are badly put on, there is much confusion, long halts are necessary, the beasts are hurt by marching in close order over rough ground in the dark, sleep by day is not so refreshing for man or camel as it is by night.

Bennett considers that 16 miles per day of eight working hours is better than greater distances, and, since continuous marching wears out the animal, periodical days of rest should be allowed. In the trot a camel can traverse 7—8 miles per hour, and in the amble 4—4½ miles. Riding camels with despatches constantly did 50 miles at 5 miles per hour. The Arabs will not on any consideration work a fatigued or galled animal, they always halt during the heat of the day, and will not work in June and July; they march their camels in herds, which tires considerably less than marching in file. In many of their practices they cannot be imitated on a campaign. They prefer to water at mid-day and once a day.

Note 13.—The officers of the Nile Expeditionary Force much discussed this question of WATERING. Orders were issued at Korti prior to crossing the Desert to water only once in 3 days but on the day of marching to let the camels take their fill of water; however the general order was to, under ordinary circumstances, water once every 24 hours. Bennett arrived at the conclusion that it is only necessary to water every other day when on dry food and when the weather is not too hot; when on green food less often will suffice; camels can be and are trained to abstinence as regards water. The same writer notes that always after death the so-called water sacs contain food, which fact he thinks rather opposes the view of their being special water receptacles. Smith opposes the view that as camels are required to go long distances and periods without water they should be constantly practised in going without.

"He should be allowed to drink whenever opportunities occur. If the camel is made to travel long distances without water he has to suffer afterwards. He can certainly travel long periods without water, owing, in my opinion, entirely to the size of the rumen; but so can cattle, as was seen when the contractor of meat drove some bullocks from Korti to Gakdal wells, and beyond, without water. * * I believe that, but for the difference in the arrangement of the foot, the bullock would travel as long as the camel. * * * Great patience should be exercised in watering camels; they will often not drink before the sun rises or after sunset and many require a long time allowed them, being very shy."

Stuart Wortley gives the following *watering rules* from the experience gained in the Nile Expedition :—

(*a.*) Before a long march do not water for three days, and then allow camels to drink as much as they like before starting.

(*b.*) At conclusion of a long march (say 4 days, without water) only give a slight amount of water, then set camels free, and

(*c.*) At end of two hours allow the animals to drink *ad lib.*

Unloose the girths if watering while saddled.

Adopt the following routine Camel management: 7 A.M. half grain, 7-30—8-30 A.M. grooming, 9 A.M.—5 P.M. grazing, 5 P.M.—6 P.M. grooming, 6 P.M. ½ grain, about 4 P.M. water.—(BYRNE.)

Skinner gives an instance where the camels had been nineteen complete days without drinking: Nott puts the amount a camel drinks at one time at 30—40 pints. The Arabs say that in summer and autumn, the camel naturally drinks every third day, in winter only when the weather is warm, then every 8 to 10 days.

Note 14.—Mr. Burt enumerates and comments on SADDLES as follows:—Of the riding saddles the *Egyptian* (weight 42 lbs.) is the best, as being least liable to get out of order and easiest repaired. The *Mounted Infantry* is a modification of it but not a success, being less comfortable and less easy to sit in, also its iron seat makes it heavier (65 lbs.). It did not fit the camel and the shoulder of the hind tree frequently gave way where the cross grain of the wood begins. The wooden cross pieces sometimes broke but were easily replaced. Bennett considered the riding saddles, though prepared by contract and in a hurry, mainly answered the purpose required. Of Pack Saddles, the *Cairo* ones were best, but those used were badly constructed and stuffed and made of bad material. Tibben and straw were used for padding. The *Sohag* saddle from the South of Siout is heavy and has little to recommend it. The *Dongola* is too small and suited only to small camels (such as the Bishareen) and light loads. It is very light but was often indifferently padded and caused many galls. Bennett preferred the *Esneh* saddle; he considers the following to be the defects of the service pattern saddle:—The tree is too weak, the saddles issued were all of one size and therefore unsuited to the smaller camels and difficult and laborious to alter (Col. Furse informs us that though the trees were all of one size the pads were not). The stuffing of coarse straw soon wore out as also did the non-durable lining. The lumbar transverse processes were subjected to pressure, the humps overcrushed and bruised both by the load and the make of the saddle and the unyielding portion of the trees. The hide lashings often gave way letting the key binding the two halves of the tree come down on the withers and cause galls.

He suggests:—that for hide lashings be substituted tarred rope (and in some cases this was adopted), to make the tree stronger and more stable, pads to be of two or three different sizes, the hind ones being lined with leather to protect the loins, the two rear pads to be made into one by joining them at the top in order to throw its due share of weight on the spine behind the hump. Breast-plates of rope or other soft material to be always issued with the saddles.

It was supposed that the saddle-tree being capable of yielding under pressure enables it to adapt itself to the shape of the back but Queriple's experience is that it should be solid at least in part, for under the present arrangement galls of the withers are constantly occurring. He thinks this is to an extent due to the natives always tying the breast-straps too tight and is of opinion the breast-strap may be discarded with advantage. Mr. Burt insists on the necessity of protection for the lumbar transverse processes. Smith says "the saddle for the camel should, in my opinion, be very differently constructed; more attention should be paid to the natural conformation of the animal. The lumbar region was not 'fitted' at all, the transverse processes of the vertebræ in an enormous number of animals becoming diseased or broken, and very large galls existing there, rendering the animals either useless, or resulting in septicæmia or pyæmia, and death." When the light division of the camel corps had to perform transport duty the parts about the hips and the sacral region became much damaged by the saddles being too large. "The arch of the ribs was also a great seat for saddle galls, some being frightfully severe. Abscesses were constantly forming, and owing to them not being operated on often became vast open wounds, the skin being completely destroyed; on removal of the saddle patches of the skin would be found adhering to the lining pads. The work of the campaign being so heavy all camels had to be used, though many were unfit to work owing to severe wounds and their general bad condition; the result being that many of them that died were found to have suffered from blood poisoning with the accompanying fever, they marched on till they dropped and died." At Assouan the Aden drivers preferred the *Aden pad.* It is four feet long, and thus longer than the Transport pack saddle; so also is the Egyptian army pack saddle which extends right down to the rump (Furse).

The Algerian French Saddle (pack) consists of two wooden forks 9 in. apart and 14 in. high, fastened together by two bands and a hame-shaped woollen bag, stuffed with esparto grass, encircling the hump. In front of the hump the tree is securely fastened to the padding. Two ropes pass under the animal (as far forward and aft as possible) to act as girths, the former of esparto, the latter of some softer substance, wool or camel hair because it goes under the sheath. Weight 25 lbs. (Byrne). Each camel should have its own saddle, and camels should be purchased with their saddles (Byrne). The pad should, when on the ground, open well like a horse collar, so as to thoroughly clear the hump, there being a clear opening of 9 to 15 inches in the centre. Rice straw is the best and cheapest stuffing, but bhoosa is generally used. Numnas were found dirty and troublesome.

On the Nile Expedition errors in loading and impractical character of loads proved fruitful sources of galls. The regulation method of adjusting the loads is by lashing the ropes round the end of the side pieces, which causes undue weight to be thrown on the trees and not enough on the centre of the back. The native practice is to suspend the loads from the middle of extra raised bars placed at the centre for that purpose. The Cairo saddle with nets and lashing is stated to have weighed about 100 lbs., and often the *net,* not gross, weight of stores was estimated in loading, this makes an immense difference in the weight to be carried by camels, and weight in itself suffices to arrest circulation in the skin and so cause sore back. The load should not exceed 300 lbs., exclusive of saddles, where long and continuous marching has to be gone through, gross weight should be considered in all issue of loads, whereas the Commissariat Department naturally are apt to consider only net weight. The estimate of weight by soldiers is sometimes so vague as to lead to 600 pounds being piled on the camel rather than 400 lbs. The biscuit and other boxes sent out from England proved too large and too weighty, they were difficult to load and liable to shift and so galled the animal (Bennett). Col. Furse agrees that these rectangular cases were a great source of galls and that sacks would be better than cases, as they can be better adjusted and prevented from swaying, which form of movement especially is liable to gall. Six biscuit boxes (57 lbs. × 6 = 342 lbs.), three on each side, constituted the load for one camel, but this forms a "deep" load, the bearing of which is not perpendicularly downwards but inwards, compressing the animal's ribs and sides. To reduce the depth only five boxes (= 285 lbs.) had to be assigned to each load, two on each side and one on the top.

Note 15.—Queriple in the Nile Expedition Reports gives some very useful experiences of Camel Management on Service, especially as regards *swimming*. The Nile was crossed by the River Column twice. "The first time on 20th and 21st February when about 800 animals were crossed in 24 hours, only two animals were lost; being on the bank opposite to the Veterinary Surgeon there was no chance of his resuscitating them, eight subsequently arrived in a very exhausted and semi-suffocated state but were given restoratives, revived, and suffered no ill effects. Mr. Queriple reported that (1) The Veterinary Surgeon should always cross before the animals and be ready to assist any animal exhausted on arrival. (2) The head and collar rope should not be used at all as any strain on it is liable to entirely close the mouth and to impede the animal's breathing by drawing the noseband over the nostrils. (3) A plain rope should be formed into a *fixed* noose round the neck. This rope should not be passed round the nose as was done in some cases. (4) Boat's crew to row slowly or the animal's head will be dragged under water. (5) Especially the heaviest camels should be supported by an inflated skin each placed on the neck and fastened to the shoulders. (6) The crossing should not be commenced when practicable before the sun is well up, and should be discontinued at such time as will ensure the animals being perfectly dry before sunset. (7) A certain number of men should be sent over by the boat taking over the first camel of the Corps. They should move saddles and loads well away from the shore lest a block occur and impede the landing. Immediately the camels come out of the water they should be walked about until perfectly dry. (8) The crossing of the animals to be left to Officers Commanding Corps and they to be responsible for proper fixing of ropes.

Six camels suffered from 'staggers' the result of crossing when the water was too cold and being tied up in the pickets to dry. Of them three had to be turned loose and deserted. Febrile catarrh (6 cases) and rheumatism (1 case) also resulted from the crossing. All the casualties occurred among camels with British Troops. The second crossing was less successful, for the instructions were not adhered to. The camels were crossed with a half hitch round the nostrils and in a very short time ten were landed dead and many others dying. Orders to cease the half hitch were signalled over the river and no more casualties occurred that day. On the second day half a gale of wind was blowing and three were drowned. Forty-seven animals reported by the boatmen 'dead' were revived by means of restoratives."

Note 16.—The AVERAGE RATION on the Nile was 10 lbs. of grain, either beans or dhourra, the latter being preferred, as beans, especially when given alone, cause diarrhœa. The fodder ration was 10 lbs. of Tibben, *i.e.*, bhoosa, bruised and broken straw from which the grain has been trodden out. Green dhourra stalk (cholum, jowari) was much liked, as also was Lupine stalk, which was purchased when possible; of dry dhourra stalk only the thin outer investment was taken (Burt). Queriple prefers as ration's 8 lbs. grain and 15 lbs. dry fodder. Feeding on grain alone the same officer found to be a cause of indigestion and diarrhœa; barley does not agree with the constitution of the camel, and the grain should always be crushed and split. Bennett draws attention to the necessity for a portable composition feeding cake for camels, but points out that the animals would require to be educated to its use. The grazing in the Soudan was good and no cases of poisoning took place (Bennett). It consisted of a tuft grass and desert shrubs, such as mimosa, and a herb like bastard cypress. Green date leaves were also eaten. Government animals often refused to graze (Burt), and it was quite impossible to allow the animals to constantly pick mouthfuls as they marched along, as native travellers permit their camels to do. Some invalids were turned out entirely for grazing but in camp it was found essential to always picket the camels in lines, especially in large camps or in the proximity of standing crops.

Note 17.—Samples of rations on Service: Nile Expedition 1884: varied. 11 lbs. barley or sorghum daily, and 10 lbs. tibben or bhoosa, if no grazing procurable.

Afghanistan, Khyber Line: 10 seers bhoosa, kurbi, or grass.

March, 3	Seers barley.
Fatigue, 2	
Cantonment, 1½	
At graze, 1	

Bolan Line:

	Grain or jowarie.	Kurbi, bhoosa, or wheat straw.
With grazing	4 lbs.	8 lbs.
Without ,,	4 lbs.	20 lbs.

Abyssinia, on first landing. Grain 5 lbs., hay 12 lbs.

In the Abyssinian Campaign, 4 lbs. grain, 30 lbs. dry fodder, and 8 gallons of water per diem was given.

In Egypt fresh beans and chopped straw were given; but beans were found too heating for the desert, so barley and cotton seed were substituted, jowari is the best grain (Dawney).

Yaldwin quotes the following Indian rations:—

(*a*). 20—25 seers missa bhoosa daily, no gram.

(*b*). 6 seers missa bhoosa + 6 seers white or straw bhoosa + 2 seers crushed and soaked gram or mote.

(*c*). 8 to 10 seers white or straw bhoosa + 3 seers crushed and soaked gram or mote.

(Barley is a poor substitute for mote, 1 lb. ata with ghi is worth twice the quantity of gram.)

Note 18.—Major H. F. Smyth, R.A., gives the following, on *camel grazing in vicinity of Suakim, Handub, and Otao—in April.*

(*Somali.*)	(*Arabic.*)
1. Ghulam.	Saa-mur.
2. Aus.	Shoosh.
3. Habow.	Haali laago.
4. Marokh.	Aagwaid.
5. Palumba.	Hanobokh. (A description of each of these plants is given by Byrne.)
6. Suda-ho.	Eh-labh.
7. Kora.	Naawaith (Babul).
8. Haarighaarig.	Baanaibh.
9. Jubbi ogi.	Toondhoop.
10. Amaneh.	Sainonth.
11. Gadh.	Ka-toot, refused by camels, of no value as food.

Note 19.—Watt enumerates some fifty *plants eaten by camels*, as follows:—

Acacia Arabica (Babul), A. Farnesiana, Ægiceras majus (Halsi), Albizzia Lebbek (Siris), Alhagi maurorum (camel thorn or Súhtar Khàr), which is collected in Pishin valley in October and November, beaten up into bhusa, and stored; Amarantus polygamus et tenuifolius, Anthrocnemum indicum (Machúr), Atriplex Stocksii, Avicennia officinalis (white mangrove), Bauhinia racemosa, Berberis (several species), Calligonum polygonoides, Carduus nutans, Carchorus antichorus, Cressa cretica, Crotalaria Burhia (Sìs), Dalbergia Sissoo, Dodonæa viscosa (aliár) said to have not suited camels at Thul, Eclipta alba, Haloxylon multiflorum, and Hal. recurvum (the salt plant most relished by the camel in India, from it Khár-sajji is chiefly made), Halocharis violaceæ, Indigofera paucifolia, Kochia indica, Lippia nodiflora, Leptadenia Spartium, Lycium europæum, Melia azadirachta (Nim), Mimosa rubicaulis, Mollugo hirta, Phœnix dactylifera (Date palm) the ground hard kernels of the fruit and the leaves are given to camels, Pistacia integerrima and P. Mutica, Prosopis spicigeria, Psoralea plicata, Quercus Ilex (the Holly oak), Rubia tinctorum (Madder), Salicornia brachiata, Salsola fœtida et kali,

Salvadora oleoides et persica, Suæda fruticosa et maritima et nudiflora, Tamarix gallica, Trianthema crystallina, et monogyna, et pentandra, Vitis carnosa, Zizyphus nummularia (Jhari) the staple camel fodder in Rajputana, Zygophillum simplex. In Australia it has been found that camels are very fond of Sterculia or native poplar (Brachychiton Gregorii) also of Swainsonias and Psoraleas. They do not care for oily scented Myrtaceæ such as Eucalyptus, Melaleuca, &c.

Byrne tells us six hours grazing a day on good ground is sufficient and if on Sallum or Minosa bush is better than any amount of tibbin or bhoosa. The Sahara Arabs avoid grazing when dew is on the ground or feeding on dew damp grass. Thus they do not turn out their camels to graze till midday from the middle of April to the middle of June. In case of a two days' halt on the first day the camel men should bring in fodder and this be used for the camels so that they can be given a thorough rest on the second day. The Kirghiz graze their camels only by day. Care must be taken that each camel gets his fair share of grain; weak or slow feeders must be fed separately.

Salt is very necessary, otherwise depraved appetite is frequent. Pallas (Mém du Museum, t. xvi., page 449,) states that the Calmuck camels in winter get as food only reeds and the bark of trees. He remarks that they thrive on the steppes in proportion to the amount of salt they obtain.

Note 20.—Tar dressing is applied to the skin in the Sahara annually in spring to prevent mange. The camels are made to sit down, a twitch put on the lower lip, the wool removed, and the animal smeared from head to foot; then, as a purge, is given 1 lb. of rancid butter boiled and mixed with three or four eggs and grease of sheeps' wool. The animal is not used for ten days after this. The process is repeated every three months, but the first application is the most thorough.

Note 21.—The Central Asian nomads in very cold weather sew a thick cloth round the animal's body. In their Central Asian campaigns, the Russians have felt the want of proper bedding, for which purpose straw, reeds, and skins were found useful.

Note 22.—The average weight is put at 10 cwt.; height to top of hump 7 feet, length 8—10 feet—(Byrne). Lombardini gives some *dimensions of camels as follows* :—

Two Bactrians stuffed, in St. Petersburg Government Museum, the measures being given in millimetres.

Height from top of front hump to ground...	1,420 & 1,880 *m. m.*
Length from nape of neck to base of coccyx measured on one side of animal...	1,920 & 2,500 ,,

Of living Bactrian 7 or 8 years old.

Length of body from point of shoulder to buttock ...	2,050 *m. m.*
Hind hump to ground ...	2,200
Length of head from occiput to muzzle ...	652
Width of forehead at orbits ...	282
Height of front hump ...	330
Do. hind do. ...	410

Male Dromedary from Constantine, 5 *years old.*

Hump to ground ...	2,050 *m. m.*
Greatest length of trunk ...	1,503
Height of hump ...	340
Middle length ...	580
Length of head ...	580
Breadth of forehead ...	342

St. Rossore female, 8 *years old.*

Hump to ground ...	1,740 *m. m.*
Neck to tail ...	2,200
Breast to hump ...	1,400
Length of head ...	440
Width of forehead ...	269

Note 23.—Examination as to fitness for service : Byrne gives the following, from observations made in Egypt :—

1. Note the brand. Fawn colour better than white. Species should suit country of operations.

2. Shape. No elbow brushing and elbow well set out and its horny prominences of medium size. Hind legs not too angular, rather straight.

3. Hump. Index to general health, age, condition; should be firm, inclined to rear rather than to front and not too large, in Sowari generally small, in baggage camels large and covered with coarse hair, also look for injuries, scars, &c.

4. Hind quarters. Broad and firm and good muscle; abdomen well rounded.

5. Girth. Deep; back and loins muscular and free from sores or scars; chest wide; rahafay large; round chest gives an unpleasant rolling gait; wide chest in Sowari lessens speed.

6. Joints (especially hock) free from puffiness. Limbs strong and well attached to trunk. Flexors fine and clean.

7. Teeth, sound molars. Eyes free from blindness, large neck; head, wide and well set on; lips closed.

8. Foot. Pad well developed, hard, sound, and free from fissures; toe nails normal.

9. Branding on the head shows animal has been treated for Kapaulee or other such disorder.

10. Paces. Should walk and trot well and not cross hind legs. In walking should show suppleness of neck and wavy motion of head.

11. Should kneel level, and get up under a 400 lbs. load easily.

12. Well nourished healthy camel has head erect, eyes clear, ears pricked, hump vertical or only slightly inclined.

13. Determine the age by teeth. At about 15 years hair on tail becomes white and from this time streaks appear in the eye. At about 20 years hollow above eyes very deep and camel has lost some of his teeth.

In the Soudan the principal causes of rejection are enumerated, by Byrne, as: bent hocks (as not being up to weight), bent knees (weak as having been overworked when young), elbow brushing, mange; skin thickening between fore legs or on outside of hind legs, as a result of disease, groin swelling, skin under belly coming down too low so as to be liable to be cut by the ground, hump too leaning or too small, wide splay action of fore legs the result of slipping up and muscle laceration indicating weakness, lifting legs very high, head fired. Loose swollen lump near external part of near fore leg or shoulder, excessive size of stifle callosity, trembling in rising or kneeling, small fore feet, thin and poor condition, ulceration under tail, elephantiasis of legs, broken jaw, sinew of hind leg movable to one side when felt by hand while camel is resting.

"SNIPE" in a valuable article (Quarterly Journal Veterinary Science in India, October, 1889) deals with this interesting subject. Among other original suggestions he tells us to:—

I. Have camel walked past and back again, then, trotted past and back again, note any lameness, dragging of hind limbs, rolling gait, friction of elbows against side called by the natives (bhagul lugé).

II. Halt the animal and walk round him examining pads, tendons, &c., and taking care not to get kicked with the hind legs or struck backwards with the fore.

III. Make him sit down. Age him, examine nostrils, eyes, head for swellings and scars; humps, various seats of saddle gall (and pluck at the hair over all such places for the dealers plug up fistulæ with mud and then gum hair over all traces of the gall). Look carefully at foot pads and nails, tail, points of hocks, and insides of thighs. Examine skin carefully for mange, and do not mistake simple eczema for it.

IV. Load with pack, or two men; cause to rise and note if he has any difficulty in doing so. Move him sharply forwards for a short distance to detect any crouching when caused to do so from weakness of loins or hind limbs.

V. If a female see that she is not pregnant.

A baggage camel should be short in the leg, deep in the girth, round in the barrel, with elbows well out from the sides; muscles of the shoulders, quarters, and thighs well developed; hump large and round. A riding camel is longer in the leg and lighter in the bone, deep in girth, and run up to the flank like a greyhound; with small head and ears, eye bright and intelligent, and all other marks of breeding. His paces should be fast and smooth and he should pick up his feet well, as a stumbling camel is dangerous.

The Kirghiz date the age of camels from the time of coupling, therefore one year must be deducted from the age as given by the owner. The camel is full grown at 7 years of age; fit for regular, but not hard, work at 6; at his prime at 9 years; and will work up to 25 years of age.

The Kirghiz rest their females three months before and three months after parturition. They breed in February and wean the young after 12 to 18 months. The male is must in December and January, so couplings usually occur in the winter.

Note 24.—Being off feed shows sick camel should be led apart on march and given oats 4 lbs. per diem for eight days by which time he will have either recovered or be dead (Byrne).

When a camel gets thoroughly low in condition he takes six months to recover.

Among means of restraint may be mentioned at twitch put on the lower lip.

Note 25.—In page 46, 9th line from bottom of page read Dhal for Tel. Rest, plenty of water, and laxative diet are said to be essential in treatment of Heat struck.

Poyser, (Q. J. V. Sc. in I., vol. I., p. 379) investigated an outbreak of what seems to have been Surra near Kalka on the Simla road. There was sudden unaccountable death of emaciated animals, *autopsy* showed 1—2 qts. of citron coloured fluid in the belly, jelly-like material in the gastro-hepatic fold, pelvis of kidney full of jelly, about one pint serum in chest and some also in pericardium, clots in heart and large vessels, muddy maroon colour of blood, jelly round base of heart, echinococcic cysts in lungs, jelly between the membranes of brain and spinal cord, brain congested. *Symptoms* in the animals reported sick were dulness, eyes watery, drooping eyelids, and slight trembling, not off feed nor cud, tolerably lively. Turpentine, chiretta, salt, change of grazing ground and carbolic acid in ʒij doses in 2—3 quarts of gruel or water for three or four days in succession were recommended.

Note 26.—Hallen reported on DANAKIL EQUINE TYPHUS FEVER

or **African Glanders** as fatal to many animals, including the camel (horses and cattle) in Abyssinia in 1867. It was contagious, typhous in type, and prevailed at all seasons on the east coast of Africa being most malignant after the rains in February, June, and July. It was probably Anthrax. *Symptoms:* trembling, panting, stupor; swelling of mouth, eyes, throat, jaws, and glands. Congestion of mucous membranes, petechiæ on gums, tongue enlarged, mouth dry, breath offensive; pulse feeble and weak, cough, choking. Thick, sometimes bloody, nasal discharge, later frothy; urine scanty and high coloured. *Treatment:* Diffusible stimulants, extensive irritants to chest walls over lungs or heart. When fever subsides, quinine ʒj—ij in ether or brandy morning and evening. Enemata if necessary, warm clothing, bandaging, green food, gruel or boiled grain, salt in food and drink, and the best practicable hygienic measures.

Note 27.—In the Soudan Expedition (1887) many hundreds of the camels were affected by catarrhal fever of an enzootic character in April. It was not very fatal. *Symptoms:* off feed, cough, fever, nasal discharge, and general unhealthy appearance. *Treatment* comprised isolation, stimulants, steaming nostrils, clothing at night, and general good nursing.

Note 28.—Rheumatism is caused by getting chilled after being heated; thus the camel often becomes incapable of movement. Frost causes much loss of camels in Central Asia mainly from this affection. *Treatment:* give stimulants and apply stimulating liniments and warm clothing to loins. Byrne recommends nitre ℥j morning and evening in a pint of water or in moistened flour or ground grain, warmth, and dietetic measures.

Note 29.—Parasites—Inspecting Veterinary Surgeon Evans, (Proceedings, Asiatic Society of Bengal, March, 1882), supplied to Lewis mature Filariæ which he obtained from the blood vessels of the lungs and mesentery, where he found them in tangled masses. These were determined to be a new species and termed Filaria Evansi. The male was 3—4½″ long by $\frac{1}{80}$—$\frac{1}{45}$″ wide at widest part; $\frac{1}{250}$″ at oral end, $\frac{1}{90}$″ at about ⅓″ lower down. Tail tapers to a blunt point and is curled into two or three coils. Two spicules; longer $\frac{1}{25}$″, shorter $\frac{1}{150}$″. Cloaca $\frac{1}{222}$″ from candal end.

Bursa small with four pairs of preanal and two of postanal papillæ; a fifth postanal papilla near tip of tail. Mouth devoid of well marked lips, œsophagus $\frac{1}{4}''$ long by $\frac{1}{200}''$ wide. Cæcal commencement of sperm tube lies near junction of œsophagus and intestine; sperm tube $\frac{1}{400}''$ in diameter. Intestine $\frac{1}{170}''$ in diameter near middle of body. Female generally double the size of a male, 6—8″ long; $\frac{1}{50}$—$\frac{1}{32}''$ across in widest part, $\frac{1}{225}''$ at mouth, which is simple and somewhat pointed. Tail bent, terminates in clubbed or funnel-shaped enlargement, width at end $\frac{1}{186}''$, but a little higher is $\frac{1}{200}''$. Œsophagus 3″ long by $\frac{1}{180}''$ wide. Intestine $\frac{1}{170}''$ diameter, anus $\frac{1}{100}''$ from caudal end, genital orifice $\frac{1}{40}''$ from mouth; here and for $\frac{1}{4}''$ is $\frac{1}{280}''$ in diameter then widens to $\frac{1}{100}''$ and sub-divided into two utero-ovarian tubes each $\frac{1}{180}''$ in width and generally packed with embryos averaging $\frac{1}{125}''$ long by $\frac{1}{4500}''$ wide; lower down ova and embryos are mixed together.

Note 30.—Colin found Pentastoma tænioides in the mesentery of a dromedary. Cobbold mentions as found in the camel, Fasciola hepatica, Echinococcus veterinorum, Cysticercus tenuicollis, Cœnurus cerebralis, and Trichocephalus affinis. Sarcoptes Cameli he terms a variety of Sarcoptes Scabiei. The throat Bot is Cephenomyia maculata. Galeodes, he tells us, is a Salpugidan and will bite severely any one who attempts to dislodge it from the bearer.

Note 31.—POISONING—A Hill camel avoids poisonous plants carefully, but a plain camel often falls a victim to poisoning.

A kind of Iris or lily of Quetta, Peshin, and Kardanai Valleys proves fatal. In poisoning by it give in one dose when milk-warm gur and red pepper of each half a pound boiled together in a seer of water.

In Transcaspian Steppes, "Kindertchouk" kills in an hour.

Watt enumerates as poisonous, or at least not wholesome to camels, Acorus calamus (bachh), Calotropis gigantea et procera, Cannabis sativa, Euphorbium neriifolia et Royleana et Tirucalli, Nerium odorum, Othonnopsis intermedia, Peganum Harmala, and Withania coagulans.

Note 32.—*Translated by Formad for the Journal of Comparative Medicine and Surgery, April* 1889. Vedernikoff, Veterinarian to the Kirghese herds in the Government of Astrakan reports (in the Archives of Veterinary Science) on the form of epizootic diarrhœa known to Kirghiz camel owners as TSCHAK. This is found in the valleys of the Caspian sea-board especially in parts of Astrakan and is supposed to have developed only within the last twenty years. In this time the character of the sea-board land has changed from flats into quick-sands. Before 1870 only isolated cases occurred and those after heavy rains followed by prolonged dryness when the stagnant rain water collected into pools which if used for watering the animals caused disease especially of the feeble and the young. Rank grass growing after subsidence of the sea water driven up by the South East winds in autumn also produces the disease. In 1881-82 the epizootic and enzootic character of the affection was first noted. In 1885 the disease raged violently sparing neither old nor young, strong nor feeble. Sometimes the suckling young became affected while the mother remained sound. In some instances whole herds were swept off, in others deaths averaged 5—70 °/ₒ. The number affected and the recoveries varied in the case of different owners. The several local outbreaks varied in fatality percentage. Vedernikoff considers the disorder a severe gastro-intestinal catarrh caused by eating food or drinking water strongly impregnated with such sea salts as chlorine, sulphur, iodine, and bromine compounds. Of these agents the chlorides (with which Caspian water is highly impregnated) irritate the alimentary mucous membrane, by absorbing liquids they increase peristalsis and secretion of mucus and water, entering the blood the sodium salt promotes formation of blood corpuscles but the potash salt lessens this production, nitrogenous interchanges are prevented by salt and digestion interfered with. The coagulability of the blood is lessened and the blood pressure increased, whereby the pulse is slowed, the heart's beat rendered irregular, the respiration less frequent, and the body temperature lowered. Weakness, diminished sensibility, and sluggish motions show the nervous system is involved. The pancreas and kidneys are hyper-stimulated. The sulphur compounds act like the chlorides but less markedly. The bromides produce more severe irritation of the alimentary mucous membrane and excite the heart and vessels, producing fall of pulse and temperature. They act like chlorides on the nervous system and glands. Iodides act as more powerful irritants, causing congestion of the gastric and intestinal mucous membrane and vascular dilatation in the stomach. Their effects on the respiration are either stimulant or the reverse. They cause increased temperature and act on the nervous system and glands like the bromides.

Symptoms: No prodromata: Three stages; 1st, mild, lasts twenty days; bowels slightly loose, dung infriable, moist, green balls of characteristic odour, faint at first. No loss of appetite or cud, a slight thirst, slight redness of conjunctiva and discharge from eyes; respirations increased to 20 per minute, pulse 40—50, temperature 38°C. 2nd stage lasts about nine days. The above symptoms become more intense. Excrements semi-liquid, greyish-green or light brown in colour; eye discharge profuse and purulent, white in colour; conjunctiva bright red, respirations 25 per minute, pulse 70 irregular, temperature 40°C., off feed and cud almost entirely; thirst more intense, patient dull, frequently lies down, turns head backward, grunts at the same time, rises with great difficulty, is sluggish in his movements and low in general conditions. 3rd stage lasts only five days; even more intense, fæces quite liquid, dark, mixed with blood and of offensive odour. Rectal mucous membrane dark red and protrudes. Eye discharge thicker, milk white, glues the eyelids together. Conjunctiva florid. Respirations 20 per minute, pulse 40; temperature 37°C. Mouth filled with foaming saliva. Off feed and cud, and no desire for water. Animal very weak, drowsy, and grunts constantly. Weak and young animals become comatose on third or fourth day. Recovery when it takes place does so between the first and second stages, it is gradual, convalescence extending over two or three months. The state of the dung is a guide in prognosis. In favourable cases the liquidity ceases, partially formed brittle balls are formed, these fuse together and are covered with an opaque layer, often with blood. Next the balls become the normal greyish green. The grunt may persist for a long time and the hump is a very considerable time before it returns. *Autopsy* shows, in addition to the external appearances above indicated: in the abdomen an absence of omental fat, marked vascular engorgement, gastric mucous membrane congested; walls of 3rd and 4th stomachs and of rectum thickened markedly, those of other parts of intestine also slightly thick. Intestinal contents of most offensive odour. Liver capsule light in colour, marble coloration of the liver substance. Gall bladder distended with dark-green thick bile. Spleen enlarged 1½ times, filled with blood, soft, and splenic pulp can be scraped easily; capsule dark violet. Pancreas enlarged, rose-red; kidneys with adherent capsules, cortex dark, medulla lighter but whole organ congested. Ureters partly thickened. Bladder much distended with light yellow urine, yielding on standing a whitish flakey precipitate. Tendon of diaphragm much congested, as also is pleura and, still more, the pericardium. Muscular portion of the diaphragm pale. Blood, in all heart cavities, liquid, and with clots floating in it. Lungs and bronchial passages congested. General congestions of all the large blood vessels. No changes of central nervous organs detected. (This record reads very like Rinderpest, but the views of the Veterinarian who records it may be correct.)

Note 33.—Lady Annie Blunt writes:—"The best way to manage camels is to keep them going at a steady pace all the morning, for they do not care to eat during the forenoon, and then, when the sun begins to decline, to let them feed as they go." This reduces their pace to 2½ m. per hour. 2 hours before sunset at least, allow them to stop and turn them loose to get all they can before dark; if there is a moon they will go on grazing half the night, otherwise they will sit quietly chewing the cud. They require no water during the winter, nor so long as they get grass during the spring; if fed on beans as in Egypt they must drink at least every 4 days in warm weather.

A camel forced to swim is very ridiculous; he hates water and roars and moans if forced to face it. Unload one by one, put one man on his back, and let six others push him down the bank, a steep slide from which he goes souse into the water, have men after them shouting and splashing water in their faces, till at last they were out of their depth, then they resign themselves

I. OLD
Side view.

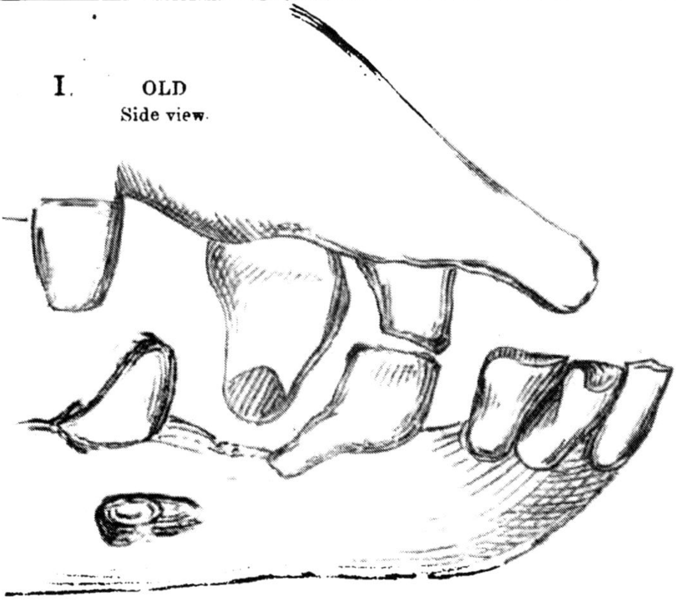

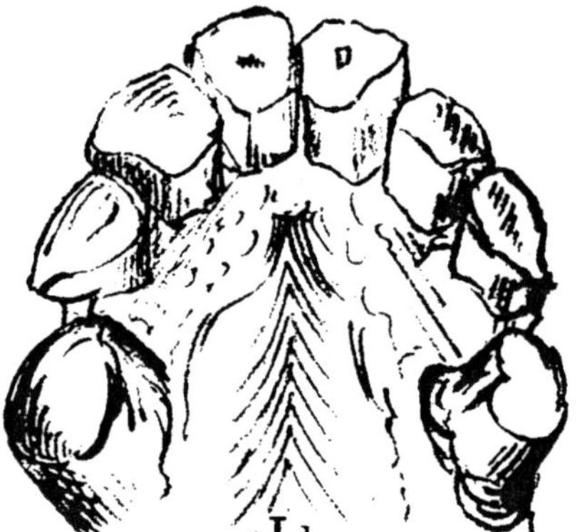

I, I.
Lower incisor from above.

I, II.
Upper jaw from below.

Pl: VIII.

ALEX: BARREN: LITHOG: MADRAS.

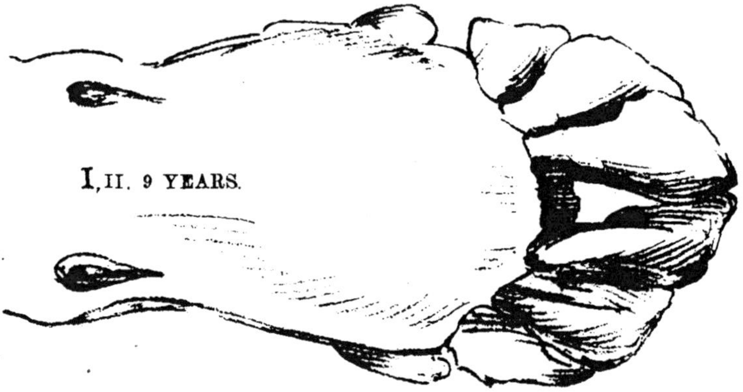

I, II. 9 YEARS.

I, III. 9 YEARS.

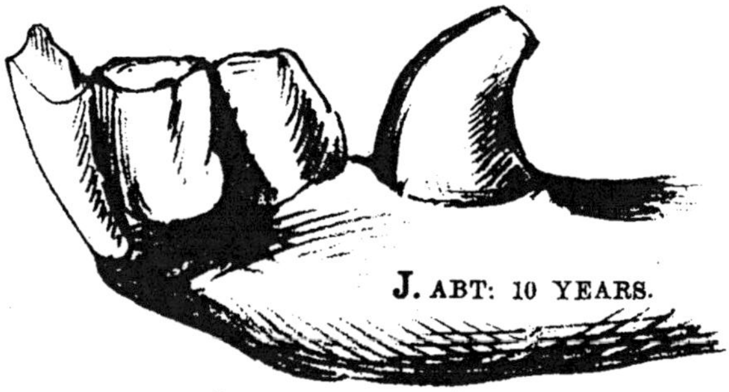

J. ABT: 10 YEARS.

Pl: VII.

ALEX: BARREN; LITHOG: MADRAS.

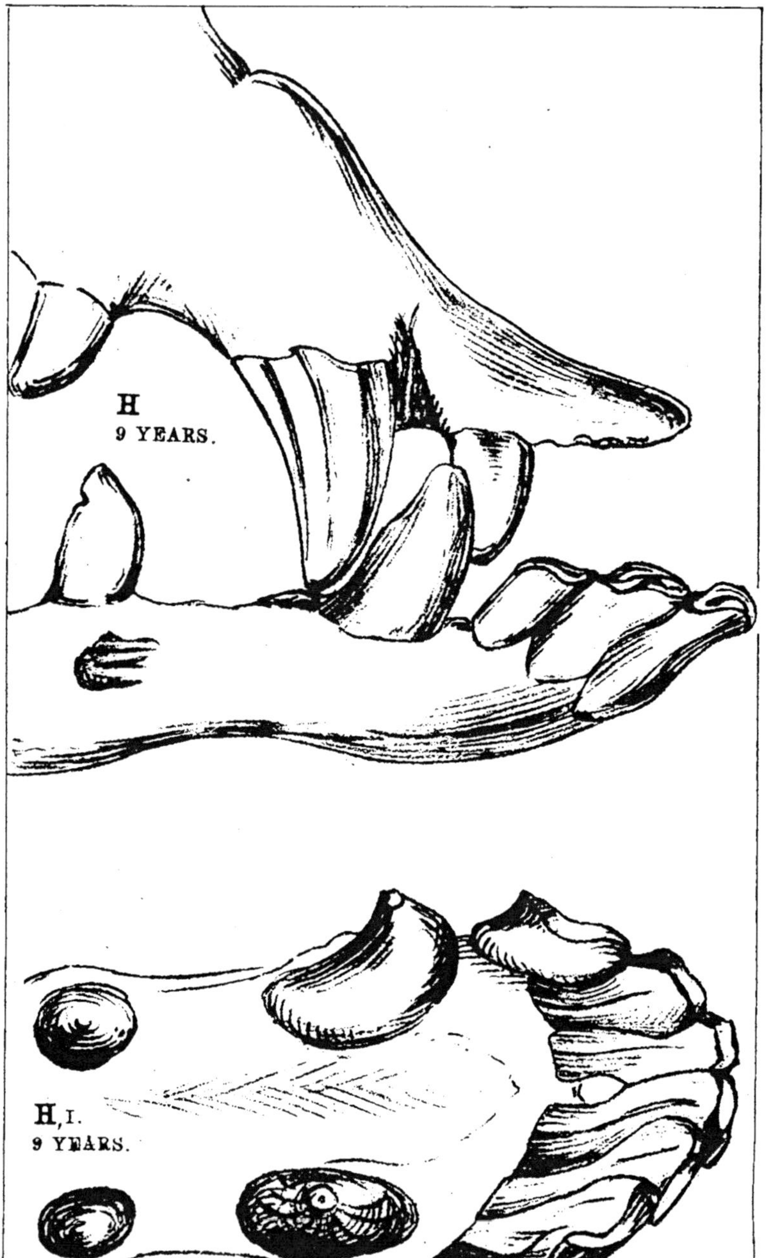

Pl: VI.

ALEX: BARREN: LITHOG: MADRAS.

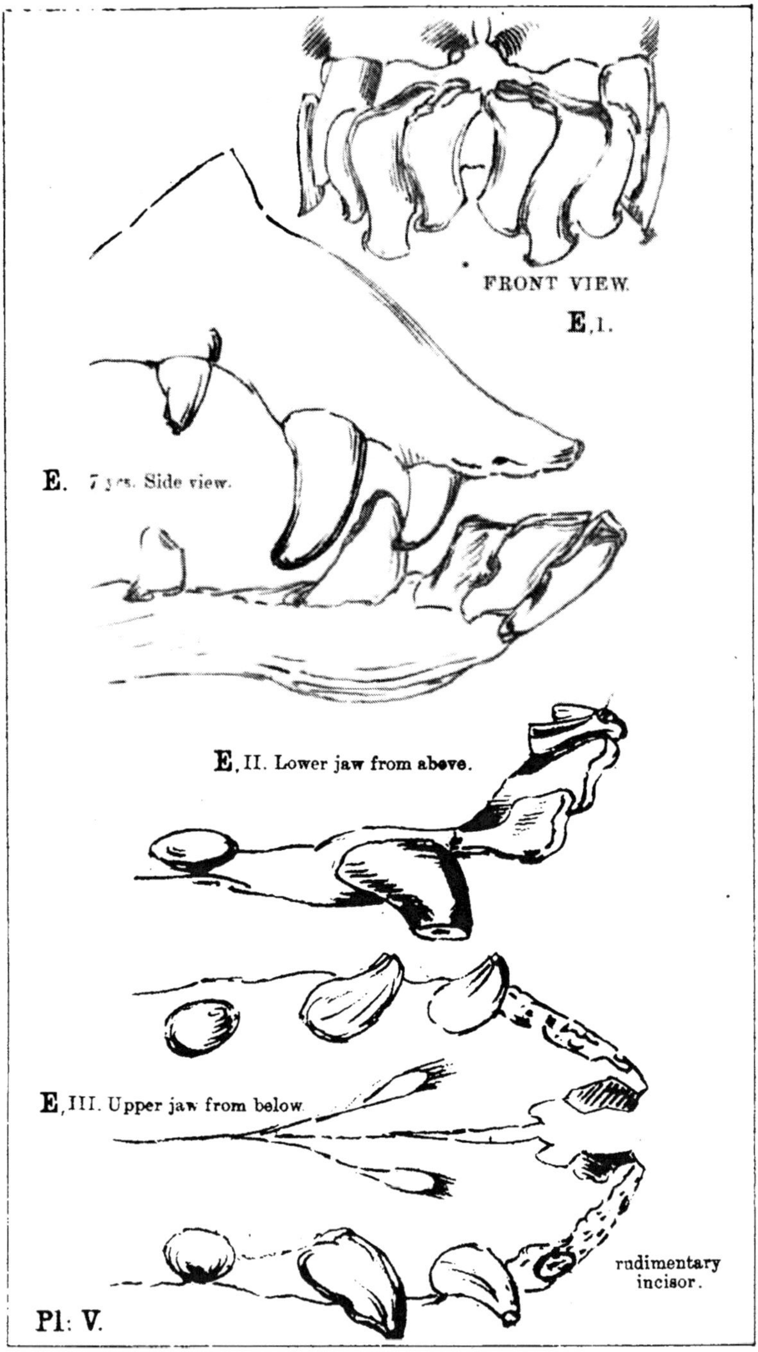

Pl: V.

ALEX: BARREN; LITHOG: MADRAS.

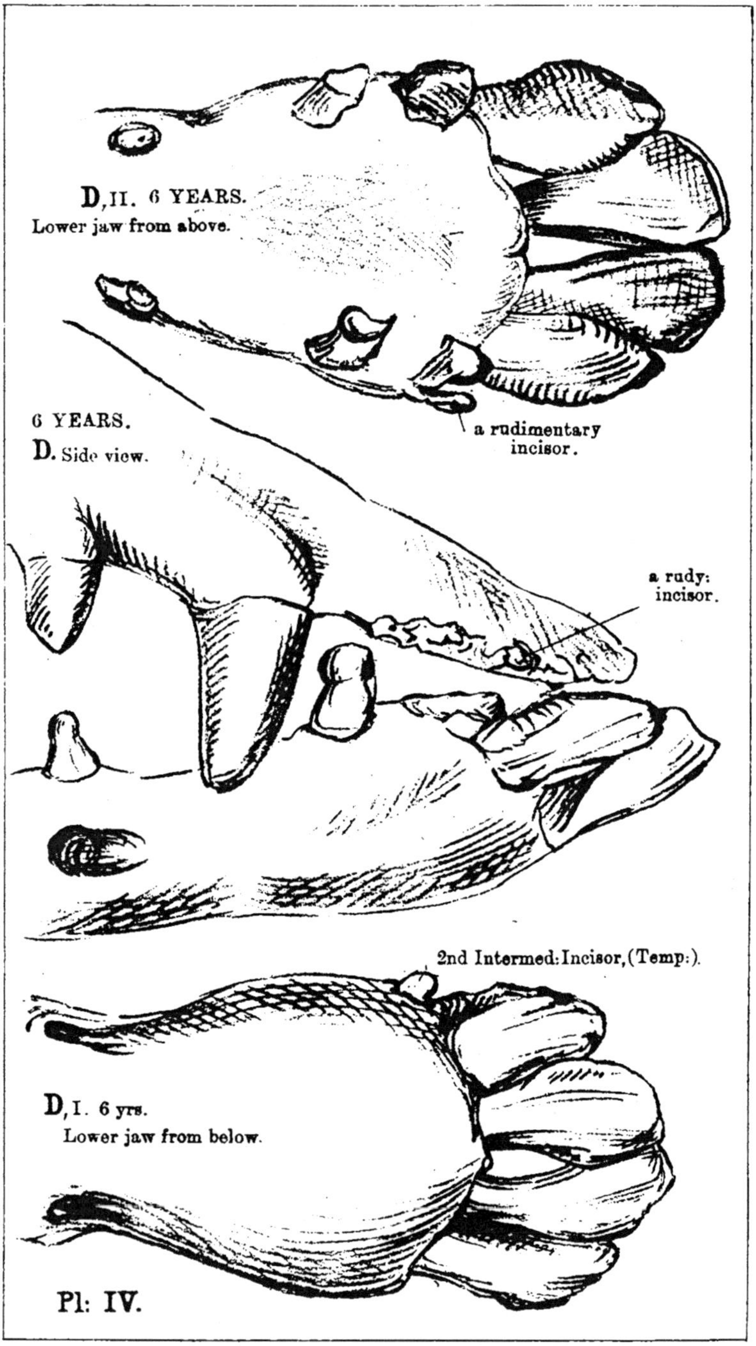

ALEX: BARREN; LITHOG: MADRAS

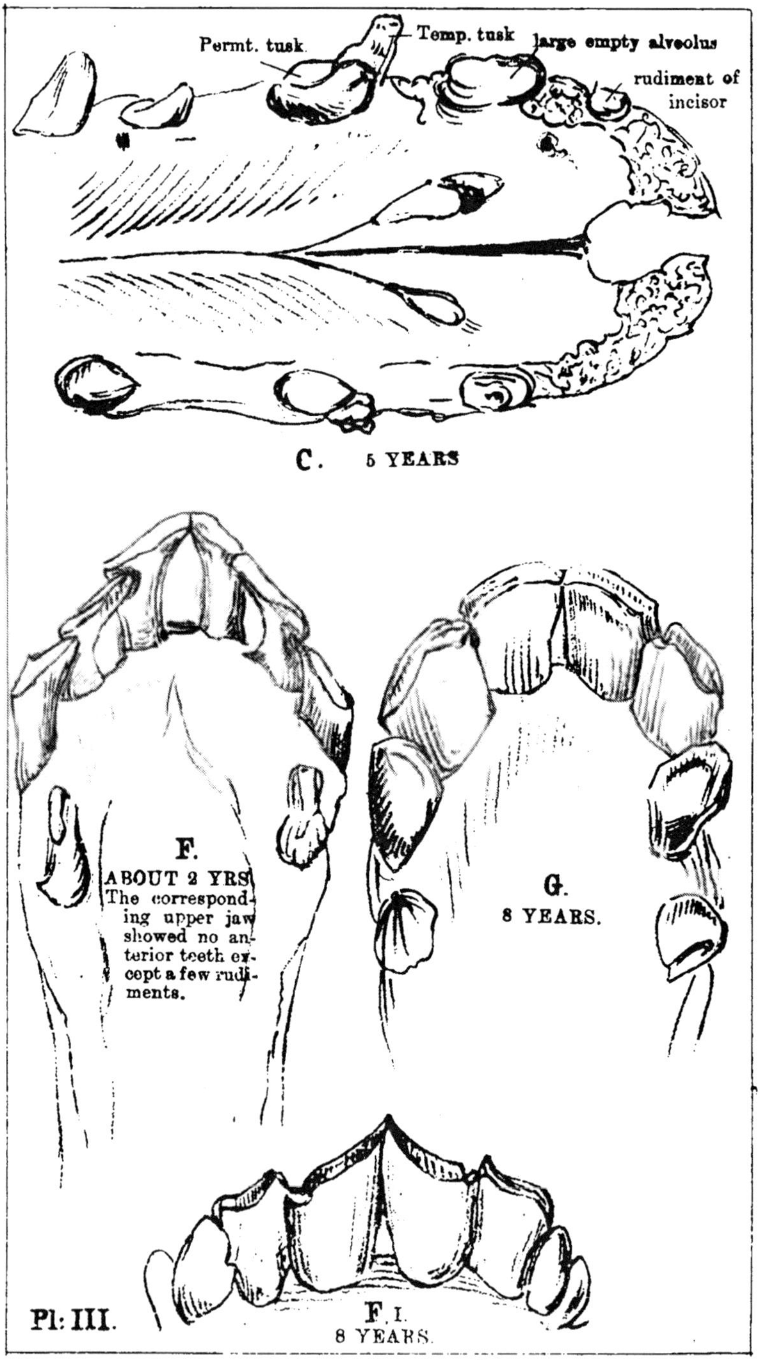

ALEX. BARREN, LITHOG. MADRAS

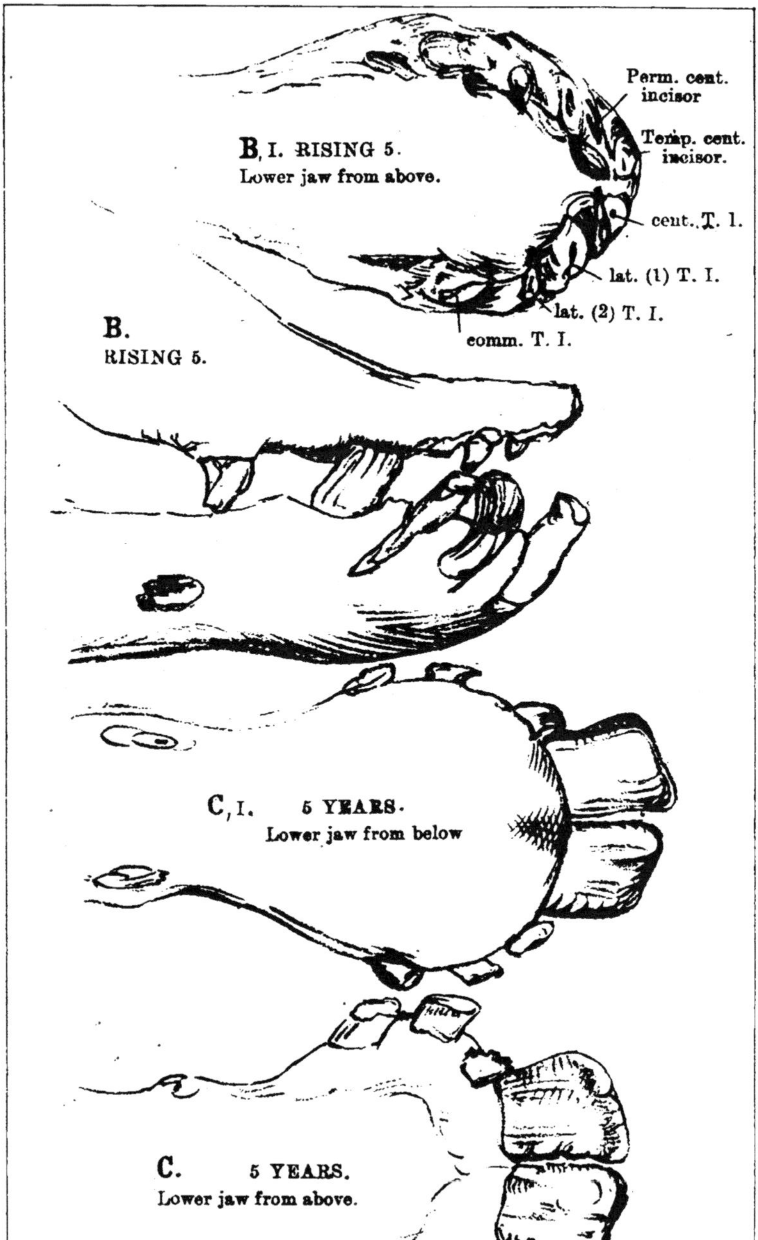

ALEX: BARREN; LITHOG: MADRAS.

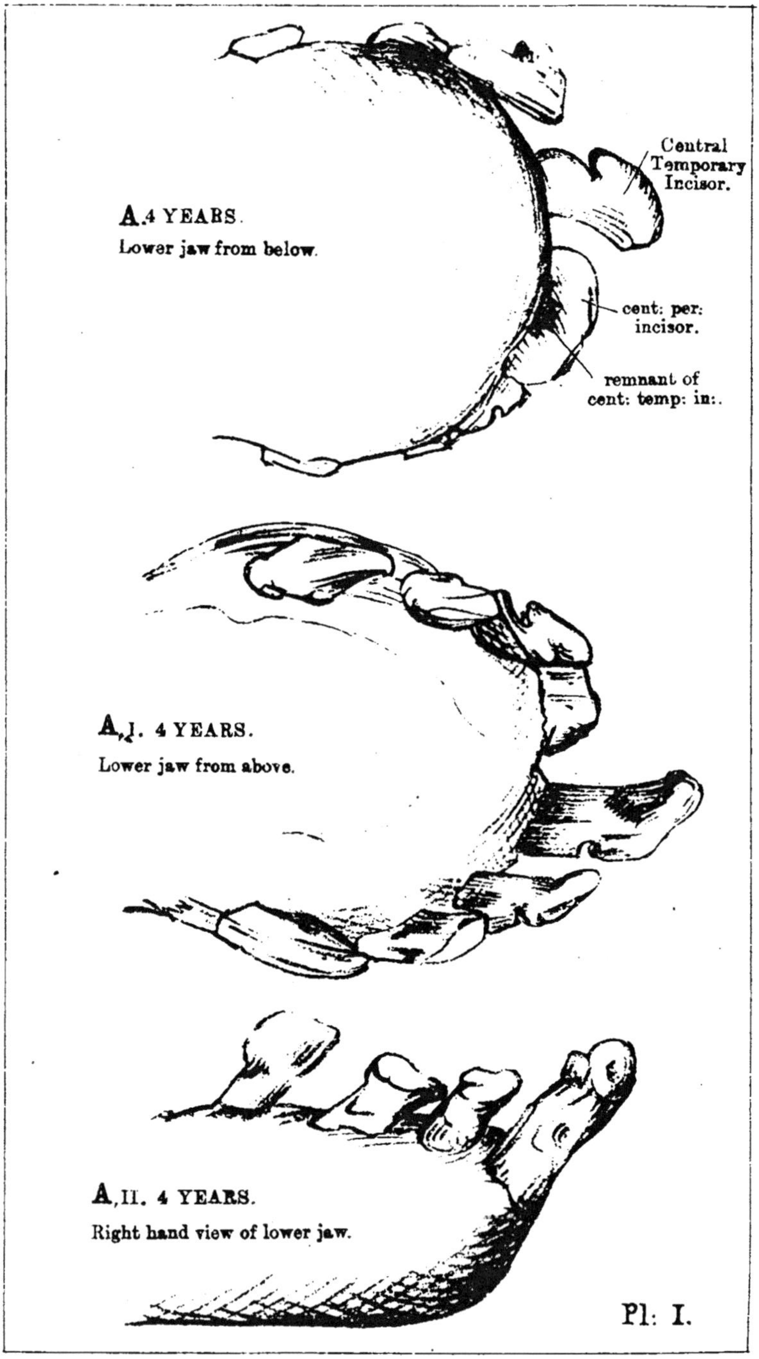

A.4 YEARS.
Lower jaw from below.

A,I. 4 YEARS.
Lower jaw from above.

A,II. 4 YEARS.
Right hand view of lower jaw.

Pl: I.

ALEX. BARKEN; LITHOG: MADRAS.

and only their noses appear. They swim steadily but slowly, and on landing bolt off scampering and kicking.

The Anazell now ride deluls instead of mares, a result of introduction of fire arms. 150,000 seems to be about the number of their camels; those from Nejd are less esteemed than the common sort; they are smaller scraggier, and give less milk.

Camel-owning tribes of Bedouins are perpetually on move. Calving time is in February and March when the tribe is at extreme south where much ghúr kudd, a thorny tree 5 feet high, stem reddish, leaves fleshy and green. After this they travel north, 2 miles per hour never exceeded, doing 8—10 miles daily.

Appendix V.—DENTITION.

The following are the conclusions to be drawn from a study of the appended plates drawn, *ad nat.* and diagramatically, from the specimens in the Museum of the Aldershot Army Veterinary School, and each examined as to the age by an expert, Veterinary Surgeon (1st Class) J. A. Nunn. The lower jaw is the main guide. *At four years of age* it contains the remnants of the central, primary and secondary intermediate, and corner temporary teeth which have become (except the latter) worn down to stumps, and they are wide apart. The outer edge of the front teeth shows a very peculiar indication of wear in the form of a deep groove where the tooth has become notched by dragging along tough fodder stalks. The permanent central incisors are now coming through and displace the corresponding temporary tooth from above and within. They come up as very broad sharp white edges (*vide* Plate I). Thus the four year old and "rising five" mouth is a regular wreck in general appearance, consisting merely, as far as teeth are concerned, of a number of ugly and inefficient stumps, wide apart, perhaps some being loosened by the growing permanent teeth which are visible as a cause of disturbance of the temporary set and have either been cut or bulge under the gum. Slight traces of the tushes may now be detectible in the form of a bulging of the gum where they will come through (Plate II, B. 1 and 2).

At five years the central permanents project squarely forward and have sharp edges serrated laterally, they have not met along the central line. The tushes are a litttle more evident, the remaining incisor are temporary and merely insignificant stumps (Plate II, C. 1 and 2). The condition of the upper jaw is now interesting. For the specimen under examination it is uneven, in that whereas there are five teeth in the right side anterior to the molars, on the left side there are but three. The five are as follows, from before backwards :—A rudiment of an incisor, which probably would not be detectible through the substance of the tooth-pad, a large alveola from which the corner incisor has dropped, a young tush replacing the corresponding worn out temporary tooth, a small wolf's tooth, and the usual large wolf's tooth (Plate III, C).

At six years of age the central and primary intermediate incisors of the lower jaw are well developed. The former meet at the inner edges of the thin broad part and slightly overlap. They also are worn at the margins and have well defined necks. The latter are very fresh looking, broad at the gum, unworn at the edges, and finely notched in a very pretty manner, their inner edges overlap the centrals, as may be seen in looking at them from above. The second intermediate is in the act of being replaced but it and the corner tooth are insignificant and invisible from below. In the upper jaw the tush and its successor in the series posteriorly are fine large teeth, the lower tush is progressing. The upper incisors are small (Plate IV).

At 7 years : In the upper jaw the tush and its incisor in front and successor behind are fresh, strong, and sharp, traces of rudimentary lateral incisors are present and the corner incisors fit in front and the tushes behind the corner lower incisor in a formidable manner. This corner lower incisor is a veritable tush in shape and in the way it becomes worn, *i.e.*, so as to form a circular or oblong table. The central and intermediates (primary and secondary) have now well defined nipping edges with marks more or less distinct ; they look crowded togethor, as they overlap, being placed *en echelon* from before backwards and outwards ; the centrals meet above and form each a small lateral table here by mutual friction (Plate V).

Judging from the conditions depicted in Plate III, the mouth *at eight years of age* is somewhat varying in its degree of forwardness. The secondary intermediates and corner incisors show little wear at this time, the laterals and centrals look very broad and their thin nipping edges slant obliquely outwards and backwards whereby the incisor line gets somewhat a serrated appearance ; centrally it is sharp and prominent, laterally where the central and primary intermediates meet it is grooved by the rubbing of hard stalks, thus results at the inner edge of each primary intermediate a prominence. So the incisor line gets a very irregular ugly look.

The mouth in full wear *at nine years of age* has a fine show of good working teeth all a little worn but not sufficiently so to in any way impair efficiency. The incisors mutually support one another and form a rough nipping margin. The lower tush in the particular instance figured has become curiously grooved behind in the form of wear peculiar to camel's teeth and due, no doubt, to the method of browsing adopted by these ruminants (Plates VI and VII).

At ten years of age the wear is a little more marked (J, Plate VII).

After this we find increased wear of each of the teeth until the condition shown in Plate VIII is attained. Here the organs are still in good working order, they are upright, firm in the jaw, worn to rounded tables on which in the incisors slight secondary dentine marks may be noted. The incisors still mutually support one another and the upper incisor meets the lower corner incisor and they form tables by mutual friction. The lower tush is not much worn.

A full mouth of permanent teeth as compared with a full mouth of temporary front teeth can be studied in Plate III, figs. F and G. The smallness, light build, and narrowness of the milk incisors is very evident ; they meet in front at an acute angle, and thus such a mouth as F, can only by the veriest tyro be mistaken for G, much less for the fine array of stout old teeth shown at VIII, I. To make assurance doubly sure we find in the two year old mouth no anterior teeth in the upper jaw except a few rudiments.

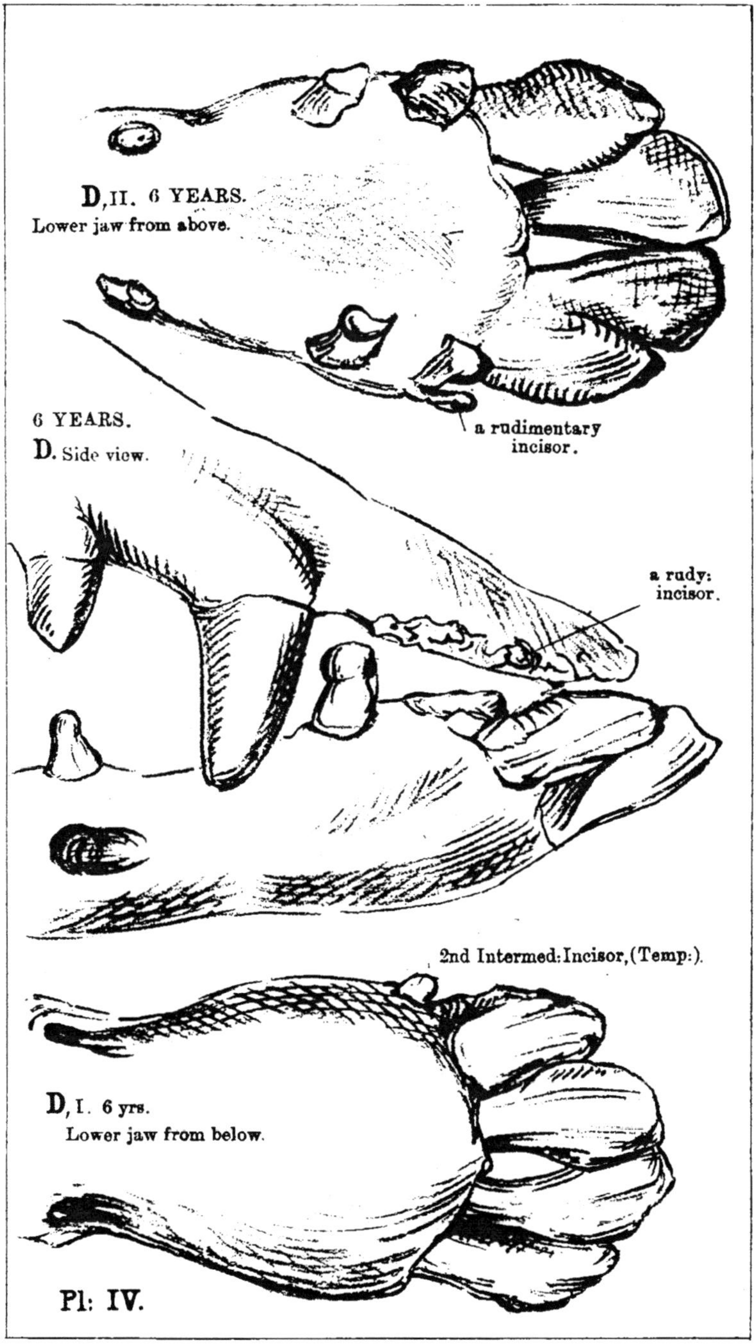

ALEX: BARREN; LITHOG: MADRAS.

same author were available to Lombardini. Gilchrist's excellent and practical works date before 1840 and thus take precedence of the writing on this subject of Graoberg'd Emsoe "on the existing Tuscan Dromedary" and "on the Naturalisation of a troop of Dromedaries" published in Paris in 1841 (the latter by the Geographical Society). Müller and Wedl in 1850 published at Vienna some studies on the anatomy of the two-humped camel, and Pancîres at Naples contributed a useful paper on the development of the molar glands of the camel (1873) while Chauveau included the anatomy of this animal in his Comparative Anatomy of Domestic Animals (2nd and 3rd editions).

In the Chinese, Arabic, and other oriental languages from remote times the camel has been noticed, especially as Mahomet was originally a camel driver and always retained his original love for the Dromedary. Some of the views of Arabs concerning, camels have been made known to us by Daumas in his version of the words of Abd el Kadir, others are merely repetitions of the views expressed in the Kurân.

What may be termed practical literature of camel management is of recent growth. Naturalists and travellers had dealt at length with the picturesque side of the camel as the "Ship of the Desert" or with his value for carriage of merchandise and the discomfort of his paces to the rider, but, after Gilchrist, the French Veterinary Officers in Algeria seem to have been the first to deal with him from a service point of view, their reports being published in the official and valuable records of the French Army Veterinary Service. Russian soldiers have from time to time noticed the uses and defects of the camel as an animal of war. Englishmen in India have contributed the bulk of our knowledge in the most systematic form, thus Charles Steel wrote of the Camel in Afghanistan to the United Service Institution of India; Leach published a useful little book on camels; Martin and some others have contributed their experience; Oliphant, Rayment, and other Veterinary Officers have dealt with the camel in their reports of active operations in the North-West of India; finally, since the British occupation of Egypt and during the warlike operations which led up to it, British Veterinary Officers have collected much information. Nor must we forget the Italians whose Veterinary periodicals since the occupation of Massowa have contained articles on this important subject and whose labours have culminated in the excellent work of Professor Luigi Lombardini, to which we are much indebted. The author of the present book has endeavoured to collect, condense, and arrange all previous knowledge of this subject.

APPENDIX VII.—MEGNIN in his *Monographie de la Tribu des Sarcoptes psoriques*, Paris, 1877, describes the sarcoptes of the camel.

FEMALE: 0·32—0·36 mm. long by 0·25—0·27 mm. broad. *Body* yellowish-white, ovoid in form and with a fairly regular margin, but having a little behind the posterior limbs three or four sharp spines, some hairs about here run out transversely and some longitudinally, and to right and left of the anus are small hairs unequal in size. No marked distinction between abdomen and cephalothorax. *Head and rostrum* conoid, compressed from above to below, and having a rounded blunt extremity. Palps with two setæ, one long at the apex, the other shorter and at the base. Throat indistinct. *Limbs*, the anterior bear each four setæ varying in size and length. Each terminates in a cup placed on a long stalk at the free extremity. The epimeres of the first pair of these limbs unite to form two prolongations, one dorsal the other ventral. The hinder limbs are ventral at fair distance from the median line with separate epimeres and each bearing a long strong seta. *Skin of back*, chitinous plastron not very distinct. Transverse striæ undulating and obscure. Small conical prominences between the epimeres of the anterior limbs and two strong hairs, behind these three circular hollows with inturned margin, then a number of transverse lines of conical papillæ with wide bases. At the posterior part two diverging series each of four spinules and midway between those on the margin is the anal opening. *Skin of belly*, striæ more distinct than on dorsum. Two circular hollows outside the anterior epimeres and somewhat behind them. Eight series of conical papillæ arranged transversely, the last forming a kind of large stria looking backwards. The spines form a V-shaped curve looking forwards. Genital openings at a large slit behind the anterior epimeres.

MALE: 0·18—0 mm. long by 0·14—0·15 mm. broad. *Body* smaller and less rounded than that of female. Cephalothorax distinct from abdomen and with well marked rings. *Limbs,* anterior, like those of female; posterior, brought nearer the central line of the body and having their epimeres united to form two arches, outer with a long seta, inner bearing small cups. *Genital organs,* near internal posterior limbs in an eliptical opening directed from before backwards containing a chitinous apparatus consisting of two parts, the sternite and the hyposternite. *Anal aperture,* retrodorsal and on the margin of the body.

APPENDIX VIII.—MATERIA MEDICA AND THERAPEUTICS.

The Nile Expedition Regulation unit pattern medicine chest was 10 inches deep, 16 inches broad, 14 inches long, and 11¾ lbs. in weight or when complete weighed 32 lbs. It contained McDougall's sheep dip, 10 lbs.; oils of turpentine and linseed of each 2 lbs. in a corked tin; carbolic acid and carbonate of ammonia of each 1 lb. in tin; also a syringe, drenching horn, enema funnel and pipe, tow, fomenting cloth, sponge, and metal dispensing bowl. The chests were fastened each by two straps and buckles, marked "Army Veterinary Department" and instructions for use of medicines were pasted inside the lid.

Queriple advocates unit chests on a more elaborate scale for use by Veterinary Surgeons in charge of camels on service containing a clyster funnel, 2 oz. syringe, firing iron, mortar and pestle, scales and weights (4 oz.), graduated glass measure (4 oz.), and bullet forceps, of each one; whale-bone probes, seton needles and handle, hanks of wire, forceps, drenching horns, of each two; needles for wire, 4; scalpels, 12. Also (as stores) canvas 10 yards, tow 20 lbs., sponges 12 per 100 camels for 6 months. Of medicines the following were most generally useful, ammon. carb., aloes barb., canth. tinct., creta præp., opii pulv., ferri sulph., acid carbol., ol. tereb., argenti nitras (Official Report).

I.—*List of Medicinal Agents showing those which are generally used in Camel Practice.*

No.	English name.	Most common Vernacular name generally Hindustani.	Uses. Internally.	Uses. Externally.	Doses internally.	Remarks.
1	Acetic acid ...	...	...	...	...	Information has been collected from all available sources and, in accordance with the idea of this work being to concentrate experience, a large number of the most useful agents in the Pharmacopœia are not described. This omission is with a double object *(a)* to show the deficiencies of existant knowledge of Camel Therapeutics *(b)* to remind the Practitioner of the drugs available for his use in emergency and of which the camel man is apparently ignorant. The agents thus undescribed are to be used as though in treatment of the ox or horse and in about similar doses. Much is to be lost and nothing to be gained by a slavish adherence to "native" methods of treatment, as they are empirical and based on ignorance of anything better and on a want of more suitable remedies.
2	Vinegar ...	Sirka ...	...	...	...	
3	Aconite ...	Kala Bitchwa ...	Sedative (seldom) ...	...	$\frac{1}{12}$—$\frac{1}{2}$ tol..	
4	Country spirit...	Arrack ...	Narcotic; stimulant.	To bruises stimulant.	$\frac{1}{4}$—1 seer	
5	Rectified spirit...	...	...	...	...	
6	Methylated spirit	...	...	...	...	
7	Aloes ...	Moosumber ...	Cathartic ...	Astringent, slightly, to ulceration and sore feet.	1—1$\frac{1}{2}$ ozs.	
8	Alum ...	Patackder ...	...	Detergent and astringent in eye, skin, and foot diseases.	...	
9	Ammonia ...	...	...	...	...	
10	Amm. Carbonate	...	...	...	...	
11	Sal Ammoniac...	Nowsagur ...	Refrigerant ...	Used in severe sprains, eye affections, and hard tumours.	...	
12	Liq. Amm Acet.	...	...	...	...	
13	Amyl. nitrite ...	...	...	...	...	
14	Aniseed ...	Sonf ...	Stimulant tonic and carminative ...	...	$\frac{1}{2}$—1$\frac{1}{2}$ lb.	
15	Caraway ...	Jeera, suffedi ...	Tonic and aromatic...	To eye affections ...	$\frac{1}{4}$—1 seer.	
16	Cummin ...	Jeera, kala ...	Tonic and aromatic ..	...	$\frac{1}{2}$—2 seer.	Useful in dysentery, in ulcerated fauces, and debility.
17	Chamomile ...	Buom ka Phul ...	Tonic and astringent.	...	...	
18	Fenugreek ...	...	...	...	...	
19	Antimony Oxide	...	...	...	...	

20	Ant. Sulphide....	Surmah ... / Surmahka kahk	Alterative ...	Detergent ...	ʒj.—℥ss.	Liable to be largely contaminated with Lead-Sulphide.
21	Butter of Antimony ...	...	...	...	...	
22	**Tartrate of Antimony.**	**Ungooree Neemuk.**	Refrigerant and diuretic.	...	$\frac{1}{8}$—$\frac{3}{4}$ seer.	
23	**Areca nut** Young ...	Chicknee supari.	Astringent ...	To ulcerated feet and in decoction as a chob	1—4 tola	
	Areca nut Old ...	Gotee supari ...	Tonic and astringent.	To swellings.		
24	**Arnica** ...	...	...	...	...	
25	**Arsenic** ...	Soomul (generally contains some chalk).	Stimulant, alterative; never given to camel. (Gt.)	Stimulant to ulcers.	...	
26	**Lal Soomul** ...	**Realgar or Arsenic bisulphuret.**	Tonic and alterative, is used externally in sloughing tail, hump, ears, and skin.	...	$\frac{1}{12}$—$\frac{1}{2}$ tola.	
27	**Munseel** ...	(**Mixture of red and white orpiment).**	Tonic and alterative; used in skin diseases.	...	$\frac{1}{8}$—$\frac{1}{4}$ tola.	
28	**Urthal** ...	**(Another Sulphuret of Arsenic)**	**As last** ...	...	...	
29	**Asafœtida** ...	Hing ...	Stimulant, antispasmodic, carminative, errhine.	...	1—4 tolas.	
30	**Lard** ...	...	...	...	...	
31	**Barley** ...	...	...	...	...	
32	**Belladonna** ...	...	...	...	...	
33	**Benzoin Tincture**	Caodalu Oodh (the gum).	Tonic, astringent ...	Detergent to wounds and skin disease.	$\frac{1}{2}$—2 tolas.	

I.—*List of Medicinal Agents showing those which are generally used in Camel Practice*—(Continued).

No.	English name.	Most common Vernacular name generally Hindustani.	Uses. Internally.	Uses. Externally.	Doses Internally.	Remarks.
34	Borax ...	Suhaga ...	Tonic and purgative in large doses ...	Detergent and suppurant.	$\frac{1}{2}$—3 tolas.	
35	Calabar bean ...	...	...	...	...	
36	Physostigmia ...	...	...	...	...	
37	Quick lime ...	...	...	...	...	
38	Chalk ...	Sea shells (sunk) Cowry shells (kowdi). } Lime stone (kulli ka choona).	Tonic, refrigerant. (Gilt). Refrigerant and diuretic in affections of urinary organs.	Detergent in ulcers and eye diseases.	$\frac{1}{4}$—1 tola } $\frac{1}{2}$—3 srs.	
39	Bleaching powder ...	...	...	...	...	
40	Camphor ...	Kapúr ...	Narcotic, anodyne, antispasmodic.	Detergent and vulnerary.	$\frac{1}{2}$—3 tolas.	
41	Cantharides ...	...	...	...	...	
42	Mylabris ...	...	...	...	...	
43	Carbolic Acid ...	...	...	...	...	
44	Cardamoms ...	Elachee ...	Carminative ...	In skin affections ...	$\frac{1}{4}$—1 seer.	
45	Ajwan or Oomam	..	Stimulant tonic ...	...	1—4 tolas.	
46	Dill ...	Mithi ...	Tonic, carminative, and (with ghee and salt) to fatten camels	...	$\frac{1}{4}$—1$\frac{1}{2}$ seers	
47	Cloves ...	...	Stimulant ...	...	ʒiij—℥jss.	
48	Date Stalk ...	Shendee ka gahbah.	Refrigerant and diuretic in urinary affections, but seldom used, as Tyre is preferred.	...	2—8 seers.	

49	Castor oil ...	Erundi ka Tel ...	Cathartic ...	...	1—4 seers.	
50	Castor Stalks ...	Erundi ka cop-lee.	Slightly purgative and tonic.	...	½—3 seers.	
51	Catechu. (White) ...	Kutha sufed ...	Tonic and astringent.	Discutient ...	⅛—1 seer.	
	Catechu. (Black) ...	Kutha kala ...				
52	Charcoal ...	...	...	...	...	
53	Chloral ...	...	...	...	...	
54	Chloroform ...	...	...	...	...	
55	Cinnamon ...	Dhal chini ...	Tonic and carminative.	...	⅛—1 seer.	
56	Cinchona ...	...	...	...	...	
57	Quinine ...	...	...	...	...	
58	Cod liver oil. ...	...	...	...	...	
59	Colchicum ...	...	...	...	...	
60	Coriander ...	Dhunya ...	Carminative, tonic—cooling.	...	½—2 seers.	
61	Copper sulphate.	Morethootha ...	Never given internally (Gilt).	Collyrium in ophthalmia, detergent, and escharotic.	...	
62	Do. Amm. Sulph	...	...	...	...	
63	Sulph Iodide ...	...	...	...	...	
64	Do. Subacetas.	Zungaul ...	...	Ercharotic and astringent.	...	
65	Creasote ...	...	...	...	...	
66	Croton oil ...	...	...	...	...	
67	Do. seeds ...	Jumal gota ...	Powerful cathartic ...	...	1—2 tolas.	
68	Cubebs ...	Kabab chini ...	Useful as carminative tonic.	...	1—4 tolas.	
		Dunki mureen ...	Tonic, stimulant, diuretic.	...	...	
69	Digitalis ...	...	...	...	...	

I.—*List of Medicinal Agents showing those which are generally used in Camel Practice*—(Continued).

No.	English name.	Most common Vernacular name generally Hindustani.	Uses. Internally.	Uses. Externally.	Doses Internally.	Remarks.
70	Ergot of Rye ...	...	...	...	...	
71	Ether sulphuric..	...	...	...	...	
72	Euphorbium ...	Shend ka Coplee.	(Stalk) cathartic and stimulant (with aloes, garlic, and wheat flour).	...	$\frac{1}{4}$—$1\frac{1}{2}$ seers	
73	Fern root ...	...	...	...	...	
74	Galls ...	Mahpul ...	Tonic, astringent, errhine.	Used for foot affections and in wounds and ulcers.	$\frac{1}{4}$—2 tolas.	
75	Gamboge ...	...	...	...	...	
76	Gentian ...	...	...	...	...	
77	Ginger (dry) ...	Sonth ...	Antispasmodic and anodyne.	...	...	
78	Do. (green) ...	Udarruk ...	Stimulant, tonic ...	...	$\frac{1}{8}$—$\frac{1}{2}$ seers	
79	Glycerine ...	...	...	...	...	
80	Gum Arabic or Acacia.	Gum Kikar ... Bark Babul ...	Astringent and refrigerant, demulcent.	...	$\frac{1}{2}$—2 seers	
81	Helebore ...	Kala Bitchwa ...	Narcotic ...	...	$\frac{1}{8}$—$\frac{3}{4}$ tolas.	
82	Hemlock ...	...	...	...	...	
83	Hyoscyamus Seeds.	Khorasani Ajwan.	Antispasmodic and anodyne, carminative, stimulant, tonic	...	1—4 tolas.	
84	Hydrochloric Acid (strong).	...	...	...	...	
84a	Hydrochloric Acid (dilute).	...	...	...	...	

85	Iodine ...	...	...	...	...	
86	Ipecacuanha ...	...	...	...	...	
87	Iron carbonate...	...	...	...	...	
88	Do. sulphate ...	Hira kus ...	Tonic ...	Escharotic in superfluous granulation.	½—1 tola.	
89	Do. iodide ...	...	...	...	...	
90	Do. perchlor ...	...	...	...	...	
91	Iron peroxide with silica, garoo.	...	Refrigerant and astringent externally in swelling and inflamed joints, bruises, sprains, &c., (Gilt).	...	...	
92	Jaborandi ...	...	...	...	...	
93	Jalap ...	...	...	...	...	
94	Juniper ...	...	...	...	...	
95	Lead carbonate..	...	...	...	...	
96	Do. acetate ...	...	...	...	...	
97	Litharge ...	Moodharsing (semi-vitrified.)	Excitant, tonic, suppurant.	...	½—2 tolas.	
98	Lead oxide ..	...	Alterative ...	...	℈j—ʒj.	
99	Sendur, lead sesquioxide.	...	Stimulant, astringent, detergent in skin diseases, and foot ulcerations, also as a hæmostatic.	...	...	
100	Linseed root and seed.	Atis. ...	Tonic useful in diarrhœa.	Emollient as poultice.	1—6 tolas.	
101	Linseed oil ...	...	...	...	...	
102	Liquorice ...	...	...	...	...	
103	Magnesia ...	...	...	...	...	
104	Do. sulphate..	...	...	...	...	

I.—*List of Medicinal Agents showing those which are generally used in Camel Practice*—(Continued).

No.	English name.	Most common Vernacular name generally Hindustani.	Uses. Internally.	Uses. Externally.	Doses Internally.	Remarks.
105	Mercury or Quicksilver.	...	...	...	...	
106	Mercurial oint...	Parah ...	Stimulant, tonic and alterative.	...	$\frac{1}{12}$—$\frac{1}{4}$ tol..	Used in preparations.
107	Mercury red oxide.	...	...	...	...	
108	Cinnabar ...	Ruschendoor ...	Never used for the camel (Gilt).	Externally in skin affections.	℈i—ʒj.	
109	Calomel ...	Para ka kahk ...	Alterative, cathartic.	Deobstruent ...	℈j—ʒj.	
110	Corrosive sublimate.	Ruskapoor (a mixture of calomel and corr. sublimate).	...	Escharotic in eye affections and ulceration, also detergent	...	
111	Mercury red iodide.	...	...	...	...	
112	Mustard ...	Rai ...	Laxative, stimulant, tonic.	To sprains and swellings, stimulant.	1—4 tolas.	
113	Myrrh ...	Hari bol ...	Tonic ...	Stimulant and digestive.	$\frac{1}{2}$—2 tolas.	
114	Nitric acid ...	...	...	...	...	
115	Nux vomica bark	Koochlay ka benj	Stimulant, tonic, narcotic; given in exposure to rain and over-work.	Used in painful swellings.	$\frac{1}{8}$—2 tolas.	
116	Strychnine ...	...	...	...	...	
117	Oak bark ...	...	...	...	...	
118	Olive oil ...	...	...	...	...	

119	Opium ...	Afim ...	Anodyne, narcotic, and antispasmodic; useful in profuse purging.	Anodyne in sprains, contusions, and eye diseases as a fomentation.	ʒj—℥j.	
120	Poppy seeds ...	...	Tonic ...	...	½—3 lbs.	
121	Do. capsules..	...	Tonic and narcotic (slightly).	...	¼—1 seer.	
122	Peppers red (Capsicum)	Lal mirich ...	Stimulant ...	In Thullee and other skin affections.	1—4 tolas.	
123	Do. black ...	Kala mirich ...	Tonic, stimulant, and carminative.	...	2—4 tolas.	
124	Do. long ...	Piplee; root, pipla mode.	Stimulant, tonic ...	Used with onions to old ulcers.	Stimulant ʒiii—℥i; tonic, 1—4 tol.	
125	Petroleum ...	See Oil of Tar...	...	...	...	
126	Podophyllin ...	...	...	...	...	
127	Caustic Potash...	...	...	...	...	
128	Carb. of Potash...	...	...	...	...	
129	Iodide of Potassium.	...	...	...	...	
130	Cream of Tartar.	...	Refrigerant ...	...	℥j—℥iij.	
131	Bromide of Potassium.	...	...	...	...	
132	Nitre ...	Shorah ...	Refrigerant, diuretic in bloody urine and excessive thirst.	Detergent in eye affections and irritable ulcers.	ϑj—℥j.	
133	Chlorate of Potash.	...	...	...	...	
134	Prussic acid ...	...	...	...	...	
135	Quassia ...	...	...	...	...	
136	Rhubarb ...	Ravul chinee ...	Refrigerant & tonic..	...	¼—½ seers	
137	Salicylic acid ...	...	...	...	...	

I.—*List of Medicinal Agents showing those which are generally used in Camel Practice*—(Continued).

No.	English name.	Most common Vernacular name generally Hindustani.	Uses. Internally.	Uses. Externally.	Doses Internally.	Remarks.
138	Savin ...	...	...	...	...	
139	Silver nitrate ...	Kari kahr ...	...	Escharotic and detergent.	...	
140	Soap, hard Country soap.	Sabun ...	Anthelmintic ...	Detergent and stimulant to wounds.	$\frac{1}{4}$—1 tola.	Used with salt, mustard, and aloes to remove slime from the bowels (Gilt).
141	Soap soft ...	...	...	...	...	
142	Carb. of Soda (impure).	Sujee kahr ...	Tonic and escharotic.	Occasionally for reducing superfluous granulations.	1—4 tolas.	
143	Sulphite of Soda	...	...	...	...	
144	Sulphate of Soda	...	...	...	...	
145	Common Salt ...	Neemak	Laxative, tonic ...	Detergent and useful for ulcers.	$\frac{1}{2}$—3 lbs.	
146	Rock Salt ...	Shamberlone..				
147	Starch ...	...	...	...	...	
148	Stavesacre ...	...	...	...	...	
149	Sugar ...	See Jaggery ...	...	...	...	
150	Sulphur ...	Ganduk ...	Stimulant, alterative (with oil).	Antiparasitic and useful for ulcers.	ʒss—ʒij.	
151	Sulphuric Acid..	...	...	...	...	
152	Sulphurous Acid	...	...	...		
153	Sweet spirits of nitre.	...	...	...	...	
154	Tobacco leaves...	Thambakoo ...	Narcotic, purgative..	...	$\frac{1}{12}$—$\frac{1}{4}$ tola.	
155	Turpentine ...	...	...	...	...	
156	Oil of turpentine	...	...	...	...	
157	Resin ...	...	...	...	...	
158	Tar	...	...	...	...	

159	Oil of Tar ...	Muttee ka tel (mineral tar).	...	Stimulant in sprains and rheumatism.	...	
160	Pitch ...	Keel ...	...	Detergent and in extensive wounds.	...	
161	Valerian ...	...	...	...	...	
162	Vaseline ...	...	...	...	...	
163	Veratrum ...	...	...	...	...	
164	Water ...	...	...	...	...	
165	Wax ...	Mom ...	...	Desiccating and cleansing to wounds.	...	
166	Zinc oxide ...	Sufid tootha ... Often calcium sulphate is sold in bazaars for this.	...	To foul ulcers, tail rot, burns, and foot diseases.	...	
167	Do. carbonate ...	(Impure) Kulcopree.	...	Slightly escharotic and detergent in diseases of eye and foot.	...	
168	Do. sulphate ...	...	...	Detergent ...	...	
169	Do. chloride ...	...	...	...	...	
170	Do. acetate ...	...	...	...	...	
171	Marking nut ...	Bhelamay (given in oil).	Stimulant after exposure to wet or cold.	Stimulant and caustic	1—4 nuts.	BAZAAR MEDICINES :—For details of this and the following drugs, see No. 2. "Indian Veterinary Manuals."
172	...	Biscoprah ...	Tonic, cathartic, anthelmetic.	...	1—8 tolas.	
173	...	Momiri ...	Tonic, aperient, narcotic.	...	⅛—1 tolas.	The doses to the camel are generally the same as those to be given to the horse.
174	Embelia ribes ...	Baobarang ...	Tonic, cathartic, anthelmetic.	...	1—4 tolas.	
175	Margosa ...	Nim (either the leaves as poultice or expressed oil.)	Tonic, antispasmodic, anthelmetic.	Stimulant ...	ʒij—℥ss..	In flatulency and rheumatism (Leach).

I.—*List of Medicinal Agents showing those which are generally used in Camel Practice*—(Continued).

No.	English name.	Most common Vernacular name generally Hindustani.	Uses. Internally.	Uses. Externally.	Doses Internally.	Remarks.
176	Papaw ...	Popaya juice ...	Lumbricifuge ...	Digestive ...	...	
177	Bael fruit ...	Behela ...	Astringent ...	...	℥v—x ...	Infusion used.
178	Tender Ink Nuts	Kakar Singi ...	Tonic and astringent.	Astringent, useful for sore feet and ulcers.	1—4 tolas.	
179	Tender gall nuts	Halre ka phul ...	Astringent, intoxicant.	Astringent ...	℥j	Terminalia tree is good fodder.
180	Cassia ...	Amaltas ...	Laxative, tonic ...	Astringent in Ophthalmia.	½—4 lbs...	Very extensively as dry powder, used in many affections —Bark
181	Tamarind ...	Ambli ...	Laxative, refrigerent, and diuretic.	...	¼—1½ srs..	(Thudwud ka chall) is tonic and astringent 1—3 tolas,
182	Butea seeds ...	Palas papras ...	Stimulant, tonic, anthelmetic, and laxative.	...	1—2 tolas.	externally as an astringent and stimulant with turmeric and salt.
183	Dikamali ...	Dikamali ...	Antispasmodic ...	To keep off flies ...	1—4 tolas.	As ointment
184	Custard apple ...	Sitaphul (leaves)	Purgative, tonic ...	Juice as a Parasitifuge.	300 leaves	
185	White oats ...	Inderjou ...	Tonic, aromatic and astringent.	...	¼—2 tolas.	
186	Kutki ...	Kutki ...	Tonic, febrifuge, emetic, anthelmetic.	...	1—4 tolas.	
187	Chiretta ...	Chirayatah ...	Tonic, stomachic, cholagogue.	...	1—4 tolas.	Useful in various debilities and to restore the tone of the bowels in cases of flatulency, diarrhœa, and dysentery.
188	Mudar { leaves, flowers and root .	Ak ...	Alterative tonic ...	Vesicant and to cleanse foul ulcers.	ʒiij—℥ij.	

189	Clarified butter..	Ghee ...	Cathartic, nutrient...	Protective ...	$\frac{1}{8}$—1 seer.	
190	Jingili oil ...	Til ka tel ...	Laxative, demulcent, errhine.	Demulcent ...	$\frac{1}{4}$—2 seers	*Phoolale ka tel*, a mixture of Til oil and Jasmine flowers is used as stimulant tonic in doses of $\frac{1}{2}$—2 tolas and externally as a stimulant.
191	Lamp oil ...	Bari arand ka tel	Unsafe ...	Stimulant to wounds	...	
192	Kerosene oil ...	Burré ka tel ...	...	Stimulant in skin disease.	...	
193	Black oil ...	Malkangani ka tel	Restorative seeds ...	Stimulant ...	$\frac{1}{8}$—$\frac{1}{2}$ seer.	
194	Colastrus nutans seeds.	...	Nutritive, demulcent.	...	...	
195	Cocoanut oil ...	Copra ka tel ...	Astringent, laxative.	Promote growth of hair.	$\frac{1}{4}$—2 seers	
196	Millet flour ...	Suttoo ...	Nutritive and demulcent.	...	Ad lib.	
197	Rice gruel ...	Congee ...	Nutritive and demulcent.	...	Ad lib ...	Wheat flour, *geong ha atta*, is given in all acute diseases in doses of $\frac{1}{2}$—2 seers as a tonic and nutritive.
198	—— ...	Bason ...	Nutritive, tonic, and excipient.	...	$\frac{1}{2}$—2 seers	
199	Honey ...	Shahad ...	Stimulant, tonic ...	...	$\frac{1}{4}$—1 seer..	*Kala sujee.* Tonic, stimulant $\frac{1}{2}$—2 tolas.
200	Jaggery ...	Gur ...	Excipient, nutritive, demulcent.	Vehicle ...	$\frac{1}{4}$ to 4 seers	
201	Palmyra sugar...	Thadh ka misri..	Tonic in urinary affections.	...	2—8 tolas.	
202	Abrus leaves ...	Gungchi ka putta.	Cathartic and tonic...	Suppurative and detergent.	1—4 seers	
203	Liquorice root ...	Meetha lukri ...	Tonic ...	...	$\frac{1}{4}$—1 seer.	Wood of Tetranthera Roxburghii is also called *Mitha lukri* and given as a stimulant tonic in doses of $\frac{1}{4}$—3 tolas, and applied externally for strains and bruises.
204	Milk ...	Dudh ...	Nutritive, emollient, demulcent.	...	Ad lib.	
205	Soap nuts .. {	Ritha Shikakae }	Laxative, diuretic, refrigerant, tonic.	Detergent ...	$\frac{1}{2}$—1 seer.	
206	Clearing nuts ...	Nirmali ...	Cooling and astringent.	Useful for sore eyes and irritable ulcers.	...	
207	Zedoaries ...	Kachur, Jangli Huldi.	Tonic, aromatic, and stimulant.	...	ʒj—jv ...	*Cleome visca* is antispasmodic and anodyne iij, $\frac{1}{4}$ lbs., tonic ℥j.

I.—*List of Medicinal Agents showing those which are generally used in Camel Practice*—(Continued).

No.	English name.	Most common Vernacular name generally Hindustani.	Uses. Internally.	Uses. Externally.	Doses Internally.	Remarks.
208	Galangals ...	Kulanjan ...	Tonic, aromatic, and stimulant.	...	$\frac{1}{8}$—2 tolas.	*Murkachur.* Tonic and carminative, used externally in skin affections.
209	Turmeric ...	Haldi ...	Tonic, aromatic, and stimulant.	Discutient ...	3—6 tol. ʒj—jv. ℥ss.	
210	—— ...	Shoree ...	Tonic, aromatic, and carminative.	...		
211	Colocynth ...	Indarayan ...	Hydragogue cathartic.	...	ʒj—℥j.	
212	Peruvian poppy..	Dhatmah pulah.	Stimulant, tonic aperient.	Detergent ...	$\frac{1}{2}$—2 seers.	Given with common salt.
213	Stramonium ...	Dhatura kala ...	Narcotic, anodyne, antispasmodic.	To irritable ulcers ...	ʒij—℥j.	
214	Indian Hemp ...	Bhang ...	Narcotic, tonic ...	...	ʒij—℥j.	Given in colic, diarrhœa, and to failing animals on the line of march. Hemp stalk, *gunjah*, is tonic, narcotic, antispasmodic, $\frac{1}{3}$—1 tolas.
215	Cocculus Indicus	Kaka mari ...	Tonic, excitant, intoxicant.	Antiparasitic and used in ulceration of ears, and tail, ulcers &c.	...	Used externally in paste with two-thirds flour, left for a quarter of an hour.
216	Columba root ...	Kaiphul ...	Tonic, astringent, and errhine.	...	$\frac{1}{2}$—3 tolas.	
217	Garlic, Onions, &c.	Lahsan, Piyaz...	Stimulant, diuretic, digestive.	Stimulant to foul ulcers, vesicant, and for boils.	$\frac{1}{2}$—3 seers onions. 1—4 tolas garlic.	

218	Sweet flag ...	Butch ...	Stomachic, aromatic, antiperiodic.	Antiparasitic and antirheumatic.	ʒjss—℥ij.	Used in Infusion.
219	Kokum butter...	...	...	Vehicle ...	...	
220	Asteracantha ...	Thal makanah...	Diuretic and tonic ...	...	1—4 tolas.	
221	Nirmullee ...	...	...	...	...	
222	Bombax root ...	Sufed musli ...	Reputed tonic, but probably inert.	...	$\frac{1}{8}$—$\frac{1}{2}$ seer.	
223	Cyperus rhizome	Nagar mòtha ...	Stimulant, diuretic, diaphoretic ...	Vulnerary ...	℥j.	
224	Oleander ...	Kanél ...	Tonic, excitant, narcotic.	Vulnerary ...	$\frac{1}{6}$—2 tolas.	As poultice.
225	Bamboo seeds and leaves.	Bhans ...	Nutritive, demulcent, tonic.	Emollient ...	$\frac{1}{2}$—2 seers seeds.	Useful in flatulency and debility. *Thabasir*, a silicious concretion from the female bamboo. Reputed tonic and cooling, is probably inert, $\frac{1}{8}$—1 tola. (*Gilt*).
226	Snake roots ...	Gandán and Ischarmul.	Antidote, stimulant, tonic.	...	℥jss.	
227	Indian Peppermint.	Pudina ...	Carminative and tonic.	...	1 lb.	
228	Moringa ...	Mungé ...	Tonic, carminative, stimulant, diuretic.	Stimulant and detergent.	1—4 lbs...	Rarely used, as fomentation or poultice.
229	Mangoe bark ...	Am ...	Tonic and astringent.	Mild astringent ...	...	
230	Plantain ...	Banana; Mózé ka jar.	Nutritive, refrigerant, and diuretic in musthi and urinary affections.	...	6—12 lbs..	Leaves used externally as eye-shades in ophthalmia.
231	Country gooseberry.	Anvula or Myrobolams.	Diuretic, refrigerant, astringent in debility and urinary diseases.	Collyrium in the form of expressed juice.	℥ss—℥jss.	
232	Radish ...	Muli ...	Diuretic ...	...	3—12 lbs.	
233	Bonduc ...	Nata Karanja ...	Tonic, astringent, antiperiodic.	Enlarged joints and hydrocele.	1—4 tolas.	Used ground in castor oil.
234	Wood apple ...	Kát Bél ...	Tonic, astringent, stomachic, demulcent.	...	1—4 tolas.	

I.—*List of Medicinal Agents showing those which are generally used in Camel Practice*—(Concluded).

No.	English name.	Most common Vernacular name generally Hindustani.	Uses.		Doses Internally.	Remarks.
			Internally.	Externally.		
235	Solanum Jacquini.	Katai ...	Tonic, diuretic, anthelmintic.	...	4—12 tol.	
236	Costus, Arabian.	Pachak ...	Tonic, narcotic, aphrodisiac.	Antiparasitic ...	$\frac{1}{4}$—1 tolas.	
237	Spurgewort ...	Kúpí ...	Cathartic, stimulant.	...	$\frac{1}{4}$—2 seers	In form of poultice.
238	Kuskus infusion	Bálá ...	Tonic, refrigerant, useful in diarrhœa.	...	2—8 lbs.	
239	Physalis ...	Nagehore uzgun.	Narcotic and tonic ...	Applied to carbuncle	$\frac{1}{2}$—3 tolas.	The leaves are steeped in warm oil and then applied.
240	Kamela ...	Kamala ...	Purgative, anthelmintic.	...	...	N.B.—Mitha tel comprises. { Til ka tel. Ulsee ka tel. Kair ka tel.
241	Lime juice ...	Nimboo ka russ.	Refrigerant, added to all metallic preparations used for this animal.	Added to ointments for eye affections and skin eruptions.	2—4 tolas.	Kurwa tel comprises. { Sarson ka tel Rai ka tel. Tara mera tel.
242	Mulberry ...	Shaitut ...	{ Leaves cooling ... Fruit heating.	...	$\frac{1}{8}$—1 tola.	
243	Thalictrum foliosum.	Hirbisee ...	Excitant and narcotic	...	...	
244	Indigo ...	Neelbuddee ...	Errhine in surdee and kapalee.	Externally to eye and ulcers.	$\frac{1}{4}$—$1\frac{1}{2}$ tol.	
245	Sweet almonds.	Bahdum mita ...	Demulcent and emollient in dysentery and kidney diseases.	...	2—8 tolas.	
246	Olibanum ...	Bahndee bole ...	Stimulant, tonic, astringent.	Externally to foul ulcers.	$\frac{1}{2}$—3 tolas.	Useful in acute diseases
247	Frankincense ...	...	...	...	...	
248	Gunpowder ...	Barut ...	Tonic, stimulant ...	To harden the feet ...	1—4 tolas.	With Euphorbium.

II.—*Some extra medicinal substances recommended for use in Camel Practice*:—

LEACH. *Gocru.*—Cooling; a prickly spreading plant.

Halon.—Very heating; a small red brown seed.

Jaman bark.—Astringent in dysentery; a large evergreen tree, leaves bronze when young, an evergreen, with thin grey bark, generally small.

Jhal.—Heating, overgrown leaves and shoots considered a good antidote to poison.

Jhan poda.—Heating; a deciduous thorny tree.

Katira.—Cooling; a gum.

Kattheli.—Heating; a thorny plant, flowers yellow, grows along the ground.

Katchri.—Heating; a small plant (fruit).

Lahna.—Heating; a grass.

Main choti.—Heating, a native medicine.

Majit.—Heating, drug which yields a red dye.

Maline.—Lice poison, a very bitter small shrub.

Pipla noor.—Heating, a small Deccan plant.

Phalicirathuar.—A prickly cactus, heating.

Phulahi.—A thorny deciduous tree of medium size, gum used in medicine; leaves and fallen blossoms used as fodder for cattle.

Smilax root.—Inert, but Gilchrist says tonic, 1—4 tolas.

Dhobi's mud.—Purgative and refrigerant, 1—2 seers.

Tyre (Dhein).—Diuretic and refrigerant, given with boiled rice and onions in superpurgation. Stimulant externally in skin affections, 2—6 seers.

Gahélone (gall stone).—Excitant, probably almost inert (Gilt) ¼—4 tolas.

Googul.—Bdellium (impure).—Tonic, astringent, and suppurant, ½—3 tolas.

Goonbede.—Rough salt with a trace of sulphur. Tonic and refrigerant, ¼—1 seer.

Imwar ka chall.—Tonic, stimulant, astringent, 1—3 seers.

Imwar ka phul.—Tonic, stimulant, and discutient; 3—8 tolas.

GILCHRIST. *Barringtonia: Sumunder pul.*—Tonic and astringent; externally suppurative, 1 to 2 tolas.

Asbestos, Sungjeera.—Tonic to old and ill conditioned camels; probably inert; detergent externally.

Chloritic Schist, Sanglaputa.—Similar to last ¼—2 tolas.

II.—*Some extra medicinal substances recommended for use in Camel Practice*:—(Continued).

GILCHRIST—(*Continued*).

Damar, Reeahl.—Externally astringent in eye diseases, ulcers, and wounds; as a paste in copious eye discharges and extensive joint swellings.

Nutmeg, Jaiphul.—Anodyne, tonic, and narcotic, and externally discutient, $\frac{1}{2}$—2 tolas.

Mace, Jowathri.—Carminative, narcotic; $\frac{1}{2}$—2 tolas.

Nardostachys, Jatamansi.—Tonic and refrigerant; given as an Errhine in surdee, $\frac{1}{2}$—3 tolas.

Kapeelá, Rottlera tinctoria.—Stimulant, tonic; $\frac{1}{4}$—4 tolas (apparently same as Kamcha).

Lahvung, Cloves.—Stimulant, tonic, as an errhine in kupallee, 1—6 tolas.

Senna, soona mupee.—Tonic and slightly purgative, $\frac{1}{4}$—2 seers.

Spear nut.—Tonic, $\frac{1}{2}$—2 lbs.

Missee (native Tooth-powder).—Consisting of galls, Ink nut, Iron preparations, &c., applied to foot diseases, ulcers, and wounds.

Mudode pulee (Screw pine).—Tonic, $\frac{1}{2}$—2 tolas.

Nagchumpah (Asclepias volubilis).—Stimulant, escharotic, and detergent for foul ulcers, tumours, abscesses, &c.

Nirbisee, Balanophora gigantea.—Stimulant, tonic, and narcotic, rarely used; $\frac{1}{8}$—1 tola.

Benjamin Gum: (Varieties *Oudth, Puttanee, Suffade, and Kaoodalee).*—Tonic; externally as detergent for irritable ulcers with country soap, onions, and salt.

Urud, black gram.—Tonic and nutritive, $\frac{1}{2}$—2 seers.

Ukalkarah, Pellitory Root.—Stimulant, tonic; $\frac{1}{2}$—2 tolas.

III.—*A few of the various Recipes given by* GILCHRIST *and others.*

KUPALEE, use simultaneously a lape to the tumour, a nahass, and a mussaul.

Lape.—1. Take linseed and dill of each ½ seer; aloes and bdellium of each ¼ seer; finely powder and mix with the juice of fifty limes and a little water, boil to consistency of an ointment, and apply.

or 2. Mix a seer each of sugar and sweet oil with 1½ seers of dill and a little water, boil and apply.

or 3. Pound well together 1 seer each of mustard, bdellium, and lime stone, with 1½ seer of jaggery, and add arrack to consistency of ointment, apply a little to the tumour and dry by holding a heated dung cake near it.

Nahass.—1. Take 3 tolas each of assafœtida, cloves, long pepper root, calumba, galls, and alum, and 2 tolas of barringtonia. Powder finely and blow one-third into the nostrils, night and morning, until the mucous discharge disappears.

or 2. Take 3 tolas each of cloves, calumba, galls, barringtonia, and pellitory, well powder and blow into the nostrils: "To be continued till the discharge stops."

Mussaul.—1. Take of gur, mudar flowers, green-ginger, garlic, colocynth, and galangal each 5 seers; dill and eera googul each 3 seers; butea seed 2 seers; powder well and add arrack sufficient to make into balls the size of an orange and give one, morning and evening, for three days then repeat daily.

or 2. Take black pepper, 1 seer, old jaggery 3 seers, dill 4 seers, and garlic 1½ seers; add arrack sufficient, and make up into orange sized balls, to be given as above.

BHAO.—1. Take powdered fennel seeds, long pepper root, cleome visca, and keermanee ujwan of each half a seer; add to them well powdered garlic ½ seer, colocynth and wonaleekajud of each a handful, mix and form into balls.

or 2 Take powdered long pepper, white oats, and kutki of each ¼ seer, also garlic ½ seer, long pepper root ¼ seer, green ginger 1 seer, and palmyra sugar ½ seer, with fennel 1 seer, well pounded; add the juice of sixty limes and well mix them, add one bottle of arrack, make into two doses.

or 3. Take bdellium, white oats, anise, kutki, and long pepper of each a seer; and of long pepper root ½ seer, add garlic 2 seers, old sugar 5 seers, arrack 3 bottles, pound and well mix. Of either of these mussauls a dose to be given at once and another every two hours.

Similar recipes are given for Soolfa, Moorghé, Zaarbádh, Cumaun, Jowla, Pæpsa, Uddharung, Garoosh, Bale nur, Balemahdha, Dhoobla, Surdhee, Jholluk ka gudday, and other disorders. The changes are rung on amounts of each ingredient and a few extra thrown in from the common stock of aromatics, possibly according as the camel man who propounded the recipes thought he would like a change in his food or drink; Brandhee, Junn, Sheerafe cropping up here and there as a variety on arrack. To repeat such trash in full would be ad nauseam, both to reader and camel; we may, however, cull a few notes from a study of the other recipes, lest per chance there be something of value in them. An unjun or ointment, for the eyes in *Bhao*, consists apparently of lime juice, cloves, assafœtida, gunja juice, and camel's ear wax. A single dose for *catarrh* is 1½ tolas of bdellium with ⅔ seer bajri flour given as a cake every evening for three days, and, as a Nahass, ¼ seer of assafœtida mixed with milk. In the recipes for *Soolfa* gall stone and bdellium find a place; and indigo, camphor, long zedoary, cloves, opium, and urine are ingredients of the Nahass. One of the prescriptions for *Moorghee* contains ink nut flowers, another the physalis somnifera. In this disorder the Nahass consists of cloves, cleome visca, barringtonia, and gall nut of each a tola, to be blown up as fine powder for three mornings, or sal ammoniac and assafœtida of each ¼ seer, sweet oil 3 seers, one-third to be poured into the nostril for each of three successive mornings. Frogs, mudar, and galls are recommended for *zarbadh*; alpinia and aconite for *Cumaun*, malkagani and kutki also for this affection; borax is prescribed for *Pœpsa*. In the disease called *choodee* take a seer each of jaggery, galangal, and embelia, add ¾ seer garlic, half a seer of henbane seeds, and ¼ seer of gopute sathwa, with arrack enough to form a mass, give one-third every morning, fomenting the head and body with an infusion of shumballee and phanee rumair leaves (equal parts). In *colic*, palas papra and mudar, stem and fruit, are combined with a miscellaneous collection of aromatics and given every two hours: or silex (thabasir) and Cleome visca are used. Rather a flinty dose is recommended for *red urine*, asbestos, silex, and chloritic schist being ingredients. In *purging* may be given a seer each of gumbeede (soda and sulphur) and omam boiled in two seers of water until reduced to one seer, or embelia ribes and salt one seer each may be given in the same way and superpurgation controlled by a seer of rice boiled with some buttermilk or a mixture of Indian hemp and onions of each one seer, poppy capsules ½ seer, and oorud ¼ seer may be tried. In *retention of urine*, white oats, black pepper, anise, and dab chiné of each a quarter seer is given daily until relief occurs. In the form of *madness associated with pendulous penis*, two seers of old tamarind juice with one seer of castor oil may be tried as being the simplest of several mussauls recommended. For *Rheumatism* a mass of fifteen ingredients each dose of which weighs twelve seers is recommended and in addition about three seers of stuff are to be poured down the nostrils! For *swollen throat glands* the following is suggested:—Take of aloes and fennel each half a seer, add ¾ seer of garlic and pound finely. Add the white of ten eggs and then a seer of marking nut mix well and apply. Hold a heated bratty to the affected part until the application dries.

Passing over some hit-and-miss recipes for surdhee, dhoobla, and other diseases we come to that given for *kharisk*. Take ¼ seer each of sulphur, Arabian costus, turmeric, and salt; powder them separately; then take ¼ seer marking nuts broken and boil them with five seers of sweet oil for a short time, throw away the nuts, but add the oil to the powdered drugs, mix and rub over the body of the animal.

The recipes from which the above are taken were gravely republished, for the information and guidance of the British troops in Egypt, in 1885; there can be no hesitation whatever in stating that the majority of them are impracticable, a considerable number are incomprehensible, a large proportion of the ingredients are unattainable especially of service (a matter of small moment as they probably were inserted for the benefit of the serwans not of the sick camels). In fact, these recipes are a mediæval barbarism like those given in Gervais Markham's Way to get Wealth or other quartos of the time of Charles II. The sooner it is recognised that the camel is not radically different in Anatomy and Physiology from the horse and the ox, that tonics for them are tonics for him, and that even their doses are tolerably safe for use with sick camels, the better. The Serwan in treating sick camels knew nothing of the use of surgical means, nor of the action of agents on the system; he relied on the teachings of his fathers, and fatalities were put down to disease, not to his attempts to cure them. For some time it has been fully recognised that surgical means as adopted for other animals are suited for the camel, henceforth let the same be admitted as regards medicinal treatment; and research be directed to determination of doses and special features of the action of particular drugs.

IV.—The following recipes are *samples of what several writers on camel diseases have recommended.* They are a little less unsatisfactory in many cases than those given by Gilchrist as recommended by the head Serwans of Hoonsoor.

1. *Phitgaya* (Leach).

Take of Babul bark, chopped small, 10 lbs.; add gur, 5 lbs. and thoroughly boil in water 20 lbs. Give half this amount morning and evening for 15 days.

or Take of garlic 40 tolas.

Bazbarang, mehti, and kaliziri of each 20 tolas; salt 35 tolas. Mix and give 45 tolas at a time every third day.

2. *Rheumatism* (Leach).

Garlic, Red Pepper, Turmeric, Dhania, — of each 10 tolas.

Onions, Salt — of each 20 tolas.

Sarson oil, 40 tolas;

Water, 10 lbs.

Boil with a sheep's head, and give the soup to camel. Repeat for seven days.

Or, in slight attack, give 1 lb. Sarson oil in hot weather or 1 lb. Til oil in cold weather, with 4 lbs. of milk.

3. *Cough* (Leach).

Take of Philiara Thowar (Cactus) 1 lb.; cut up in thin lengths, tie in a cloth, covered with mud, place for an hour in hot ashes, take out, cool and break up and give with ghur, 2 lbs. daily for 3 days.

Or Kaliziri, 20 tolas soaked in tobacco water or hooka water for twelve hours. Give the grain first and the water afterwards. — Give daily for a week.

Or Kattheli and Ak leaves of each 1 lb., Haldi 10 tolas. Pound and boil in water 5 pints, until it becomes 2½ pints, then strain and cool. Give daily for 3 days.

4. *Cough* (Burn).

Poppy seed, Goor, — of each half a pound.

Aqua, lbs. ij.

Boil and give in four parts one every evening.

5. *Pneumonia* (C. Steel).

Henbane, 6 tolas.

Dhatura, 1 tola.

Turmeric, 24 tolas.

Mustard seed, 24 tolas.

make into 18 balls, and give 1, 2, or 3 daily.

6. *Heat Apoplexy* (Leach).

Give ½ pint brandy with 2 lbs. of sugar three times a day. Subsequently try.

Garlic, Mehti, Kaliziri, — of each 20 tolas.

daily for 8 days.

7. *Sun Fever* (Leach).

Sarson, 1 lb.,

Salt, 20 tolas,

broken up small and soaked for 24 hours in water, 1 ghurra.

Or Butter, 1 lb., Honey, 20 tolas, Black Pepper, 10 tolas. — Daily for three days

8. *Indigestion* (Leach).

Give a seer of warm Ghee;

or

Majit, 20 tolas boiled in water, 5 pints, with some pieces of Jehr

Sojhna until one seer of water has evaporated, then cool;

or,

Kamela, 10 tolas followed by a lota of warm water;

or

Ajwan and soap of each 10 tolas, with salt, 1 lb., ghur 2 lbs., and sujji, 5 tolas,

or

Ghur, 2 lbs.,
Salt, 20 tolas,
Soap, 10 tolas,
Katchiry, 5 tolas,
} boil in water 2 lbs., and give when cool.

9. *Colic* (Burn).

Ol. lini Ojv., followed by Ammoniæ Carb., ℥js.; Arabs fire on belly.

10. *Tympany* (Burn).

Country Soap, ℥iv. Ajwan, ℥iv. Boiling water, Oij.

11. *Flatulent Colic* (Leach).

Take Beef 4 lbs., red pepper and garlic, of each 20 tolas, onions and salt and sarson oil, 40 tolas; Dhania, 10 tolas. Well boil in water, 10 pints, and remove bones. Give daily for 7 days.

12. *Retention of Urine* (Leach).

Take Katira, 10 tolas,
Nitre, 5 tolas,
Borax, 2½ tolas,
Soak for 2 hours in water, 4 pints, and give three times a day until well.

13. *Diarrhœa* (Leach).

In mild cases give 4 lbs. mote flour in 2 lbs. ghee daily for three days. In severe cases give 10 tolas bhang with 2 lbs. Jamar leaves and 1 lb. sugar, pounded up and mixed with water. When due to bad feeding give 20 tolas Bél fruit in 2 lbs. ghur boiled in 10 lbs. water to half bulk, then cooled, daily for three days, or give in the morning a ghurra full of Mendi leaves soaked all night in water.

14. *Dysentery* (Burn).

Linseed or Castor oil, Ojv.

Powdered opium ʒj.,
Calomel, ʒj.,
Powdered Catechu, ʒij.,
Congee, Oij.,
} three times a day.

Or Opium, ʒij—iij.,
Catechu, ʒij—iij.,
Rum, 6—8 ℥.,
Water, sufficient.,
} daily.

15. *Weakness from overwork* (Leach).

Give Salt,
Mehti,
Kaliziri,
} of each 20 tolas,
with Baobarang 10 tolas, every eighth day, and

Ghee, 2 lbs.,
Milk, 4 lbs.,
Black pepper, 10 tolas,
every four or five days;

or

Turmeric, 10 tolas,
Ghee, 4 lbs.,
three or four times per month.

16. *After severe injury internally* (Leach).

Alum, 20 tolas, followed by 1 lb. of sarson oil in hot (til oil in cold) weather daily for seven days.

17. *Tonic in Abscess* (Leach).

Kaliziri,
Coarse sugar,
Ajwan,
Salt,
Panir,
} of each 20 tolas

Dose 20 tolas every evening for five days in water.

On the sixth day give

Kaliziri,
Garlic,
Salt,
Mehti,
} of each 20 tolas,

as one dose, in balls of convenient size.

18. *Stimulant tonic for Cold* (Leach).

Kutki,
Kaliziri,
Mehti,
Baobarang,
Garlic,
Manchoti,
} of each 10 tolas,

Salt, 2 lbs.,

pound, give 20 tolas daily in evening for seven days, follow with

Pipla mor, 5 tolas,
Gur, 2 lbs.,
daily for 4 days;

or

Alum, 10 tolas, milk, 4 lbs., daily for 3 days;

or

Keril wood charcoal, 5 tolas with sweet oil, 60 tolas, poured down the nostril daily for two or three days.

Give Gur and Halon of each 1 lb. in milk boiled, 10 lbs. daily for three days.

19. *Chimukh* (Burn).

Majit,
Sweet oil,
} 2 lbs. of each.

Give one quarter every morning; on fourth day if not relieved give 2 oz. of indigo.

20. *Sore Neck* (Burn).

Bilamah leaves, tara mera oil, and sulphate of copper. Mix (equal parts?) and apply twice daily.

21. *Wound ointment* (Leach).

Marking nut,
Turpentine,
} of each 5 tolas.

Acorus root, 2½ tolas.

Garlic,
Red lead,
} of each 10 tolas.

Kerwa oil 40 tolas,

or one made by boiling red pepper in Kurwa oil. Apply three times a day.

22. *Contagious skin disease* (Burn).

Petroleum or Oil of Tar, Oj,
Common oil, Ojii,
Sulphur, enough to form a mixture like thick cream.

23. *Mange* (Burn).

Take Train oil, 4 parts,
Sulphur, 1 part,
rub in well, leave on for three days, then wash off with soap and water.

24. *Internal treatment for mange* (Leach).

Ghee or Sarson oil, 2 lbs., weekly for a month, and then
Luhson, 20 tolas,
Salt, 20 tolas,
Water, 1 ghurra,
allow to stand for 24 hours, give daily for seven days (this is called "Tel Karna") and is given as a matter of routine management in the beginning of Spring.

25. *In poisoning* (Burn).

Gur, ½ lb,
Red pepper, ½ lb,
Water, 2 lbs,
boil together and give when milk-warm as a dose.

Mindful that the diseases of Camels have frequently to be treated by non-professional men, and also to avoid the imputation of having pushed down the old system without substituting a new, we have given a Therapeutical table, and now give a series of Formulæ such as seem best suited to the emergencies of Camel practice. In doing this we shall be not unmindful of what was of value in the old system but shall unhesitatingly strike out what is inert, superfluous, filthy, or otherwise manifestly erroneous. We shall also aim at that simplicity in selection of drugs, in compounding, and in dose which is absolutely essential to successful practice. Even on this system our methods will seem rough and clumsy in comparison with the refined modes of surgery and medicine in the present day, but we have written to very little purpose if we have not succeeded in making it clear that Cameline Pathology is as yet but little advanced and that intratracheal injection, hypodermic medication, neurotomy, and other methods of modern Surgeons would, at present in it be as much out of place as an Elizabethan wing appended to the Taj Mahal. We must progress gradually to get sure results.

V.—RECIPES FOR GENERAL USE IN CAMEL PRACTICE.

1. *Stimulant Mass* or "*Gurrum Masalah.*"

Take of Powdered Ginger, }
Turmeric powder, } of each half an ounce
Asafœtida, }
Rum, enough to moisten.

Give in pellets the size of a small orange.

2. A *Stimulant Tonic drench*, or "*Pick-me-up.*"

Take of Solution of Ammonia, half an ounce, Arrack, six ounces, Asafœtida, half an ounce. Gruel up to a quart. Give as a drink, and repeat in two to four hours as required.

3. *Febrifuge Mass.*

Take of Common Salt, }
Nitre, } of each one ounce.
Sulphur, }

Jaggery, sufficient to make into a convenient mass. Give in pellets the size of a small orange.

4. *Tonic Masalah.*

(*a*). Take of Sulphate of Iron, two drachms.
Chiretta powdered, one ounce.
Ginger powdered, one drachm.

Gingili oil sufficient to give a convenient consistency.

Or (*b*). Take }
Chiretta powdered, }
Sweet flag, } of each half an ounce.
Kootkee, }
Jaggery, }

Mix and give as a bolus.

5. For cases of *poisoning with Acrid Shrubs*:—

Take of Wood charcoal, two ounces,
Chalk, one ounce,
Milk, a quart.

Mix and give as a drench.

6. In *Sore-throat.*

(*a*). Take of Opium infusion, four ounces.
Spirits of Camphor, two ounces.
Jaggery, four ounces.
Water, enough to make a quart.

Mix and give slowly as a drench or gargle.

(*b*). Externally apply with friction,
Cantharides powdered, one part.
Spirits of Turpentine, one part.
Ghee, eight parts.

---

7. In *Simple Colic.*

(*a*). Take
Opium gum,
Asafœtida,
Powdered ginger,
Jaggery.
} of each two drachms and make into a ball, to be given at once.

May be repeated in four hours if necessary.

Or (*b*). Take of Rum, half a pint.
Wood ashes, one ounce.
Ginger, half an ounce.
Turpentine, one ounce.

Water as much as is required for convenience in administration as a drink.

Or (*c*). Take of Tincture of Opium,
Solution of Ammonia,
Tincture of Asafœtida.
} of each an ounce and a half.
Rum, half a pint,
Cold water, a pint and a half.

---

8. In *Costiveness.*

(*a*). Take of Ghee, two pints.
Tamarind, one ounce.
Cassia pulp, two drachms

Mix and give as a drink.

(*b*) Take of Aloes, one ounce.
Ginger, two drachms
Rum, four ounces.
Water, a pint and a half.

Mix and give as a drink.

9. In *Diarrhœa*.

(*a*). Take of Gum Opium, two drachms.
Gum Catechu, four drachms
Chalk, powdered, one ounce.
Jaggery, four ounces.

Mix into a mass and give in balls the size of an orange.

(*b*). Take of Gum Benzoin, half an ounce.
Ajivan seeds, one ounce.
Powdered galls, two drachms.
Warm water, a quart.

Mix and give as a drink.

10. In *Dysentery*.

Take of Gentian Root powdered, four drachms
Infusion of Chiretta, four ounces
Liquor Calcis, four ounces.
Powdered galls, four drachms
Water, a pint and a half.

Mix and give as a drink—repeat daily.

11. For *Intestinal or Gastric parasites*.

Take of Sulphate of Iron, one ounce.
Kutki, four drachms.
Palas Papra Seeds, two ounces.
Treacle, as much as necessary.

Powder and make into four doses, one to be given daily.

12. For *Hepatic Congestion*.

Take Vinegar, } of each four ounces.
Chiretta infusion, }
Sal Ammoniac, one ounce.
Water, a quart.

Mix, administer, and repeat daily.

13. For *Weak heart*.

Take Digitalis powdered, } two drachms of each.
Gentian powdered, }
Rum, half a pint.

Mix in water, one pint, and give as a dose.

14. For *Catarrh.*

Take Nitre, Sulphur, and Common salt } of each half an ounce.

Mix as a powder in the feed.

15. For *Cough.*

Take Alum powdered,	two drachms.
Belladonnæ Ext.,	one drachm.
Tepid water,	a quart.

Dissolve and give as a drench, slowly.

16. For *Pneumonia.*

Take of Spirits of Nitrous Ether, Spirits of Turpentine,	of each one and a half ounces.
Chiretta infusion,	four ounces.
Oil of Til,	one pint.

Mix and make into a drink; repeat daily.

17. For *Pulmonary Apoplexy.*

Take Spirits of Ammonia, aromatic, Spirits of Turpentine, Spirits of Nitrous ether, } one ounce of each.
Rum, half a pint.

Mix with water one pint and give forthwith.

18. For *Parasitic bronchitis* (*Penhale.*)

Take of Acid Carbolic,	twenty drops.
Oil of Turpentine,	one fluid drachm.
Chloroform,	half a fluid drachm.
Oil of Olives,	two drachms.

Mix and inject into the trachea—repeat daily for three days.

19. For *Hæmaturia.*

Take of Iodide of iron,	one drachm.
Kutki powdered,	four drachms.
Arrack,	four ounces.
Water,	one quart.

Mix and administer daily as a drink.

20. For *Dysuria.*

Take of	Nitre,	one ounce.
	Turpentine,	half an ounce.
	Resin,	half an ounce.
	Liquorice root,	two ounces.

Mix with sufficient Treacle and give as a mass.

---

21. For *Rutting.*

Take of	Ghee,	half pound.
	Wheat flour,	one pound.
	Onions,	quarter pound.
	Sugar,	quarter pound.

Give daily one quarter of the above as feed.

---

22. For *Brain derangements,* as a Sedative.

Take of	Aconite root,	two drachms.
	Belladonnæ ext.,	one drachm.
	Water,	a quart.

Give as a drink.

---

23. For *Eczema.*

Take of	Soluble phenyle,	one part.
	Water,	twenty parts.

Wash the affected skin daily with this.

---

24. For *Mange.*

Take of	Sulphur,	two pounds.
	Quick lime,	one pound.
	Water,	sixteen pounds.

Boil together and stir continuously until the ingredients are combined.

---

25. For *Wounds.* *(a)* Camphorated oil (Gilchrist).

Take of	Jingli oil,	1 pint	mix and dissolve.
	Camphor,	3 ounces	

(b) Dikamali ointment (Hawkes).

Take of Dikamali, bees' wax, and gingli oil, each two ounces.
Powdered gall nuts, half an ounce.

Boil the galls in oil, add the Dikamali, then melt and strain through a cloth; add the wax and keep still till cold.

---

26. For *Galls:* Astringent lotion.

Take of Sulphate of zinc powdered,	} of each one ounce.	
Acetate of lead powdered,		
Ghee	one pint to one quarter pint.	

Mix and apply frequently.

---

27. *Stimulating liniment* for abscesses, sprains, &c.

Take of Liquor ammoniæ,	4 ozs.	mix and shake up thoroughly.
Olive oil,	1 pt.	
Oil of turpentine	4 ozs.	
Common oil,	1 pt.	

---

28. For *Ophthalmia.*

Take of Nitrate of Silver	1 drachm.
Rain water,	4 ounces.

Instil into the eye a few drops daily

---

29. A *Chob.*

Take of Aloes, wax, dammar, and grease equal parts and of catechu four parts—melt together and apply as an ointment (Hawkes).

---

30. A *Foot poultice.*

Take of Chlorinated lime, one part; linseed meal, one part, bran four parts—hot water to make of proper consistency—apply when hot.

INDEX.

Page

A

Abscess ... 111
„ chest ... 111
„ groin ... 112
„ neck ... 112
„ outside thigh 112
„ over eye ... 112
„ subcutaneous 112
„ tonic for ... 191
Acaricides ... 95
Acarus Cameli ... 92
Adaptations, anatomical... 9
„ to desert xiv
Aden camels ...134,137
„ pad ... 146
Administration of medicines ... 43
Afghan camels ... 2
„ campaigns.. 2,7
Age, as told by teeth 160
„ determination of 26
Agheen bhao, ... 100
Agim ... 133
Ahreen Bhao ... 86
Aker ... 56
Akra ... 56
Algerian camels .. 6
„ saddle ... 146
Alimentary canal... 59
American fossil camels ... 163
Anæmia ... 45
Anatomical adaptation to uses ... 9
Anchylosis, Vertebral ... 114
Anthrax ... 47
„ vaccination 49
Apoplexy ... 88
Apparatus, nervous 85
„ pedal... 115
„ respiratory... 72
Arab's aphorism ... 1
Ascites ... 64
Asia Minor, camels of ... 2,4
Atrophy, limb muscles ... 115
Attendants ...28,127
Auscultation ... 37

Page

B

Baàreer ... 133
Back, sore ... 106
Bactrian camel ...2,133
Bagga ... 4
Baibiron ... 133
Bajri camels ... 3
Bakhti ... 133
Bale ka murz ... 112
Bar ke unt ... 3
Barr ... 48
Bazaar medicines... 195
Beloochi camels ... 4
Bhai ... 56
Bhao ...64,80,88,185
Bhao ka murz ... 86
Bikanir camels ... 4
Bil ... 48
Bishareen ... 134
Bisova ... 56
Bissel ... 53
Bite of a camel ... 44
Bleeding ... 41
Blindness ... 115
Blood ... 45
„ diseases ... 45
Boils ... 113
Bone, spavin ... 114
Bones ... 131
Booghdee ... 138
Boss galls ... 105
Bot ... 76
Brahui camel ... 141
Brain derangement 197
Branding, Government... 103
„ sores ... 102
Breeding ...29,31
Bridges, camel ... 17
Bronchitis, chronic. 80
„ parasitic ...80,196
„ verminous..80,196
Buddha Bhao .. 80
Bullet wounds ... 102
Bumnee ... 104
Butchers' meat, camel flesh as ... 132

C

Cænurus cerebralis 87
Cairo saddles ... 144

Page

Calculi urinary ... 82
Camel ... 3
„ attendants ... 127
„ bridge ... 17
„ Compensation Committee.. 30
„ corps ...118,124
„ employed along Nile ... 134
„ flesh ... 132
„ fodder ... 125
„ grazing ... 150
„ guns ...14,139
„ hybrids ... 3
„ in South Australia ... 2
„ lines ... 22
„ loads ... 138
„ losses on service ...5,136
„ management.. 147, 160
„ pox ... 53
„ sowars ... 14
Camping ground ... 25
Cancer hump ... 110
Canker of ear ... 115
Capacity, intestinal 60
Cartilage of heart.. 72
Castration ...25,83
„ arguments for 128
Catarrh ...74,196
„ nasal ... 73
Catarrhal fever ... 156
Cathartics ... 42
Causes of saddle gall 106
Cephalitis ... 86
Cerebral congestion 85
Cerebritis ... 86
Chandni ... 87
Chandri ... 113
Cheechuck ... 58
Chest abscess ... 111
„ diseases of 78
Chhallie ... 47
Chhaliyan ... 113
Chimukh ... 191
Chob ...118,198
Choodee ...54,187
„ ka murz ... 62
Choufulli Dagh ... 112
Chronic bronchitis.. 80

Entry	Page
Chronic lung disease	80
Chursah ...	20
Circulatory system.	71
Cold ...	191
„ struck ...	56,86
Colic ...	187,190,194
Concretions, tonsillar ...	67
Congestion cerebral	85
„ of liver	70
Constipation ...	64
Contagious skin disease ...	192
Contract Camel Transport ...	6
Contusions ...	103
Convoys, camel ...	13
Cooling mussauls...	45
Copulation ...	83
Corps, camel ...	118,124
Costiveness ...	64,194
Cough ...	73,189,196
Crimean campaign..	5,7
Crossing rivers ...	160
Crupper galls ...	105
Cumaun ka murz...	86
Cuppray ...	54
Cutaneous system..	88

D

Entry	Page
Dalon se nikal gaya	54
Danakil Fever ...	156
Dansna ...	73
Debab fly ...	101
Debility ...	45
Defects of camel as an animal of Transport ...	14
Delta camels ...	135,137
Dentition ...	27,160
Dewanah kootha ka murz ...	55
Dhadbund ka murz	87
Dhoobla ...	46
Dhudkay ...	86,88
Dhundee ka murz...	83
Diaphragm ...	114
Diarrhœa	64,129,190,195
„ epizootic...	158
Digestive system ...	59
Dimension of camels	152
Diseases ...	32
„ of blood ...	45
„ „ chest ...	78
„ „ foot ...	117
„ „ young camels...	83
Dislikes of camels...	10
Dislocation ...	114
„ neck ...	114
Disorders, generative...	82
„ urinary	81
Distomum ...	71
Doaia ...	47
Dolool ...	133
Dongola camels ...	135
„ saddle ...	144
Doses ...	43
Dragging out nose peg ...	75
Draught camel ...	14
Dromedaries ...	6
Duration of life ...	28
Dust julab ...	66
Duties of camel corps	120
Dysentery ...	64,190,195
Dysuria ...	82,197

E

Entry	Page
Ears ...	115
Economic value of camel ...	1
Ectozoa ...	100
Eczema ...	89,100,197
Egyptian campaign	6
„ saddle ...	144
Elastic pad, inflammation of ...	117
Elbow gall ...	105
El magoub ...	112
„ mooroos ...	118
Emphysema infectuosum ...	49
Encephaloid hump..	110
Endurance of camel	4
Enemata ...	42
Enteritis ...	64
Epizootic diarrhœa	158
Esneh saddle ...	144
Examination as to fitness ...	27,152
Excreta ...	37
Eye ...	115

F

Entry	Page
Farcy ...	54
Fastening ropes ...	23
Febrifuge mass ...	193
Feeding ...	17
Feet, sore ...	118
Fever ...	35
Fever catarrhal ...	156
„ relapsing ...	46
Fibroma ...	115
„ pedal ...	118
Filaria ...	80
„ Evansi ...	58,157
Firing ...	40
Fistula, foot ...	117
„ hump ...	110
Flatulent colic ...	63,190
Fluke in liver ...	71
Fly ...	101
Fodder for camels...	125
Fodders ...	19
Fomentations ...	42
Food ...	18
Foot and mouth disease ...	52
Foot, diseases of ...	117
„ poultice ...	198
„ puncture ...	117
Formula, spinal ...	113
Fossil camels ...	163
Founder ...	118
Fracture ...	114
„ jaw ...	114

G

Entry	Page
Gad fly ...	15,101
Gadik ...	112
Gahasha ...	62
Gait of camols ...	29
Galeodes ...	101,157
Galls ...	103,105,198
„ hump ...	110
„ saddle ...	106
Ganda ...	34
Garab ...	88
Gathar ...	112
Gear ...	23
General signs of ill-health ...	35
Generative disorders ...	82
Geographical distribution ...	xii
Ghariz ...	111
Ghizeh camels ...	135
Gid hydatid ...	87
Gland, temporal ...	82
Glanders ...	53
Globules of blood...	45
Glossitis ...	62
Godi ...	112
Gomri ...	112
Gooroosh ...	111

Page
Government branding ... 103
Grain for camels ... 126
Grazing ...18,150
Groin abscess ... 112
Grooming ... 21
Guns, camel ...14,139
Guptul hudda ... 64
Gurrum masalah ... 193
Guttud ka murz ... 64
Guttural pouches... 68
Guzmah ... 117

H

Hæmaturia ...82,187,196
Hair, shedding of. 15
Ham muscles torn... 115
Hazara camels ... 4
Heart ... 71
Heat apoplexy ...88,189
„ struck ... 46
Heca Belau ... 71
Hejeen ... 133
Hekar ... 111
Hepatic congestion. 195
Hepatitis ... 71
Hernia, umbilical... 69
Hewa ... 88
Hill camels ... 2
History of the camel 163
Horn on camel ... xv
Hoven ... 63
Hubbi ... 54
Huk ... 54
Hulwa ... 131
Hump ...xv,110
Hurva ... 87
Hydatids ... 57
„ in liver ... 71
„ „ lungs... 81
Hydrophobia ... 55

I

Impaction of the rumen ... 64
Indigestion ...69,70,189
Inflammation of elastic pad... 117
„ „ encephalon 86
„ „ palu ... 62
Influenza ... 74
Injuries of the lower jaw ... 105
Internal temperature ... 36
Intestinal measurements... 60
„ parasites... 70
Itch ... 88

J

Jakar jana ... 56
Jali ... 31
Jaw, fractured ... 114
Jehun ... 100
Jenuk ... 87
Jesalmir camels ... 4
Jhool ... 24
Joints swollen ... 115
Jolay ka murz ... 87
Joluk ka gudday... 112
Joogal ... 63
Jowaki camels ... 2

K

Kababeesh camels.. 135
Kajuria dagh ... 111
Kapaulee ...74,112,185
Karachna ... 73
Khanhog ... 47
Kharisk ...88,187,197
„ mussauls ... 19
Khéléâa ... 133
Khivan campaigns. 5,6
Khoorka ... 73
Kinds of camels ... 133
Koodkay ... 73
Kookra ... 62
Kumree ... 87
Kupalee ...74,112,185
Kuppas ... 131
Kussooree ... 56
Kutchwa ... 115

L

Laceration, ham muscles .. 115
„ nose... 104
Lachrymants ... 40
Lameness ... 117
Lapes ... 40
Laryngitis ... 73
Laxatives ... 42
Legs, levelled ... 115
Length of camel ... 26
Levelled legs ... 115
Lice ... 100
Ligamentum nuchæ ... 114
Limb muscles, atrophy of ... 115
Lines, camel ... 22
Literature of the camel ... 163
Liver ... 70
„ congestion ... 70
„ disease ... 195
„ fluke ... 11
Loading ...23,26
Loads ...11,146
„ of camels ... 138
Locomotory system 113
Losses of camels on service ... 136
Lung disease, chronic ... 80
Lutchuk ... 115
Luxation of shoulder ... 114
Lymphangitis ... 56
„ traumatic. 128

M

Madness with pendulous penis ... 187
Maggot in nostrils.. 75
Mahdeebale ... 112
Maia ... 133
Malole ... 63
Management, military, of camels 138
„ of camels ... 160
„ „ on service.. 163
Mange ...88,187,192,197
„ treatment ... 95
Marches ... 142
Marching ... 12
Mata ... 53
Materia Medica ... 38
„ „ and Therapeutics ... 166
Means of restraint.. 43
Medicine chest ... 166
Medicines ... 168
„ administration of... 43
„ Bazaar... 195
Megrims ... 85
Mehari camels ...133,138
Military camel management ... 130
Milk ... 84
Minor surgical conditions ... 102
Mongolian camels... 5

Page
Moorghee ka murz ...85,185
Mooroos ... 118
Mori ... 52
Mounted Infantry saddle ... 144
Mule *v.* Camel Transport ... 140
Mumps ... 54
Mussauls ...18,39
Must ...10,26,127

N

Nahass ... 39
Names of camels...27,30
Napoleon's camel corps ... 2
Nasal catarrh ... 73
Native camel doctors ... 7
Neck abscess ... 112
„ dislocation ... 114
„ glands, tumour of... 111
Ner breed ... 5
Nervous apparatus.. 85
Nile, camels used along... 134
„ Expedition...142,147
Nôk, 133
North West Provinces camels ... 4
Nose laceration ... 104
„ peg dragged out... 75
Nostrils, maggots in... 75
„ ulceration of 75
Nurbale ... 112

O

Occasionally used drugs ... 183
Œstrus cameli ... 75
Ointments ... 40
Ophthalmia ...115,198
Organs of special sense ... 115
Oudh camels ... 4
Overgrown toe nails ... 117
Overworn sole ... 118

P

Paces ... 115
Pack saddle ...23,144
Pad gall ... 105

Page
Pœprah ... 79
Paepsa ... 187
Pahari camels ... 2
Pakdar ...54,78
Palu ...59,61
Pan ... 88
Pancreas ... 70
Papesa ka murz ... 79
Papillæ of cheek ... 66
Paraplegia ... 87
Parasites...65,70,156,157, 195
Parasitic bronchitis 196
„ diarrhœa.. 130
Parotiditis ... 62
Pathan camel ... 141
Peace services ... xi
Pedal apparatus ... 115
„ fibroma .. 118
Penchees ... 66
Pendulous penis ... 83
Pentastoma ... 157
Percussion ... 37
Persian camels ... 4
Pharyngobolus ... 75
Phipri ... 47
Phitgaya ... 54,188
Phora ... 111
Phthisis tuberculous. 81
Phudmuth ... 82
Pinsee ka murz ... 54
Placenta ... 83
Plants eaten by camels... 150
„ poisonous 157,158
Pleuropericarditis... 79
Pleuropnemonia ... 79
Pneumonia 78,80,189,196
Pockdarie ... 54
Poisoning 58,157,192,193
Postures of camel 115
Pro-camelus ... 163
Procurability of camels ...29,136
Products of the camel ...xiv,131
Prognosis ... 37
Pulan ... 23
Pulmonary apoplexy ...80,196
Pulse ...36,72
Punctured foot ... 117
Punjab camels ... 3
Pupday ... 79
Purana purgaya ... 54
Purchasing camels. 26
Purging ...64,187

Page

Q

Qualities of the camel ... 8
Quittor ... 117

R

Rabies ... 55
Rahafay ... 105
Rail transport of camels ... 139
Rajputana camels.. 4
Randuk ... 112
Range of camels ... xii
Rate of marching... 12
Rations ... 18
„ on service... 149
„ up the Nile. 148
Ratta ... 4
Recipes ... 193
Records of Suakim ...120,124,138
Red urine ...187,196
Renal calculi ... 82
Regulation medicine chest, Nile 166
„ rations... 18
Regulations for purchasing ... 26
Rejection of camels, causes of ... 153
Relapsing fever ... 46
Requisition camel transport ... 6
Respiratory apparatus ... 72
Respirations ... 37
Restraint, means of 43
Retention of urine ...81,187,190,197
Rheumatism 56,156,187, 189
Riding on camels ... 29
„ saddles ... 144
Rinderpest ... 52
„ supposed 158
Rivers, crossing of ...17,147
Roads suited for camels ... 16
Roosne ka murz ... 82
Ropes of load ... 23
Routine examination... 27
„ camel management... 20
Rumen, impaction of ... 64

Page

Rus ... 63
Rusoli ...112,113
Rutting or Must...10,26, 197

S

Saddle gall ...106,145
Saddles for camels. 124, 144
Saddling ... 22
Sarcoptes cameli..92,165
Sarpo ... 117
Scindi camels ...
Sea transport ... 139
Sedatives ... 43
Seemuck ... 115
Seistan camels ... 4
Seroot fly ... 101
Service rations ... 149
Serwans ...7,28,127
Severe injuries ... 191
Shearing ...22,24
Shoulder luxation... 114
„ sprain... 115
Sick transport ... 139
Sink ... 23
Skeleton ... 113
Skin disease, contagious...192
„ dressing, Sahara 151
Skins ... 131
Slitting the ear ... 41
Snuff ... 39
Soale ... 63
Sohag saddle ... 144
Sohawa ... 4
Sole overworn ... 118
Sooka zaarbadh ... 57
Soolee ... 66
Soolfa ... 185
Soolfa ka murz ... 80
Soozark ... 82
Sore back ... 106
„ feet ... 118
„ neck ... 191
„ throat. 62,194
Sores from branding 102
Soudan campaigns. 6
„ expedition. 156
Soudani camels ... 134
Soundness, examination for ...152,154
Sowars, camel ... 14
Spavin ... 114
Special sense organs 115
Spinal formula ... 113

Page

" Splitting up " ... 114
Sprained shoulder.. 115
Sprains ... 115
Stimulant mass ... 193
„ tonic ... 191
Stimulating application... 45
„ liniment... 198
Stomach ... 59
Stomatitis ulcerativa ... 83
Strangles ... 54
Strongylus filaria... 80
Suakim Records.120,124, 138
Subcutaneous abscess ... 112
Sukhbund ... 64
Sul ... 63
Sulfa ka murz ... 62
Sun fever ...35,189
Surdee ... 73
Surgical conditions minor ... 102
Surra ... 46
„ supposed ... 155
Symptoms ... 35
System circulatory. 71
„ cutaneous .. 88
„ digestive... 59
„ locomotary. 113
Swimming camels17,160
Swollen joints ... 115
„ throat glands... 187

T

Tabanus bovinus ... 101
Tahkne ... 117
Tail amputation ... 104
Tak ... 56
Taloocher camels ... 4
Tapping the belly 64
Teeth ..59,67
„ as indicative of age... 160
Temperature internal ... 30
Temporal gland ... 82
„ „ Inflammation of... 112
Temporary parasitic ectozoa ... 101
Tetanus ... 87
Thall camels ... 3,4
Therapeutics ... 38

Page

Thermometry ... 36
Thigh abscess ... 112
„ dislocation... 114
Thullee ... 117
Toe nails overgrown 117
Toks ... 138
Tonic for abscess .. 191
„ masàlah ... 196
Tonsillar concretion 67
Traditional method of treatment of mange ... 97
Transport by rail and sea... 139
„ of sick... 139
„ value of camels 140
Traumatic lymphangitis ... 128
Tread of the camel... 117
Treatment ... 38
„ of mange 95
„ of saddle gall... 108
Trichocephalus ... 65
True mange ... 92
Tschak ... 158
Tsetze fly ... 101
Tubercular phthisis 81
Tuberculosis ... 56
Tumour of neck glands ... 111
Tumours ... 115
Turkestani camels.. 5
Tuyer ... 5
Tup surga ... 85
Twitch ... 155
Tympany ... 190
Typhus fever, Danakil ... 156

U

Ulceration, nostrils 75
„ tail ... 104
Ulcerative stomatitis ... 83
Ulcers ... 127
Umbilical hernia ... 69
Unjuns ... 40
Urethral calculi ... 82
Urination, halt for.. 26
Urinary disorders... 81
Urine, retention of.. 81
Uses of parts of camel ... 131
Uterogestation ... 83
Uvula ... 59

Page

V

Vaccination for Anthrax ... 49
Vahee golah ... 70
" ka durudh... 56
Value of camel ... ix
" " " for transport... 40
Varieties of camel.2,3,53
Variola cameli ... 53
Venesection ... 72
Verminous bronchitis ... 80
Versatility of camel xiii
Vertebral anchylosis ... 114
Vertigo ... 85
Vices of camels ... 10
Vomition ... 63

W

War services ... xi
Water, carriage of.. 123
" sacs, uses of. 68
" tank theory. x
Watering of camels.xi,20 143
Weak heart ... 195
Weakness ... 190
Weight of a camel. 157
Whipworm ...65,130
Whitlow ... 117
Wool ... 131
Wound ointment ... 191
Wounds ...102,187
" eye ... 115
" healing of. 128

X

Y

Yahcud ... 111
Yield of milk ...1,31
Young camels, diseases of ... 83

Z

Zahmat ... 52
Zarbadh ...56,187
Zerbad ...56,187
Zhob Valley Expedition ... 141
Zillay Baaz ... 62

INDEX TO AUTHORITIES.

Page

Abdul Kadir ... 164
Aelian ... 164
Agnelli ... 53
Anderson (Dunlop) ... 34
Aristotle ... 164

Baines ...109,138
Baker, Sir Samuel ... 101
Bennett ...69,81,96,103,108,143,144, 147,148,149
Blumenbach ... 164
Blunt ... 160
Boisse ... 132
Bruce ... 102
Buffon ... 164
Burke ...48,49,72
Burn 97,101,102,103,104,135,107,110 112,115,117,118,104,135,136,140, 144,146,150,151,152,153,155,156, 189
Burnaby ...5,10,12,29
Burt ...90,105,140,144,145,148,149

Carbuccia ...96,101,119
Cautley ... 164
Chatin ... 84
Chauveau ... 165
Clayton ...89,92,94,96,97
Cobbold ... 1C1
Colborn ... 101
Colin ...32,36,45,60,61,66,115
Cuvier ... 164

Daubeuton ... 68
Daumas ...1,13,15,21,164
Davidson ... 108
Dawney ... 149
Diodorus Siculus ... 164
Dragendorf ... 84

Elliot ...14,97
Evans ...46,47,58,156

Falconer ... 163
Fenton ...75,138
Fleming ...5,53,89
Fogliata ...69,70,79
Formad ... 158
Furse ... 137,142,144,147

Galton ... 10,11
Garrod ... 59
Gervais ... 92
Gesner (Conrad) ... 164
Gilchrist ...19,24,32,35,38,41,42,43, 48,52,54,55,56,57,62,63, 64,70,71,73,74,75,78,79, 80,81,82,83,85,86,87,88, 96,104,106,109,111,112, 114,115,117,164,183,185
Giles ... 2,21
Gordon ... xiv
Graoberg D'Emsoe ... 165
Grodekov ... 136

	Page
Hallen	... 156
Hamley	... 5
Haslam	...50,51,92,93,94,96
Hodgson	...52,56,63,64,71,78,87,112, 115,118
Home	... xv,68
Humboldt	... 136
Ivanin	... 6
Jones	...140,142
Kostenko	...1,5,12,13,14,19,21,25,28
Larrey	...55,82
Leach	...13,19,23,24,25,26,32,35,40, 41,54,56,63,73,80,85,95,101, 103,111,112,165,185,188, 189,190,191
Leidy	... 163
Leo Africanus	... 164
Letang	... 15
Lewis, Dr.	... 58
Linnæus	... 164
Lombardini	...66,67,68,69,79,80,82, 83.84,92,93,97,101, 110,152,163,165
Lord	...109,138
Mahomed	...1,ix,132
Malleson	... 5
Marochetti	... 84
Martin	...7,11,16,17,19,23,25,94,165
Marvin	... 4
Masson	... 53
Maxwell	... 14
Megnin	...92,93,165
Meyrick	... 3,11
Milne Edwards	... 164
Moses	... 132
Miller	...66,164
Nactigal	... 132
Napier, Sir, Charles	... 138
Niebuhr	... 164
Nitzsch	... 70
Nott	... 144
Nunn	...3,18,28,30,31,47,48,52,54,56, 57,63,74,87,88,89,96,112,160
Oliphant	...2,7,16,26,30,32,47,49,53, 57,75,78,80,85,89,91,92, 97,101,105,136,163,165
Otto	... 68

	Page
Palgrave	...xii,133,134
Pallas	... 151
Palmer	... 133
Pancires	... 164
Pasteur	... 49
Peel	... 116
Phipson	... xv
Piot	... 81
Pliny the younger	... 164
Porse	... 164
Potto	... 12
Poyser	...141,155
Prejevalsky	... 3,5
Pringle	...12,141
Queriple	...75,86,96,140,141,142,145, 147,148,167
Raymont	...33,75,98,115,165
Richardi	... 66
Rudolphi	... 70
Sani	... 83
Santi	... 164
Savi	... 164
Skinner	... 144
Smith, S. M.	...69,89,140,143,145
Smyth	... 150
"Snipe"	...101,154
Steel, C.	...3,7,21,26,27,32,57.58,78, 82,117,165.189,xv
Steel, J. H.	... 125
Stewart, Col.	... 4
Strabo	... 164
Symonds, T. J.	... 62,70
Tassy	...11,18,54,78,81,85,114,118
Vallon	...1,6,7,8,10,81,85,91,92,110, 114,117
Vedernikoff	... 158
Von Linstow	... 87
Walters	... 6,137
Warren	... 12,20
Watt	...131,150,158
Wedl	...66,164
Wilson, Sir, Charles	... 142
Wolseley	... 9
Wortley (Stuart)	... 143
Yaldwin	... 3,11,13,16,19,21,22.25,46, 56,58,93,96,149

ERRATUM.

For "Byrne" in many places read "Burn."

Breinigsville, PA USA
16 March 2011
257802BV00003B/97/P

9 781164 538066